KT-428-098

CASUALTIES OF THE NEW WORLD ORDER

Casualties of the New World Order

The Causes of Failure of UN Missions to Civil Wars

Michael Wesley
Asia-Australia Institute
University of New South Wales
Sydney

First published in Great Britain 1997 by
MACMILLAN PRESS LTD
Houndmills, Basingstoke, Hampshire RG21 6XS and London
Companies and representatives throughout the world

A catalogue record for this book is available from the British Library.

ISBN 0–333–68244–0

First published in the United States of America 1997 by
ST. MARTIN'S PRESS, INC.,
Scholarly and Reference Division,
175 Fifth Avenue, New York, N.Y. 10010

ISBN 0–312–17478–0

Library of Congress Cataloging-in-Publication Data
Wesley, Michael, 1968–
Casualties of the new world order : causes of failure of UN
missions to civil wars / Michael Wesley.
p. cm.
Based on the author's thesis (doctoral—University of St. Andrews)
Includes bibliographical references and index.
ISBN 0–312–17478–0
1. United Nations—Armed Forces. 2. Civil war. I. Title.
JX1981.P7W43 1997
341.5'84—dc21 97–3798
CIP

This book is printed on paper suitable for recycling and made from fully managed and sustained forest sources.

10 9 8 7 6 5 4 3 2 1
06 05 04 03 02 01 00 99 98 97

Printed and bound in Great Britain by
Antony Rowe Ltd, Chippenham, Wiltshire

To my parents

Contents

Preface viii

Glossary x

1 Introduction 1
The Weaknesses in United Nations Missions 2
The Logic of Civil War Conflict Dynamics 15
UN Missions in Civil Wars: A Framework for Analysis 21

2 Mediation 29
Bosnia-Herzegovina: Speaking into a Hurricane 31
El Salvador: A Timely Success 49
Conclusion 62

3 Peacekeeping 66
Handling Scorpions in Somalia 68
Purchasing Peace in Mozambique 81
Conclusion 93

4 Election Monitoring 96
The Angolan Elections: War by Other Means 98
Corralling the Khmer Rouge in Cambodia 109
Conclusion 122

5 Conclusion 125

Notes 133

Bibliography 162

Index 189

Preface

To be beginning to teach, research, and write on International Relations in the mid-1990s is a daunting task. These are times of great change and uncertainty in the international system, and yet they are also fascinating. This does not only result from the ending of the Cold War and the receding of ideological confrontation from international politics. In many ways the nuclear balance is maturing and becoming less stable at the same time. For the first time, Western great powers are being joined by other great powers with different cultural systems and readings of international politics. And while all this is happening, even the sovereign state, which serves as the lodestone of our thinking about international politics faces an uncertain role and future.

Part of the international scenery at the end of the Cold War was the real reactivation of the UN. For years it had been a shadowy player, carrying connotations of irrelevance and faded memories of great power confrontations and the speeches of great statesmen. But in the 1990s pictures of peacekeepers flooded the broadsheets and the UN became a subject of much conversation and debate. In some ways it was like a return to the past, but in others it was a vision of the future. Then everything started to go wrong. Impotence in Bosnia, brutality in Somalia, and prostitution in Cambodia turned visions of hope into diatribes of condemnation. The UN learnt once again that being flavour of the month is a very short experience in international politics.

This book is a study of the reasons why so many UN missions to civil wars have failed. It sets out to prove, through analysing how and why UN missions are mounted, that there are common causes for these many failures. Rather than being an inherent failing of the missions, these weaknesses derive from the misuse of the missions by UN member-states, who fail to understand civil wars, but dispatch UN missions anyway for cynical and selfish reasons. While it is a book that looks for weaknesses in UN missions, it is not intended to be a criticism of the talented people and brave personnel who mount, support, and carry out these often impossibly difficult tasks. Neither is it a criticism of the representatives of the member-states in the UN, who are only carrying out the instructions of often cynical governments. Members of all of these groups of people proved most generous with their time during the research for this book. If it blames anything for mission failures, this book blames the structure of the international system, which causes states to behave as they do.

This book began as a doctoral thesis at the University of St Andrews. The experience of writing it at an ancient university in a country half a world away from my own was one of the most formative of my life. This opportunity would not have been possible but for the encouragement, help, and support of a number of people. Foremost were Professor Paul Wilkinson, my supervisor, and also Dr Joanne Wright and Dr Keith Bryett who encouraged me to take the plunge. Associate Professor Glyn Davis provided excellent advice, encouragement, and criticism for converting the thesis into a book. I must also thank my sister Nasim and brother-in-law Willis for their kindness and support both in London and in Sydney. The research for this book took me to three continents, and I am extremely grateful for the hospitality of a number of people: Tony Warren and Kate Reynolds in Canberra, Mr and Mrs Gil and Janet Galloway in New York, Mr and Mrs Fred and Naomi Wray in Virginia, Nigel and Josie Ralph in London, and Cyril and Barbara Wright in Northern Ireland.

For their help and time during my research, I must thank Lieutenant-Colonel Damien Healey ADF, Lieutenant-General John Sanderson ADF, Sir David Hannay, Mrs Sally Morphett, and Ms Carol Edwards at the FCO, Ms Rima Bodcosh and the staff at the Dag Hammarskjold Library, Ms Joan Seymour, Jose da Silva Campino, Lamine Sise, and Michel Pelletier at United Nations Headquarters, Ms Alex McLeod at the United Nations Information Centre in London, and the staff at the British Library. Needless to say, the responsibility for any mistakes in this book is entirely mine.

For providing me with finance during my research I must thank the CVCP, the University of St Andrews, and the Rotary Foundation for scholarships. My thanks also go to my colleagues and friends in the Department, Deans Court, and St Andrews, who made my years there enriching in ways other than just academically. I must also thank Professor Stephen FitzGerald, Mr Larry Strange, and the staff at the Asia-Australia Institute, University of New South Wales, for their forbearance while I was completing this manuscript.

This book would have been impossible without the love, confidence, pride, and wise and caring encouragement and advice of my parents. It is impossible to express the sustenance their love provided, and the freedom that their assurances of underwriting me financially gave me during these years. It is to them, with my love, gratitude, and respect, that this book is dedicated.

Glossary

ANC	African National Congress
ARENA	*Alianza Republicana Nacionalista* (El Salvador)
ASEAN	Association of South East Asian Nations
CAC	Cessation of Armed Conflict Mechanism (Mozambique)
CCF	Ceasefire Commission (Mozambique)
CCFA	Commission for the Formation of the Armed Forces (Angola)
CD	*Convergencia Democratica* (El Salvador)
CGDK	Coalition Government of Democratic Kampuchea
CMVF	Joint Verification and Monitoring Commission (Angola)
COPAZ	*Comision Nacional para la Consolidacion de la Paz* (El Salvador)
CORE	Committee for Reintegration of Demobilized Personnel (Mozambique)
CSC	Supervisory and Monitoring Commission (Mozambique)
FALA	Unita's Military Wing
FDR	Democratic Revolutionary Front (El Salvador)
FMLN	*Frente Faribundo Marti para Liberacion Nacional* (El Salvador)
Frelimo	*Frente de Libertacao de Mocambique*
Funcinpec	National Front for an Independent, Neutral and Peaceful Cambodia
ICFY	International Conference on the Former Yugoslavia
JIM	Jakarta Informal Meetings on Cambodia
KPNLF	Khmer People's National Liberation Front (Cambodia)
LAS	League of Arab States
MPLA	*Movimento Popular de Libertacao de Angola*
NADK	National Army of Democratic Kampuchea (Khmer Rouge)
NATO	North Atlantic Treaty Organization
OAS	Organization of American States
OAU	Organization of African Unity
OIC	Organization of Islamic Conference
ONUMOZ	United Nations Observer Mission in Mozambique
ONUSAL	United Nations Observer Mission in El Salvador
PAC	Pan Africanist Congress of Azania (South Africa)
PAVN	People's Army of Vietnam

PCC	Paris Conference on Cambodia
Renamo	*Resistencia Nacional Mocambicana*
SCR	Security Council Resolution
SNC	Supreme National Council (Cambodia)
SoC	State of Cambodia
SWAPO	South West African People's Organization
TNC	Transitional National Council (Somalia)
UK	United Kingdom
UN	United Nations
US	United States
UNAMIC	United Nations Advance Mission to Cambodia
UNAVEM II	United Nations Angola Verification Mission
UNDPI	United Nations Department of Public Information
UNFICYP	United Nations Peacekeeping Force in Cyprus
UNIFIL	United Nations Interim Force in Lebanon
Unita	*Uniao Nacional para a Independencia Total de Angola*
UNITAF	Unified Task Force (Somalia)
UNOSOM II	United Nations Operation in Somalia
UNTAC	United Nations Transitional Authority in Cambodia
USC	United Somali Congress
USC-SNA	United Somali Congress-Somali National Alliance

1 Introduction

After the Cold War, the extensive use of the United Nations' mediation, peacekeeping, and peacebuilding machinery has seen a high rate of failure. This record begs serious and systematic investigation. Other policy instruments – and UN conflict resolution missions are as much policy instruments of the Organization's member-states as taxation laws or public transport upgrades are of domestic governments – that exhibited such a low success rate would long ago have been subjected to vigorous and repeated political and academic scrutiny. Yet the record of the UN's negotiators, peacekeepers, and civilian experts remains almost exclusively attended by ignorance, misunderstanding and rancorous media debates. This book searches for the common sources of the failure of UN missions since the end of the Cold War. It concentrates on missions to civil wars, the predominant recipients of the UN's post-Cold War attentions. The argument denies the cacophony of claims that the failings of its missions demonstrate the UN's obsolescence; or that they result from the ideological radicalization of the body, or from corruption and waste, or from an excessive and inefficient bureaucracy. The following political-military analysis proposes that the failings of UN missions derive from significant structural weaknesses that lie within the missions and their method of dispatch by UN member-states. It explains that the recent high rates of failure of UN missions result from their repeated injection into the conflict dynamics of civil wars, which possess certain common attributes that expose, and then accentuate, the missions' inherent weaknesses. The major contention of this argument is that the difference between UN missions' failures and successes is determined by whether the mission carries these weaknesses, and whether the conflict dynamic of a civil war is able to aggravate them sufficiently to frustrate its mandate or bring about its withdrawal. If the conflict dynamic is able to reveal and worsen these weaknesses where they exist, the mission will fail. If the conflict dynamic shows particular pliability or the mission proves free of weaknesses or especially resilient, it will succeed.

The argument of this book is presented deductively. It begins with conceptual analyses which identify the common weaknesses of UN missions and the common features of civil war conflict dynamics that are most likely to aggravate these weaknesses. In so isolating these features of UN missions and civil wars, the analysis focuses on an interaction between protagonists: the sponsors and agents of the UN mission, and the civil war's belligerents. It relies on an assumption of rationality, by identifying the actors' interests and capabilities as the motivations of their actions and the sources of the missions' strengths and weaknesses.[1] The remainder of this chapter conducts these analyses of UN missions and civil wars. From their results an analytical framework is constructed which juxtaposes UN mission weaknesses and those features of civil war conflict dynamics that are likely to expose and aggravate those weaknesses. The validity of the argument is tested in Chapters 2 to 4 by applying the framework thematically to case studies of UN missions.

Rather than being a comprehensive account of recent UN missions, these case studies are used for an analytical purpose. This is to conduct a single search among the missions for commonalities in the causes of their failures. Further, the objective of the study is to find the aspects of civil wars that repeatedly act upon these common weaknesses to cause the missions to fail. But the study does not only examine failed missions. In each of the mission types examined – mediation in Chapter 2, peacekeeping in Chapter 3, and election monitoring in Chapter 4 – a more successful mission is examined alongside a failed mission. The successful missions serve as a kind of an experimental control, by being searched for the existence, or rather the absence, of the weaknesses believed to be common to failed missions. If these weaknesses are absent from the successful missions and present in the failed missions, and if certain aspects of the civil wars are common to the failed missions but absent from the successful missions, this will support the validity of the contention of this book, that the failures of UN missions are attributable to common structural weaknesses that are especially vulnerable to resistant civil war conflict dynamics. Chapter 6 draws common themes out of the weaknesses found in the six missions surveyed, and speculates on how these can be practically eliminated.

THE WEAKNESSES IN UNITED NATIONS MISSIONS

There are significant differences between the types of missions the UN dispatches to address civil wars. Yet a common thread of disappointment, rejection, and failure to deliver mandates runs through all mission types charged with terminating or dampening internal conflicts – from mediation, through peacekeeping, demobilization and election monitoring. This questions whether each mission's failings derive from peculiarities in its mandate, resources, or personnel, as much as it suggests that all mission types are apt to share common weaknesses. It further suggests that these weaknesses have a profound source, from within the UN's organizational dynamics, and from this profound source they imbue all aspects of the missions dispatched – mandates, resourcing, leverage, personnel, and support. The following discussion of the logic of the UN's responses to recent civil wars seeks both to reveal the sources of these weaknesses in the coalitions of its member-states that dispatch the missions, and also to demonstrate how these weaknesses affect the performance of the missions. The motives of UN member-states for responding to contemporary civil wars through the UN are examined first, and identified as the most deep-seated location of the weakness of UN missions. Second, the weaknesses in the structures of the mounting and authorization of UN missions are shown to follow from the motives of the member-states. Finally, it is demonstrated that the weaknesses of UN missions, as they manifest themselves in the field through lack of influence, inappropriate mandates and resourcing, and fragmenting endorsement from within the UN, flow directly from these more profound sources.

The most basic fact about the UN is that it possesses no capability for major purposive independent action. This is because its constituent member-states all jealously guard their sovereignty, defined both as their independence of action internationally and their exclusivity of control domestically. Any grant of power to the UN to take significant independent action within the international system would limit this independence of state action,[2] and could possibly even challenge their internal control.[3] Consequently, member-states at all times retain strict control over the UN's actions, by ensuring that all of its significant initiatives are dependent upon them for endorsement, resources, personnel, direction, and tenure. No UN mission can be activated or dispatched without the agreement of a majority of the member-states present in the authorizing forum. Within the Security Council, the main forum authorizing the missions launched after the Cold War, this calculation has the added complication of requiring on substantive questions the assent or abstention of each of its five great power members: the US, the People's Republic of China, the Russian Federation, the UK, and France. This means that every UN mission is dependent on a delicate diplomatic balance of agreement between its sponsoring member-states, and that this balance of agreement is ultimately determined by the complementarity of the motivations and perceptions of these member-states.

Any state's actions in the international system – and within the UN, a microcosm of the international system – are motivated first and foremost by self-interest. The absence of any authoritative higher body to regulate the actions of strong states and protect the interests of weaker states, as a domestic government arbitrates relations within its borders, requires all states to be self-reliant to ensure their security from domination and to advance their interests. Adding a more emphatic dimension to this pursuit of self-interest is a fundamental consideration in the actions of all representatives and governments of member-states: the security of their tenure. Even with greatly varying levels of representative accountability between political systems, states' representatives within the UN are to differing extents concerned to maintain the acceptability of their actions according to whatever indicators or considerations their power is based on, be it popular endorsement, attention to religious, sectional or ethnic interests, economic success, internal or external security, or the satisfaction of the military. These considerations, as well as vast differences in culture, political system, historical experience, and geostrategic security, impact significantly on how UN member-states view civil wars, and how these views determine their actions. The first corollary is that each member-state's perception of a civil war and its policy imperatives are highly individualistic, and will most likely alter over time.[4] The second consideration is that each member-state will formulate its policy response to this perception primarily in terms of its self-defined self-interest, rather than by considerations centred around the interests or effectiveness of the UN. A coalition of such self-interested states with diverging views would be a tentative basis for any mission dispatched to address a civil war, but translates into an even more significant weakness when combined with the usual ambivalence of member-states' perceptions of civil wars.

The most widespread member-state perception of post-Cold War civil wars, which translates into a crippling weakness at the core of UN missions, is that their minor status as security concerns is judged insufficient to stimulate a massive unilateral or collective response. In terms of a simple cost-benefit analysis, civil wars today do not offer the geostrategic benefits or pose the risks to ideological blocs or spheres of influence – as they did during the Cold War – to justify the enormous material, political, and moral costs of intervention and counter-insurgency.[5] Concerns raised by civil wars can be identified, but none of these can be said to be compelling. Perhaps the least compelling are member-state concerns over the impact of civil wars on the collective interest. Just after the Cold War there appeared a proliferation of statements by leaders that each state's security depended on the general stability of the international system.[6] Among the great powers there was a general recasting of security doctrines after the disappearance of identifiable security threats. This prompted them to reconfigure their armed forces towards a greater ability to respond to minor threats like civil wars that represented 'weak links' in the fabric of the international system, targets of opportunistic interventions by adventurist middle powers,[7] and potential detonators of wider conflicts.[8] While such considerations seem to have been part of some of the motivations to intervene through the UN in civil wars, they are unlikely to have informed many hard policy choices, nor did they command wide currency among UN member-states.

Other, more concrete perceptions and considerations of states contemplating civil wars are highly individualistic. For the superpowers and their immediate clients there was a definite and compelling reason to try to resolve civil wars that survived the end of the Cold War. To these states, many of these civil wars had hitherto served as proxy sites for their struggle. Now that the superpowers' and clients' antagonism had passed, these civil wars – in Afghanistan, Cambodia, El Salvador, Nicaragua, and Angola – threatened to sour new, cooperative relationships. Now that these states were concerned with new, post-Cold War security, economic, and internal reform agendas, these proxy wars and their clients had become embarrassing and unnecessary.

Many of the civil wars that exploded after the Cold War, often as a direct result of the crumbling of authoritarian structures or the receding of superpower spheres of control, presented more concrete threats to those that were their more immediate neighbours. Some civil wars based on ethnic chauvinism threatened the cohesion of neighbouring states with similar ethnic divisions by encouraging their own ethnic groups; others threatened to spread the conflict by drawing sympathetic or outraged ethnic or religious kin in neighbouring states into competitive interventions. The internal security of overcrowded and poor neighbouring states was at times threatened by massive movements of refugees fleeing the brutality of the ethnic cleansing strategies of the combatants.[9]

States have been motivated to respond to civil wars by very real pressure exerted by domestic public opinion. Even the least democratic states have been motivated to respond by domestic outrage at genocide or mistreatment of ethnic or religious kin,[10] while the more democratic have been motivated by public concerns for human rights in civil wars. The common source and conduit of this public pressure is most often the media, which grows ever more efficient at reporting the horrors of civil wars and graphically and emotively depicting their gruesome details.[11] At times, governments have responded to such public pressure to advance their own interests, as admitted by US National Security Advisor Anthony Lake: 'humanitarian actions nurture the . . . public's support for our engagement abroad'.[12]

These states' perceptions about civil wars have an effect on their motivations to respond, which in turn has a profound impact on implanting weaknesses in the eventual UN mission. These perceptions place civil wars in a difficult category as stimuli to international action, making them sufficient to demand a response, but insufficiently threatening or inviting to command a significant commitment of resources, casualties, or international goodwill. This is a calculation that has repeatedly prompted states to resort to multilateralism in order to share with others the costs and liabilities of interventions in civil wars. The Gulf War acted as a timely advocate of multilateralism in the post-Cold War era. It was a cheaper and more legitimate way of securing a range of often diverse foreign policy goals between states with as different interests as the United States and Syria.[13]

After the Cold War, the UN became the preferred forum for this multilateral coordination for several reasons. Legitimacy was primary among these. Accompanying the decline in the legitimacy of intervention in other states since the end of the Second World War has been the steady assumption by the UN of a unique capability to confer 'collective legitimation', or the 'politically significant approval . . . of the claims, policies and actions of states',[14] by reference to the '. . . universal principles that are invoked rather than national special interests'.[15] Responding through the UN, therefore, allows concerned member-states to intervene in civil wars without incurring significant losses of international goodwill. If such actions are sanctioned by the international community through the UN, the *motive* for intervening is justified in terms of the collective good. If the intervention is implemented through an organization primarily dedicated to international peace and security using broadly multilateral forces from Western and non-Western states, the *form* of the intervention is legitimized in terms of its non-partisan nature. If the objectives of the intervention are agreed upon by an international forum with near-universal membership, the *interests* of the initiative should be above suspicion. And finally, if the conduct of the operation is accountable to the UN, then the *method* of the intervention is the responsibility of all.

Responding to civil wars through the UN also offers member-states more tangible economies. By coordinating responses through the UN, member-states are able to spread the costs of launching the intervention while deriving the same benefits as would be gained from a unilateral intervention in which they bore all the expenses. Among governments forced to cut defence and foreign policy budgets by publics demanding to see the domestic benefits of the 'peace dividend' at the end of the Cold War, the opportunity of sharing the costs of intervention with other states, and 'hiding' the expenses of the initiative among already existing contributions and commitments to the UN, becomes irresistible. Not only material costs can be defrayed through the UN: political costs, especially if military action is required, can be minimized by UN action. UN peacekeeping is calculated to result in fewer casualties than other forms of intervention; it is also cheaper in terms of military hardware. As the political cost of battle casualties rises, especially in post-industrial small-family societies,[16] governments are increasingly unwilling to risk these costs for non-compelling objectives like resolving civil wars. These multilateral missions have also been used by governments to defend their military establishments from demands for even greater cutbacks.[17] Acting through the UN also provides a safety-net for states to avoid political costs by providing a convenient scapegoat to blame if the mission runs into trouble or fails. The high rate of activation of UN mechanisms to address civil wars – between 1988 and 1994 more UN missions were dispatched than in the previous 43 years of the UN's existence – testifies to member-states' new-found perceptions of its usefulness to furnish legitimacy, and spread the costs of responding to the less compelling concerns of civil wars.

Acting through the UN necessitates forming a coalition of member-states to endorse and then resource and direct the mission. Coalition-building within the UN carries a logic of its own, which, when combined with the individualistic perceptions and motivations of the sponsoring states to the civil war involved, entails distinct consequences for that mission. Not every member-state is interested in every problem, or becomes involved in every mission. Each initiative is the result of a different ad hoc coalition of those member-states that are most concerned with the problem addressed or the solution proposed. The members of the relevant decision-making forum each have their own interests and conceptions of international order which are invoked to varying degrees by different civil wars, and which determine their active interest, benign acquiescence, or degree of opposition to the UN response.[18] The nature of the coalition is in this way determined by the nature of the threat and the proposed response.[19] As the coalition is formed, the partners that are initially chosen are those that show a sufficient community of interest with the coalition initiators to support and contribute to the initiative. By no means does this mean that all members of UN coalitions agree on the initiative completely. Often member-states which do not agree with the perceptions of the civil war, or with the proposed response, are included, either because they have a significant interest in the conflict and its outcome, or because the requirement of consulting with significant states is vital to ensuring the initiative has the legitimacy of broad and significant endorsement.[20]

The missions dispatched to address civil wars are based solely on their sponsoring coalition. It is this coalition that meets to agree on and determine the nature of the problem confronted; the UN's responsibilities in regard to the problem; the mandate of the mission; the nature and structure of its implementing mechanisms; its personnel and resourcing; and determines the tenure and direction of the mission as it progresses. Any problems with the functioning of these sponsoring coalitions will translate into weaknesses in the missions based on those coalitions. The nature of UN coalitions, and the member-states that comprise them, carry inherent problems. Most of these problems result from a combination of states' diversity of perceptions on a given issue; their pursuit of self-interest; and their concern to minimize cost and commitment when dealing with non-compelling threats. One class of problems that can result from this combination of conditions flows from most coalitions' rigidity and vagueness of decision-making. If a coalition is formed from a wide variety of perceptions and interests, the negotiation of an agreed course of action can be a long and tortuous process as a large diversity of interests have to be accommodated. Often this requires the negotiation of complex formulas of side-payments and compensations to subsidize rewards, or to compensate coalition members for damage to their interests.[21]

This can have two very different consequences for the coalition and its mission. One is that the formula negotiated can become very rigid: coalition members will be more willing to continue with an unsuccessful course of action than to engage in the costly process of renegotiating a change in response. The other is that the mandate negotiated can become extremely vague, as the coalition leaders are forced repeatedly to resort to ambiguity and dilution of the response to achieve agreement with dissenting members of the coalition. The difficulty of achieving the initial consensus in the group can also result in the opposite effect to rigidification of response: it can act to divorce the sponsoring coalition from the needs of its mission, thereby making the sponsoring coalition's responses to adverse conditions pusillanimous and prevaricating. If the mission runs into difficulties, rather than sacrificing its cohesion, a coalition may modify the mandate or objectives rather than disturb the agreement within the group. This can lead the coalition to settle for a less optimal response that still carries substantial rewards.[22] A desire to resolve a civil war can thus be downgraded to a policy of containing and de-escalating by a pragmatic coalition that would rather be content with a less than ideal outcome than with expending further resources on renegotiating the parameters of the mission.

Another class of problems with UN coalitions arises from the self-interested motivations of the member-states and the non-compelling stimuli of civil wars. Anarchy in the international system, and its attendant requirement of self-reliance for states, makes them ever-mindful of their position in the system relative to that of other states. Even when acting multilaterally to address a low-level security concern like a civil war, member-states remain primarily concerned with promoting their own interests, and preventing any damage to their security or position within the international hierarchy of power. This entails that even in a cooperative relationship, states remain obsessed with relative gains: 'states in cooperative arrangements . . . worry that their partners might gain more from cooperation than they do . . . a state will focus both on its absolute and relative gains from cooperation, and a state that is satisfied with a partner's compliance in a joint arrangement might nevertheless exit from it because the partner is achieving relatively greater gains.'[23]

For these reasons, along with considerations of tenure, member-states of a coalition will constantly calculate the effect of the mission on their self-interests, and act primarily according to those self-interests. There is thus a constant reassessment of their commitment to the coalition, its mission, and its mandate, by all of the members of the coalition. Any developments in the mission – whether positive or negative – once it has been launched can affect the coalition members' interests in such a way as to cause them to reassess their commitment to the mission, and destroy the delicate diplomatic balance underpinning the operation. The auspices of the UN makes it easier for member-states to be more fickle than they would be in other alliances. Defaulting on UN coalitions is more easily done, because often nothing more than a temporary alliance of expediency over a relatively minor concern is at stake. Such a breakdown in diplomatic consensus will not harm the UN structure, which has acted as a constant forum of shifting alliances and coalitions throughout its history.[24]

For these reasons, the most fundamental weakness in UN missions dispatched to civil wars arises from the nature of the coalitions of member-states that launch them. The rigid control by member-states over UN actions makes UN missions heavily dependent on sponsoring coalitions of member-states. Because of the widely diverging perceptions and competing self-interests of their member-states, these coalitions are usually an unsuitable base for launching a mission intended to undertake the enormously difficult task of resolving or terminating a civil war. The coalition is often too fragile and state-centric to function effectively as a directing and supporting base for the mission. The fragility of the coalition can translate directly into a vague mandate for the mission, followed during implementation with uncertain political support and even criticism from within the coalition. This has demonstrably retarded UN missions' capacity for concerted action in support of their mandates.

Often these unstable coalitions based on compromise also lack states willing to assume leadership and responsibility for the mission. Because most states will see a civil war as a moderate security concern, coalitions usually become collections of states eager to minimize their contributions and responsibility for the mission. This emphasis on parsimony of contribution can result in UN missions being under-resourced or inadequately equipped to perform their mandates. These problems at the base of UN missions addressing civil wars are fundamental weaknesses. As will be seen in the discussion of the framing and mounting of UN missions, and then in their mechanisms of influence on the ground, the weaknesses flowing from their state-centred, parsimonious, and self-interested member-states imbue all levels of UN missions.

As the UN coalition moves from coalition-building to defining its response to the civil war, the state-centrism of the organization poses further impediments to the mission's eventual effectiveness. Because the sponsoring states of a mission are primarily concerned with their own interests, they often either devote insufficient time to understanding the conflict they are about to address, or are more concerned with considerations other than those that are relevant to the resolution of the civil war. This leads the coalitions assembled within the Security Council or the General Assembly to rely on preconceptions of conflicts that have evolved from within the UN over time, and then to rely on prefabricated UN responses to respond to these problems. Often these preconceived assumptions about the conflict are based on experiences of inter-state war, and are seriously flawed views of the actual civil war. They can be responsible for the dispatch of missions which are inappropriate for securing the objectives they have been set. This is mainly because the UN, its perceptions of conflict, and its mechanisms for addressing conflict, have evolved from the interactions of states, to be effective in resolving conflicts between, rather than within, states.[25] The discussion of civil war conflict dynamics will show the ways in which intra-state conflict differs from inter-state conflict, and how these differences are likely to frustrate mechanisms designed to resolve inter-state tensions and hostilities. It is therefore necessary to examine how UN assumptions often lead self-interested states to misperceive the dynamics of modern civil wars, and how these misperceptions lead to inappropriate mission types and inadequate equipping of these missions.

UN member-states' three major assumptions about civil wars are, not surprisingly, based on a range of considerations arising from their pursuit of self-interest, and based on the weight of their experience. Their primary concerns with preserving the tenure of their governments and their control over their societies, as well as with preserving their own states from outside attack or intimidation, lead states to adopt a position that war is an illegitimate method of acquiring political power or influence, internationally or domestically. Overlaying the primary motivations behind this conviction are commitments to popular endorsement of governments,[26] which in turn inform the basic philosophy and structure of the UN,[27] and member-states' ostensible commitment to rejecting war or intimidation as a method of gaining foreign policy objectives. This normative motivation of the UN's member-states automatically leads to a number of often faulty aspects being automatically factored into their response to a civil war. It leads to an obsession with stopping the fighting before any other conflict resolution is contemplated, regardless of the context or goals of the war, and often indifferent to the terms of, or conditions obtaining after the ceasefire.[28] It also often leads the UN to assemble a mission and commit it to the civil war too early, so it can stop the fighting, but before it has given sufficient thought to the actual resolution, as opposed to the termination or suppression, of the conflict.[29] While it may temporarily stop the suffering, such ill-conceived responses can fail, often destroying any genuine opportunities to resolve the conflict.[30] This can also have serious ramifications for missions that are often inappropriate to the conflict situation and, like UNFICYP in Cyprus or UNIFIL in Lebanon, become trapped patrolling interminable ceasefire lines while the bases of the conflict simmer on, untouched by the original mission. This conviction can also often lead to the solution to the civil war advocated by the UN being based, irrespective of the demands or ideology of the belligerents, on an advocacy and assumed acceptance of ideals of universal suffrage, majority government, power sharing, civil–military separation, respect for human rights, and the peaceful adjustment of claims. How appropriate these aspects are to states without democratic traditions, long-wracked by civil war, will be seen in the later case studies.

The second major conviction of UN member-states dealing with civil wars derives from their obsession with remaining 'the principal actors in the international system, and the chief bearers of rights and duties within it'.[31] This leads UN coalitions to insert into their prescribed solutions to civil wars an almost universal requirement that the outcome must preserve the sovereignty and territorial integrity of the state experiencing the internal conflict. The UN's member-states are adamant that they are not prepared to suffer a balkanization of their fellow-members as the result of an epidemic of civil wars:

> the UN seeks to preserve the nation-state as the very foundation of international life . . . And subnational, ethnic or tribal factions cannot expect to undermine the political unit in which they exist while claiming the privileges of a sovereign nation-state.[32]

This conviction leads UN coalitions to formulate solutions that will ultimately result in a single legitimized government with full control over a unified, centralized, and territorially complete state.[33] This can lead to UN missions receiving unrealistic mandates, based on their sponsoring coalitions' insistence on the prevention of the breaking-up of a state made unviable by ethnic, religious, or other divisions.

The third major assumption about civil wars common to most UN coalitions can be attributed to perceptions of conflict based on states' predominance of experience with war between states, rather than within states. This is that wars, whether civil or international, are disputes over non-divisible or scarce commodities. This leads to the belief that the conflict can be resolved, and the fighting stopped, by substituting peaceful methods of apportioning the commodities in dispute for the parties' resort to war. This is most often the purpose of the missions dispatched to civil wars by the UN, to offer 'peaceful substitutes for the technique of violence, and to encourage – if not insist upon – their utilization by the parties to the disputes'.[34] Often the civil wars the UN addresses are much more complex conflicts. They can combine ethnic fear, urban–rural rivalry, significant historical enmities, and often the complete rejection of the other party's right to exist. Such sentiments are rarely present in the *realpolitik* of inter-state war. These three UN member-state assumptions and perceptions, and underlying self-interested motivations, dictate that the approach of UN coalitions to resolving civil wars is nearly always normative in terms of advancing a preferred solution dictated by member-states' convictions, rather than being genuinely problem-solving, and based on a close study of the civil war and an appreciation of its dynamics.[35] Unfortunately for a majority of missions, the assumptions and perceptions of their sponsoring coalitions of the civil war are flawed, and their convictions often lead to their introduction into inappropriate contexts to secure unrealistic mandates.

Compounding the weaknesses of UN missions introduced into civil wars with unrealistic mandates are the inappropriateness of the mission-types set by the sponsoring coalition, and the inadequacy of the mechanisms of influence available to those mission types. Preconceptions of the conflicts lead to the use of prefabricated responses: fact-finding missions, mediation proposals, peacekeeping, peacebuilding. Sponsoring coalitions are unwilling to expend the effort of formulating different responses, and unwilling to spend resources, sovereignty, or goodwill in experimenting with different multilateral mechanisms. The lukewarm response to, and then rejection of, the proposals of Secretary-General Boutros-Ghali and others[36] for a standing UN Rapid Response Force, used for a range of new initiatives from preventive deployment to peace-enforcement, is testament to the parsimony and sovereignty obsession of the UN's member-states. The preconceived mission types that are sent to resolve civil wars – mediation, peacekeeping, and peacebuilding – have, for the most part, been developed for, and to deal with, conflicts between states. These mission-types possess several mechanisms of persuasion or coercion over belligerents, designed to enable the UN to influence those warring states towards its preferred resolution of the conflict. Often they are inappropriate for influencing belligerents in civil wars.

Traditional UN conflict resolution mechanisms rely heavily on the moral suasion, the organization's ability to dispense collective endorsement or condemnation by a majority of the world's states:

> collective approbation is an important asset and collective disapprobation a significant liability in international relations . . . a state may hesitate to pursue a policy that has engendered the formal disapproval of the Assembly not because it is prepared to give the will of that organ priority over its national interest but because it believes that the adverse judgement of the Assembly makes the pursuit of that policy disadvantageous to the national interest.[37]

The publicization of the non-cooperation of a belligerent party with a UN mission, the censuring of a party with a General Assembly or Security Council resolution, and the according or withholding of recognition, are all mechanisms of influence open to the UN through collective approbation or disapprobation. They are designed not to affect that party's military position, but rather its moral standing and broader perception by onlookers, thereby influencing the morale of its soldiers and supporters, encouraging the resolution of its rivals, and providing its opponents with propaganda material.[38] However, the influence of the moral opinion of the UN has more effect on member-states than on other entities.[39] Insurgent movements and embattled incumbent regimes, locked into a conflict for power and survival, are likely to be little affected by considerations of UN approval or the publicity of their non-cooperation with a UN mission.

The other common methods of influence of UN missions over belligerents are also ill-suited to applying pressure to the parties to a civil war. These include the application of sanctions, and the increase or discontinuation of aid or other assistance, either by the UN or member-states. If effectively applied and maintained with a watertight sanctions regime, the interruption of supplies to a civil war party can have devastating effects on its military position, thereby making it more compliant. However, this influence is proportional to the party's dependence on external aid; insurgent movements in particular can be extremely self-sufficient.[40] Moreover, only external flows of resources that are visible and able to be interdicted are available to the UN for the application of pressure on a civil war party:

> sources of supply and military equipment [to civil wars] are usually clandestine. The fact that they're usually clandestine means that the UN can't interdict them very successfully by normal legal means. So one can have one's doubts whether . . . [an] arms embargo on [a civil war belligerent] . . . has very much effect because people don't go around the world saying they were selling arms to them in the first place.[41]

For these reasons, the mechanisms of influence with which the UN's prefabricated conflict resolution missions are equipped are often quite inappropriate for ensuring the compliance of civil war parties with the mandate of the UN mission.

Recognizing these vulnerabilities of UN missions introduced into civil wars, a number of writers, led by Secretary-General Boutros-Ghali, advocated the use of force for the purposes of peace-enforcement by UN missions to ensure belligerent compliance in civil wars: '. . . when established rules of engagement are no longer sufficient, United Nations forces may need authorization to use force'.[42] More than authorization is needed, however. The multilateral, lightly armed, small forces dispatched on UN conflict resolution missions do not possess the equipment, cohesion, or training to mount the type of concerted military operation needed to impose their will on either insurgent guerrillas or incumbent troops. The diverse quality, training, languages, and equipment of national contingents in the multilateral force paralyses these missions' ability to operate as a coordinated military force. The constant referring of orders back to national capitals for authorization by the different contingents have made it almost impossible for UN force commanders to wield their multilateral forces as cohesive instruments.[43] The UN itself is ill-equipped to direct military operations, possessing little military expertise and concerned more with administration than with logistics, tactics, or staff work.[44] Neither are the threats posed by civil wars usually serious enough for member-states to be willing to expend the resources and risk the casualties of a Desert Storm-scale multilateral military effort for objectives 'concerned with matters beyond the limited horizons of their interests'.[45] Coercion of a civil war belligerent entails all of the costs of either an inter-state war or of a major counterinsurgency operation, a burden that neither the UN nor its member-states are likely to assume lightly, and certainly not for a non-compelling security concern like a civil war.

This brief analysis has shown that the weaknesses that originate in the state-centred self-interest and diversity of interests within the coalitions that mount UN missions permeate all levels of the mission. The base of the mission is inherently fragile and obsessed with its own diplomatic agreement, often irrespective of the requirements of its mission on the ground. The sponsoring coalition responds to civil wars according to its own preconceptions and convictions, at times by dispatching a prefabricated mission-type to deal with a conflict the sponsoring coalition scarcely understands, and with which the mission is inappropriately equipped to deal.

In simple terms, then, the weaknesses of UN missions stem from a preoccupation with considerations external to the conflict at hand, which produce a strong tendency towards misdiagnosis of the conflict and the prescription of an inappropriate response. Often the sponsoring coalition dispatches these ill-equipped mission-types over the contrary advice of fact-finding missions and UN departments. The next section analyses civil war conflict dynamics in order to isolate those aspects that are likely to expose and intensify the weaknesses in UN missions. This is designed to show that UN missions fail to achieve their objectives when the civil war aggravates their weaknesses enough to frustrate the mission's objectives; and that those missions that succeed are in some way appropriate to the demands of the situation, either because of a unique robustness or appropriateness of mandate or design within the mission, or because of a singular pliability in the civil war conflict dynamic.

THE LOGIC OF CIVIL WAR CONFLICT DYNAMICS

There are as many differences among civil wars and their respective protagonists as there are civil wars: an enormous variety of ideology, terrain, extent, number of protagonists, and technology of warfare. Yet even given these differences, all civil war conflict dynamics share continuities that are significant to the success or failure of UN missions sent to resolve or contain them. These continuities all flow from the commonality of the struggle for control or alteration of the state.[46] The following analysis will demonstrate that the situation of warring for the power to determine the future of the state imparts a particular desperation on the struggle, and a singularly instrumentalist and opportunist logic on the political and military calculations of the belligerents. This in turn entails that the protagonists' political considerations will be primarily conflict-based, and that their calculations about the future and form of their struggle will be determined by a rational calculation of the constraints and opportunities that confront them at any given time. A significant corollary of the immediate influences on the protagonists' calculations is that international considerations play a negligible role in these calculations. Each of these conditions entails specific consequences for UN missions sent into civil wars. If the conflicts have been misperceived by a UN coalition, and an inappropriate mission-type has been sent to the civil war, it is likely that the mission will not achieve its objectives. Weaknesses in the acceptability of the solution it proposes will most likely be aggravated by weaknesses in its ability to compel the belligerents to comply with its mandate. The resulting helpless position is likely then to be exploited by the extremely opportunistic civil war belligerents to advance their own prosecution of the war.

The most basic structure of a civil war is the relationship between its belligerents. Most usually this comprises one or more insurgent movements struggling for an increase in political power, or a change in the structure, control, composition, or extent of the political system of the state; and usually – but not always[47] – an incumbent government fighting back in order to maintain its political control of all of the state, or to increase the influence and pre-eminence of its supporting ethnic, religious, or socio-economic group within the society. This structure gives the conflict dynamic and the motivations and actions of its protagonists a compelling logic. It is driven by the belief among all the protagonists that defeat will cause their destruction physically and as a political entity. Once a group begins insurgent violence against a state, it violates the contract of the domestic political society: by rejecting the government's monopoly over the use of violence and sovereign authority, it absents itself from protection under the law. It becomes literally outlawed, fought with not the police but the army, and tried not under domestic criminal law, but under treason laws.[48]

For the incumbent government, the stakes are just as high. An insurgent challenge threatens more than its existence: it questions its sovereign authority over the extent of its territory and population, the legitimacy of its monopoly over the use of force, and its prerogative to represent the state internationally. A violent internal challenge also weakens and divides the state, making it an easier target for an opportunistic third-party intervention. A military challenge to the state often prompts the abandonment of some of the structures and guarantees of civil society: the internal use of the army, the suspension of some civil rights, a certain militarization of the society, and an emphasis on total victory.[49] The importance of the stakes – control of the state, its resources, and sovereign prerogatives – means civil wars are usually fought with particular seriousness and brutality, and the consequences of defeat, capture, or surrender are usually extreme. Unlike a state that wages war, a civil war protagonist has no pre-existing recognized antebellum territorial area to withdraw into upon defeat or capitulation, thereby avoiding total annihilation. Often the insurgency and counter-insurgency strategies of the protagonists purposively aim to provoke, and make propaganda capital out of, the others' brutality towards its supporters and the general population.[50] Thus the brutality and zero-sum nature of the stakes of a civil war make protection and survival a vital objective for the protagonists, to complement their initial objectives to seize or maintain power. Both the insurgents and the incumbents are primarily reliant on their military effectiveness for both of these objectives. In a civil war violence is the primary means of advancing their own political power and undermining their opponent's, while soldiers and supporters are best protected from attack by the use or threat of violence.

The importance of the stakes, control of the state, and the wages of defeat, annihilation, impart the consequences of anarchy onto the positions of civil war protagonists, similar to those attending the position of states in the international system. For a civil war belligerent, there is no higher authority to which it can appeal for protection or advocacy in its struggle. It becomes self-reliant for advancing its interests and protecting its existence. Because the consequences of failure in pursuing self-interest in anarchical systems are domination and destruction, units promote their interests with an urgency and conviction less commonly found in a hierarchical system. The most basic motivation of units in a self-help system is physical survival and continued viability: 'In anarchy, security is the highest end. Only if survival is assured can units safely seek such other goals as tranquillity, profit, and power.'[51] Civil war calculations are thus in a major way influenced by basic considerations of the survival of the protagonist and its supporters, who 'have nothing to gain and everything to lose by giving up. In fact, once the banner of revolution has been raised and blood has been shed, it is no easy matter to give up. The rebels [and also the incumbents] begin to fight for whatever reason; they continue because they must.'[52]

Similarly, civil war belligerents must rely on themselves to advance the objectives for which they are fighting. These political objectives can range from the desire of an incumbent government to retain its power, sovereignty, and territorial integrity, to the goals of insurgents to seize control of the administration of the state, exclude other groups from the ability to shape or control the state, exempt themselves and their supporters from the jurisdiction of the state, or gain a general improvement or recasting of social, economic, or political conditions of existence for a sector or the whole of society. Civil war belligerents have a range of political interests – strategic and tactical, overt and covert, primary and secondary – of varying levels of importance and influence.[53] These interests are not ordered by a fixed hierarchy of importance; rather 'every action involves a trade-off, and the effort to achieve one objective inevitably involves costs with respect to some other desired goal'.[54] The relative importance of these interests are determined by the constellation of opportunities and constraints a protagonist faces at any given time, and each action is a result of a rational calculation and compromise between its diverse concerns. As protagonists in an anarchical, self-help system, civil war belligerents' concern to ensure their survival and to optimally promote their interests determines their behaviour. As their prime instrument of advancement and protection is war, political considerations of constraints and opportunities presented by any given situation govern their decisions on the conduct of war or peace.

Civil war protagonists differ from other adversarial groups in a society by their use of violence against each other. Often the option for violence is chosen by the insurgents because of frustration with other methods of changing the system, or because of a real or perceived threat to their survival from other groups in society. Incumbent governments often respond violently because of the seriousness of the challenge or because efforts at conciliation have failed. Once locked into the embrace of war, the insurgents and incumbents cannot rely on any higher authority for advocacy or protection; they become, like states in the international system, reliant for their protection and conquest of power on their ability to wage and threaten war or mobilize international protection. If they renounce war, they deprive themselves of the one reliable instrument of self-help available to them, and abandon themselves to the brutal logic of domination and destruction that attends all units in anarchical systems. However, if an opportunity arises offering self-protection and advancement of interests more effectively by abandoning war, a rational belligerent will take that option.[55] Similarly, if the continuance of the war threatens its survival and political goals more than the abandonment of hostilities, a rational belligerent will choose peace. Civil war belligerents' use of war for self-help, then, is more accurately conceived as a continuum between war and peace.

Civil war protagonists' intimate linking of political interests and war as an instrument for advancing and protecting those interests follows Clausewitz's maxim:

> War is nothing but a continuation of political intercourse with an admixture of other means . . . this political intercourse does not cease by the war itself . . . it continues to exist, whatever may be the form of the means which it uses, and . . . the chief lines on which the events of the war progress, and to which they are attached, are only the general features of policy which run all through the war until the peace takes place.[56]

War is therefore a policy instrument, and often the most effective policy instrument available to incumbents and insurgents: 'the use or threat of physical force is the most elementary way of asserting power and controlling one's environment'.[57] As a policy instrument, war, in all of its manifestations between total war and total peace, is subordinate to the political calculations advancing that policy: as 'an instrument of policy, it must necessarily bear its character, it must measure with its scale: the conduct of war, in its great features, is therefore policy itself'.[58]

The highly political nature of the conduct of war and peace in civil wars dictates an intimacy in relations between military means and political objectives often greater than in inter-state war. Not only does '. . . the political cause of [the] war [have] a great influence on the manner in which it is conducted',[59] but the influence is reciprocated, dictating that the political objectives are tailored to a level achievable with the military means open to each belligerent.[60] In this way, political calculations and interests are profoundly influenced by the conduct and fortunes of war: 'As war is dominated by the political object, therefore the value of that object determines the measure of the sacrifices by which it is to be purchased . . . As soon as the required outlay becomes so great that the political object is no longer equal in value, the object must be given up, and peace will result.'[61]

Civil war belligerents' interests are not set, but respond to the stage and success of the war, depending on the ideology, interests, and cohesion of the movement. Military setbacks can result either in a radicalization, or, more often, in a modification of objectives. Each belligerent's interests range in degrees of importance and negotiability. Primary among their concerns are survival, underlying ideological motivations, and basic goals. These interests will be the foremost ingredients of any calculations of policy arising from military setbacks, or the dangers or opportunities presented by a new development. In this way, the configuration of the belligerent's military fortunes, environment, and new developments, which determine the opportunities and constraints it confronts at any time, will influence the priorities of its interests, and regulate its conduct of war and peace for gaining or protecting those interests.

A consequence of the political use of war and of the importance of the stakes for which it is waged, is that the calculations determining the conduct of the war are opportunistic in the extreme. Each new situation is appraised of its constraints and opportunities, and responses are calculated to advance a protagonist's interests or to damage those of its opponent.

> War is always a bargaining process, one in which threats and proposals, counterproposals and counterthreats, offers and assurances, concessions

> and demonstrations, take the form of actions rather than words, or actions accompanied by words . . . The critical targets in such a war are in the minds of the enemy as much as on the battlefield; the state of the enemy's expectations is as important as the state of his troops.[62]

As their primary means of self-help, civil war belligerents manipulate their waging of war and peace and their selection of tactics in a way designed to infiuence not only their enemies, but all of their interlocutors, in such a way as to advance their interests. This includes UN missions introduced into the civil war environment. The instrumental way in which the civil war belligerents calculate the threats and opportunities presented by their presence, and determine their responses to the UN mission accordingly, has serious ramifications for the success or failure of those missions, and for the importance of the weaknesses in those missions.

The instrumental way in which UN missions are appraised by civil war belligerents gains added importance for their success or failure because of the lack of any other reliable mechanisms for influencing the calculations or behaviour of the belligerents. The preceding section demonstrated their weakness in imposing economic or military sanctions against civil war protagonists. Yet neither can UN missions rely on their status as representatives of the UN in civil wars, as they can when intervening between member-states. Pragmatism born of the struggle for survival makes civil war parties largely unconcerned by considerations of reputation, goodwill, and international responsibility that affect the behaviour of states. They are seldom affected by threats of approbation or disapprobation by the UN. Particularly the insurgent movements escape the moderating influence of international opinion or constituent preferences:

> Governments are very sensitive to what public opinion and what other governments as well as the heads of certain powerful international agencies will think of their actions because they're the people they have to live with if not depend on in the future. A guerrilla group which may have some other interest, which may in some cases be mercenary in character, is less interested in that kind of consideration. So you don't have the normal type of leverage.[63]

This means that the traditional mechanisms of influence used by UN missions to influence the behaviour of belligerents – legitimacy, recognition, moral suasion, obligations to the Charter, custodianship of international law, diplomatic contacts, and the ability to influence international opinion – are less effective in influencing the behaviour of civil war belligerents. These are real weaknesses, and if combined with a mission-type that is inappropriate to the conflict situation, can not only frustrate a UN mission's achievement of its objectives, but expose it to exploitation or attack by the protagonists in a civil war.[64]

The belligerents' opportunistic calculations will also determine their reaction to the introduction into the conflict of a UN mission. Because of their reduced influence in civil wars, most UN missions rely on the protagonists' calculations that the peace process offers a better way to advance their interests than continuing the war. If the UN mission is not so perceived, it is vulnerable to being ignored, exploited, or attacked. If not seen positively, the weaknesses of UN missions, in inappropriateness of mission design or mandate, in influence mechanisms, in the impact of their presence, and in their diplomatic support and cohesion, are open to exploitation by opportunistic civil war belligerents. If these weaknesses are exposed by the inappropriate introduction of a mission into a civil war, they will be used to frustrate or repel the mission. If the mission design is appropriate to the conflict, or if special conditions overlay the weaknesses and give the mission a special robustness, the mission will most likely succeed. The next section constructs, out of these two analyses of UN weaknesses and civil war conflict dynamics, an analytical framework for locating common weakness in UN missions, the potential of the civil war's protagonists to expose and exploit these weaknesses, and to determine the impact of this dynamic on the mission's level of success.

UN MISSIONS IN CIVIL WARS: A FRAMEWORK FOR ANALYSIS

The weaknesses most likely to be present in UN missions are vulnerable to common aspects of civil war conflict dynamics. When the calculations of the belligerents motivate them to attack or exploit these mission weaknesses, they are likely to frustrate the mission's ability to resolve the civil war. In this way, mission weaknesses and civil war calculations exist in a dynamic relationship with an observable effect on the success of UN missions. This section constructs a framework that allows the identification of whether weaknesses exist in UN missions, the action on these weaknesses by the conflict dynamic, and the effect of the presence or absence of this interaction on the missions' levels of success. The framework argues that the level of vulnerability of the UN mission to exploitation or rejection by the civil war's protagonists is determined by the mission's objectives, the appropriateness of the response formulated, the effectiveness of the mission design, the links of UN members to the belligerents, and the durability of the mission. Whether each of these aspects of the mission will become a vulnerability in the civil war is determined by the belligerents' interests, military position, changes in tactics in response to the mission, dependence on external support, and morale and cohesion. The following five sections compare the UN's and the belligerents' objectives; the appropriateness of the mission's presence in the military balance; the strength of the mission design with alterations in the belligerents' tactics; the existence of UN members' links to the belligerents with the belligerents' reliance on external support; and the mission's durability with the belligerents' morale and cohesion.

Objectives

Every UN mission that is dispatched is given instructions on what it is expected to achieve, either in the form of a set of guidelines, a mandate, or provisions of a peace treaty. The objectives of the UN mission can be its most fundamental vulnerability or strength, as determined by how achievable and appropriate they are to conditions on the ground. These objectives will be directly derived from the UN coalition's diagnosis of the conflict, as distorted by all of the assumptions and motivations attending the consideration of civil wars. The objectives are further determined by the coalition members' preoccupation with their international position and domestic tenure. The achievability of the mission's objectives is based on the accuracy of the diagnosis and the presence of extrinsic or irrelevant or clashing interests among the coalition members. The objectives can also be affected by the extreme state-centrism that pervades the UN, and the self-perception of most states as the custodians of international order.[65] This means that the objectives set each mission will usually be in the form of an authoritatively stated normative vision of a preferred outcome as informed by the sponsoring coalition's diagnosis of the conflict and assumptions and interests. Compounding any difficulties in the achievability of these objectives can be varying degrees of vagueness that result from the negotiations of disagreeing coalition partners.

The achievability of the objectives of the UN mission is determined to a large extent by the willingness of the belligerents to cooperate with the mission. This is because UN missions rarely have sufficient military power, resources, or sanctions to create the conditions for their own success by influencing the belligerents and the conflict environment. Belligerents' cooperation or opposition to the UN mission's objectives is based on their calculations of how the mission will impact on their self-interest and survival. Their reaction when confronted by a UN mission or any other actor is determined by a cost–benefit calculation of the opportunities and dangers of the situation. Operating in an anarchic relationship makes the belligerents 'self-regarding', in that they view all interactions and interlocutors in terms of opportunities to advance, or the dangers posed to, their own interests. The consequences of self-help make each belligerent dependent on its own use or promise of violence or restraint to advance its interests and control dangers.[66] If the UN mission's objective denies the interests for which it has been fighting, or threatens its existence, the belligerent will most likely react to remove the danger. If the belligerents can see an opportunity to advance their interests through the peace process recommended by the UN, they are likely to calculate that cooperation with the UN mission is in their best interests. Thus it can be seen that the basic diagnosis of the conflict, and the normative objectives set by the coalition, can be either a vulnerability or an advantage for the mission. This is decided by whether the objectives are relevant to any possibilities for advancement or safety existing within the belligerents' calculations. As will be seen in the rest of the framework, the basic liability of objectives that are disagreeable to one of the belligerents, can trigger the exposure of other weaknesses, and the use of these to exploit or frustrate the mission.

Mission Presence and the Military Balance

Often the accuracy of the diagnosis, and the achievability of the objectives, determine the appropriateness of the UN intervention. Whether the conflict can be resolved in the way envisaged by the UN coalition in the mission's mandate is usually linked to whether the presence of the UN mission is acceptable to the belligerents. The appropriateness of the UN presence usually depends on whether, as assumed in all UN conflict resolution missions, it is possible at that time to substitute instead of war a peaceful method for apportioning the disputed bases of the conflict. Again, the assessment of whether this is a desirable presence and proposal is the prerogative of the belligerents. If they opt for trying to achieve their goals through cooperating with a UN intermediary, the intervention will be welcome and appropriate; if not, the UN presence will be seen as an irritating impediment to military and political progress, or as a danger to the movement. A UN mission can also be a useful opportunity for manipulation by uncooperative belligerents. This is a situation where the mission is welcome, but still inappropriate – it is exploited by the belligerents, usually to the frustration of its original instructions. The other method in which UN missions can become unwelcome is by appearing to be unduly helpful to a belligerent's opponents. The loss of impartiality of a UN mission can result from its mandate, or from its manipulation by one of the parties in the conflict. For these reasons, the inappropriate introduction of a UN mission can be a significant liability, by encouraging the belligerents to either exploit it or frustrate it.

The appearance of each new factor in the conflict – including a UN mission – causes all rational belligerents to recalculate the opportunities and dangers posed by their environment, and the impact of the new factor. The appropriateness of the UN mission, and the acceptability of its offer to act as an intermediary in place of the war, is determined by the belligerents' perception of whether such an offer presents an opportunity, an impediment, or a threat, to their interests. Primary in the calculations about the wisdom of abandoning or persevering with the war, is the success of the war, and the belligerent's military position and momentum. Each belligerent will question whether the continued use of violence will be the most effective course in promoting or protecting its interests. Furthermore, it will appraise the UN mission's proposal to see whether the promotion and protection of its interests will be better served through the UN intermediary than through violence. Thus a militarily secure or preponderant belligerent will most likely reject the UN mission as either an obstacle to the achievement of its objectives or an unwelcome intervention trying to cajole it into a disadvantageous peace. But if the military balance is characterized by 'mutual or painful stalemates marked by recent or impending catastrophe; [when] both parties' efforts at unilateral solutions . . . are blocked . . . bilateral solutions . . . are achievable'.[67] In other words, if a continuation of the war is more dangerous to a belligerent's interests, or more threatening to its survival than entering a UN-brokered peace process, the belligerent is likely to enter that peace process, if all of its concerns about safety are satisfied. Hence the belligerents' military positions strongly determine their reaction to the presence of the UN mission. If the mission promises to rescue them from sudden catastrophe or impending defeat, they are likely to cooperate with the mission, despite other weaknesses within the mission. The success of the mission despite these vulnerabilities, however, depends on a similar decision to cooperate among *all* of the protagonists in the civil war. If any of the belligerents see the UN mission's presence as an impediment or threat to its military success, it is likely to work to frustrate or exploit the mission.

Mission Design and Belligerents' Tactics

The design of the UN mission is usually based on templates of previous UN interventions: mediation, peacekeeping, peacebuilding. Any variations in the mission design – its mission agenda and timetable, its level of armament and strength, its number and origin of personnel, its status of forces agreement, its rules of engagement – are determined by the sponsoring coalition's desired resolution of the war. An important influence on mission design is the parsimony of the sponsoring member-states, and their perception of the importance of the threat. The mission design can be a significant vulnerability or strength for the UN mission, because it determines the levels and effectiveness of the mission's influence mechanisms over the conflict dynamic. The mission design determines the mission's access to force, diplomatic pressure, and sanctions. Whether the mission design becomes a liability for the mission is closely linked to the appropriateness of the intervention: if the intervention is acceptable to the belligerents, inadequacies in its design can either be managed or rectified. If, however, the mission's presence is seen instrumentally or adversely by any of the belligerents, weaknesses in the mission's design become tangible targets for attacking, marginalizing, or exploiting the mission.

Among the belligerents, the type and configuration of the mission determines how they react to it. If a UN mission offers a realistic peace, and is configured to deliver that peace, they are more likely to take seriously the option of cooperating with it. If it is obviously a token response from the sponsoring coalition, trusting and cooperating with it will be seen as a risky option. Whatever their calculations, belligerents will always adjust their tactics to factor in the UN mission. The tactical modifications will be calculated to take advantage of the opportunities and to minimize the dangers of the UN presence. The greatest modification in tactics is the abandonment of war by a belligerent that decides to cooperate with the UN mission. This decision is usually linked to the belief that the peace process proposed by the UN will advance and protect its interests more effectively than the continued use of violence. Furthermore, a belligerent will only submit to a peace process that it sees as giving it a reasonable chance of attaining its objectives, and which will protect it if it does not succeed in gaining, sharing, or retaining political power. If the mission is calculated to be a threat or impediment, the belligerent's tactics will be modified to allow it to either attack the mission, as another, weaker, combatant in the conflict; or to marginalize the mission, by withholding its cooperation with the peace process; or to exploit the mission for its own purposes, by making military use of ceasefire lines and protection zones, hijacking UN personnel and supplies, or using the mission to manipulate international actors. Thus the belligerent's choice of strategy and tactics determines whether, and how, it will take advantage of the UN mission design's vulnerabilities.

Links and External Support

One of the most potent mechanisms of influence a mission has over the civil war conflict dynamic is UN member-states' use of sponsoring links to modify protagonists' behaviour. This can be a powerful method of offsetting the vulnerabilities of UN missions, by forcing the belligerents to forgo strategies of attacking or exploiting mission weaknesses: 'internal disputants have . . . found themselves under considerable pressure to settle . . . the UN Security Council . . . has shown a willingness to get involved in a variety of situations, cajoling, pushing and sometimes threatening parties towards the negotiating table'.[68] There are several conditions for the existence of these mechanisms of influence, however. The first is that member-states have or have had a sponsoring link with a belligerent, that can be manipulated in a way that allows it to pressure a behavioural change. The second is that the member-states are willing to use their individual or collective influence over the belligerents they supported in such a way as to provide the UN mission with leverage over them. This condition is affected by member-states' self-interest as well: their readiness to manipulate these links on behalf of the UN depends on their calculations of whether the success of the UN's mission is more important than the unilateral interests that initially prompted the sponsorship of their client. If member-states calculate the UN's success is not more important, this can create serious problems for the mission, often resulting in these states continuing to sponsor the belligerents in opposition to the UN mission.

Among the belligerents, dependence on external supporters can determine the pliability of the conflict dynamic to settlement by the UN mission. The extent and manipulation of these support conduits determines the leverage of the mission, either to protect its vulnerabilities from attack or exploitation, or to influence the belligerents to cooperate with the conflict resolution process. If a belligerent is independent of external links, this source of leverage is unavailable to the UN. If these external links do exist, the most common way of exerting pressure through them is to threaten to cut off support to non-cooperative clients, a move that can have serious consequences for a belligerent's military position. This factor inevitably affects a belligerent's calculus of war and peace, and isolation is likely to increase its cooperativeness. However, external sponsors can also apply much subtler methods of pressure and persuasion, by issuing ideological directives, or unilateral guarantees, or even by offering to increase the flow of resources to that client. On the other hand, the continued support and supply by a sponsor of a belligerent defying or exploiting a UN mission can act to strengthen its morale and military position, thereby hardening its opposition to the mission, and its determination to exploit its weaknesses. So the extent of UN member-state links to civil war belligerents can be either a factor giving the mission resilience, or an added liability for the mission.

Mission Durability and Belligerent Morale and Cohesion

The durability of a UN mission can be a modifying factor on the targeting or exploitation of its weaknesses, by giving that mission a resilience to achieve some of its objectives despite the existence and aggravation of significant weaknesses. On the other hand, a fragile mission will be frustrated or repulsed by a few attacks against its vulnerabilities. The durability of UN missions seems to be strongly connected to the extent of agreement between the members of its sponsoring coalition and troops and resource contributors on the problem at hand. As stated above, the extent of agreement determines the clarity of the mandate and the purposiveness of the mission. However, even within the most cohesive coalitions, members constantly reassess their commitment to the mission according to the events affecting the mission and the conflict, and their impact on the members' interests. These reassessments, and the levels of agreement and commitment within the coalition, can lead either to the desire and commitment to press ahead; the pusillanimous downgrading of the response to preserve the diplomatic agreement; or unilateral withdrawal from the coalition or mission. The level of concerted direction that a mission derives from the nature of its sponsoring coalition can be a modifying factor in the influence of mission vulnerabilities on success levels, by determining whether the mission will be completely marginalized or exploited, or whether it will battle on in adverse circumstances and achieve partial success.

Like external links, morale and cohesion can influence belligerents' calculations and cooperativeness. If morale is low and cohesion problematic, belligerents are likely to be more receptive to the peace process and the influence of the UN mission. If morale is strong and cohesion favourable, a protagonist is likely to have the confidence and strength to attack or exploit the mission's vulnerabilities. The morale and cohesion of each belligerent affect calculations of its position in the military balance, its ability to promote and protect its interests through the continued effective use of violence, and its internally defined ability and willingness to fight on. Morale can be seriously affected by war-weariness and threaten the impending implosion of the belligerent's military machine. It can also be bolstered by successes or new opportunities, or hardened by new dangers, to fight on. Excessive factionalism can serve as a warning of the impending weakening of the belligerent's military forces and looming catastrophe in its military fortunes. It can also be a stimulus for extremism and recalcitrance in response to military adversity. Extremist factions, opposing the leadership's commitment to peace and compromise, may launch attacks against the delicate structures and guarantees of trust at the start of the peace process, thereby destroying the process by provoking retaliation by former opponents against their entire movement. Factionalized or decentralized belligerents can also find it difficult to enforce compliance with the terms of peace agreements on all of their cadres, often ruling out the peace option. Thus the morale and cohesion of the belligerents can also act to modify, or aggravate, the vulnerabilities of UN missions.

Thus each possible mission weakness identified has a corresponding source within the conflict dynamic that determines its vulnerability to attack or marginalization. In this way, this framework will be used to search for weaknesses within UN missions and their aggravation by aspects of the civil war, and to assess how this relationship affects the mission's progress. The framework should also show whether these weaknesses or conflict features are cumulative or whether they modify each other. The case studies highlight the other, pervading weakness of UN conflict resolution missions – that to completely succeed, they need the cooperation of all of the belligerents. In applying the framework to the case studies in the following chapters, it becomes clear that it usually only takes the adverse calculations and non-cooperative behaviour of one of the belligerents to target and act on a mission's weaknesses to frustrate its mandate.

If weaknesses exist and are prey to aggravation by civil war dynamics in failed missions, it will support the argument of this book. If the weaknesses are absent or fail to be exposed by the conflict dynamic in successful missions, it will further support the argument of this book. The argument is that the failures of UN missions are directly attributable to common, structural weaknesses that are especially vulnerable in civil wars. As will become clear in the succeeding pages, it is distracted and self-obsessed UN member-states and their close involvement with the design and dispatch of UN missions, that are primarily culpable for these common structural weaknesses.

2 Mediation

After the issue of calls for an end to the fighting, mediation is often the UN's conflict resolution mechanism of first choice. The frequent use of this mechanism in part reflects the ease of dispatching a mediation mission. The briefcase and suit of the mediator contrasts sharply with the blue helmets and armoured personnel carriers of peacekeepers as they enter a civil war; yet as they begin their work, they begin to exhibit many of the same features and vulnerabilities shared by all UN missions. This chapter searches for the weaknesses identified by the analytical framework, and the consequences of their exposure to resistant aspects of the civil wars, within an unsuccessful mediation mission and a successful one. If the weaknesses are present and vulnerable to resistance from the conflict dynamic in the unsuccessful mediation mission, but are absent or not accentuated in the successful mediation, it will begin to establish the responsibility of these structural weaknesses for UN mission failures in civil wars.

Mediation, whether in international or civil wars, is a voluntary, peaceful intervention[1] designed to affect the conflict situation towards a peaceful resolution.[2] A mediator enters the dispute to establish, as an intermediary, a non-military channel of interaction between the disputants. Mediation is an attempt to substitute negotiation for warfare as a method of apportioning the disputed commodities at the base of the conflict.[3] A UN mediator is most commonly dispatched as a representative of either a UN forum or of the Secretary-General. Mediation missions carry a number of advantages for the organization dispatching them that have resulted in their repeated use by the UN. They are much cheaper and easier to organize than other types of UN missions, such as peacekeeping forces or peacebuilding teams. This means that for the organization and its member-states, they demand a low level of commitment and resources, while their speed of dispatch allows the UN and its members to be seen to be responding in some way to the latest outrage or conflict. Mediation missions are also extremely flexible in what they can be sent to do, and are often most appropriate for the early stages of a violent or bitter conflict. For this reason, they are sometimes sent to explore whether a solution is able to be brokered at that stage of the conflict. If a solution can be found, the UN relies on the mediators to secure an agreement that its peacekeepers and peacebuilders can oversee the implementation of.[4]

While a mediator's mission is to some extent experimental, he or she also must be mindful of the mandate that the UN wishes to be carried out.

Mediation missions are never sent without being given a detailed set of instructions on the conflict and its preferred form of resolution. These instructions emerge either informally from the Secretary-General in consultation with concerned states, or from resolutions authoritatively stating the principles upon which a peace agreement should be based. While usually reflecting a desire for a peaceful, acceptable solution, these instructions are also shaped by the UN's diagnosis of the conflict and the interests of its member-states.[5] The mission is designed to use its detachment from the conflict to break up the conflict dynamic and reach a creative solution: 'Redefining the issues in conflict, or finding a formula for its resolution or management is the key to its termination, with parties frequently finding a solution hidden in the morass of bad relationships or in constructing a solution from the pieces of the conflict itself.'[6] A mediator, through providing a non-military form of interaction between the disputants, is able to provide alternative perceptions and costings of the conflict: 'Parties involved in a conflict . . . are not likely to have sufficient knowledge either of the sources of their conflictual relationships, or of the options available to resolve them. In the absence of adequate knowledge, there can be no accurate costing of policies, or of the consequence of behaviours.'[7] Most UN mediators approach the resolution of the conflict deductively, by devising a general formula for negotiation that is designed to alter the parties' terms of reference towards the dispute from a zero-sum equation to a mutually benefiting trade-off of items of differing value.[8] Mediators try to gain the parties' agreement on the definition of the conflict, the formula for negotiation, and the principles susceptible to agreement. Then, according to a cumulative timetable of negotiations, they try to negotiate trade-offs and agreements on matters of increasing specificity. They attempt to maintain the strict confidentiality of the negotiations, as a way of deflecting public scrutiny, maintaining a dispassionate atmosphere, and allowing greater flexibility and creativity during negotiations.[9] Such a discrete channel of talks can also allow belligerents to make concessions without risking their reputations, support, or future bargaining positions.[10]

While these mechanisms give mediators a high level of control over the process of the negotiations, the nature of mediation gives them little control over the outcome. [11] The mediation relationship is highly consensual: it is non-coercive in process, and the extent to which former belligerents are bound by its result depends on their satisfaction with the outcomes.[12] To have any chance as the beginning to a resolution of the conflict, the peace talks and agreement need to include all major participants in the conflict. This arises from the 'double veto' which underlies all peace talks, wherein both parties can block a negotiated solution if it does not satisfy them, but can also prevent a unilateral solution from taking place if it excludes them.[13] From the point of view of the belligerents, negotiating an end to the war takes place as a cumulative process of making conditional commitments: each undertakes to carry out certain measures if opponents are faithful in implementing those measures that they have agreed to.[14] Often belligerents will be more inclined to participate in mediated talks because of their consensual nature, knowing that they can withdraw from the talks at any time without risking any military or political resources. For this reason, belligerents often enter negotiations as an experiment, to see what they are able to gain from the peace talks, and to gauge how much their opponents are prepared to concede.

These characteristics, of both the UN mediators and the belligerents entering mediated talks, impart a certain character on mediation missions to civil wars. The high level of consensuality of the process makes the missions more vulnerable to belligerent non-cooperation and exploitation as they try to negotiate an end to certain civil wars. While these peculiarities exist in mediation, these missions share many of the same vulnerabilities as other types of UN missions. These will be searched for first within the mediation missions in which the UN participated in Bosnia, and then in the UN mediation mission to El Salvador. The existence and location of these weaknesses will be compared between the cases, particularly in the extent to which they were prey to the respective conflict dynamics, in what way they were responsible for the failure of the Bosnia negotiations, and whether they were absent from the successful El Salvador mission.

BOSNIA-HERZEGOVINA: SPEAKING INTO A HURRICANE

In March 1992, ethnic Serbs began a secessionist insurgency against the Republic of Bosnia-Herzegovina,[15] which had recently voted for independence from Yugoslavia by referendum,[16] and been granted diplomatic recognition by the EU, the UN, and most of the international community.[17] Fighting against being absorbed into a state dominated by other ethnic groups, the Bosnian Serbs embarked on a project of carving a 'greater Serbia' from the constituent republics of the former Yugoslavia.[18] The Bosnian Serbs felt betrayed by the international community, which they believed had consigned them to minority status and possible genocide in the newly independent republics. Initially with the help of the Yugoslav National Army (JNA), they were able to quickly seize and hold 70 per cent of Bosnia, and link these areas with Serbia and the Krajina region of Croatia.[19] In the areas they controlled, they carried out widespread policies of ethnic cleansing, to rid them of Muslims, Croats, and undesirable Serbs.[20] The other ethnic groups in Bosnia, the Muslims and the Croats, organized a makeshift defence against the ferocity of the Bosnian Serb assault. Heavily outgunned, outsupplied, and out-trained by the Bosnian Serb army (VRS), they clung tenuously for over three years of war to pockets of the 30 per cent of Bosnian territory they were able to deny to the VRS. The Bosnian Muslim and Croat armies slowly mobilized into mass conscript armies, but their essential vulnerability to the VRS's weapons predominance was perpetuated by the UN arms embargo around the former Yugoslavia.[21] This stalemate was to last, virtually unchanged, until the Bosnian Serbs were weakened by sustained NATO airstrikes in September 1995, and suffered substantial losses of territory to a combined Bosnian Muslim–Croat offensive. The changed circumstances were to lead all of the parties to sign the Dayton Peace Accords in November 1995.

The UN, concerned with the growing security threat and humanitarian tragedy of the war in Bosnia-Herzegovina and the destructive effect of the conflict on the cohesion of the international community, engaged in a frantic effort to mediate a solution from the beginning of the conflict in March 1992. In the first weeks of the war in Bosnia, the Security Council initiated the mediation process by requesting the Secretary-General to dispatch his Special Envoy[22] to assist the peace efforts of the EU.[23] In this capacity, Special Envoy Cyrus Vance had already met with Muslem, ethnic Serb, and ethnic Croat leaders in Sarajevo on 6 March 1992, obtaining their agreement to seek a peaceful settlement of their differences. By September 1992, the EU and the UN had established the International Conference on the Former Yugoslavia (ICFY) in London as a formal mechanism to coordinate their mediation efforts. Co-chaired by the UN Special Representative and the EU Envoy, the ICFY consisted of a Steering Committee and six Working Groups meeting in Geneva to 'prepare the basis for a general settlement and associated measures',[24] in support of the efforts of the mediators. In this way, UN mediators played a collaborative but significant role in efforts to mediate an end to the war in Bosnia. They were involved in three significant mediation initiatives: the Vance–Owen Plan, the Serb–Croat proposal, and the Contact Group Plan. Each of these failed to gain Bosnian Serb agreement. By late 1994, the UN's mediation role was largely moribund, having been repeatedly frustrated by Bosnian Serb obduracy. Thereafter, mediation was largely conducted by the Western Contact Group and carried out by US diplomats. It was Richard Holbrooke, as US Special Envoy, who finally brokered the Dayton Peace Accord. The UN's lack of success points to serious weaknesses in the mediation mission, and ultimately the unsuitability of a UN mediation initiative to bring an end to the conflict. The application of the analytical framework to the Bosnia negotiations will reveal the location and extent of the weaknesses in the mission, how vulnerable these were to aggravation by the conflict dynamic of the Bosnian civil war, and what effect these weaknesses had on the ultimate failure of the UN to mediate a solution in Bosnia.

Objectives

The most fundamental faultline in the UN's mediation mission to Bosnia originated in its sponsoring coalition within the UN. The states in this grouping brought widely diverging interests in Bosnia to each meeting, coupled with a timidity about getting too closely involved with the war. The sources of these member-states' motivations are complex. At one level, the states in the Bosnia grouping were motivated by their own interests, as impacted on by the war, and considerations like relative gains[25] and duties and obligations within alliances. Eager to test their new security independence after the Cold War, the EU states originally claimed the response to the crisis was the 'hour of Europe'. Acquiescing to a new stridency in German foreign policy,[26] the members of the EU recognized the sovereignty of the seceding Yugoslav republics, eventually carrying the US and the UN reluctantly with them, and to some extent hastening the onset of hostilities. Seeing its attempts at conflict resolution fail, the EU called for UN involvement in October 1991.[27] The Europeans in the Security Council, headed by Britain and France in the Permanent Five, thereafter formed the core of the sponsoring coalition of UN mediation efforts. From this genesis, Britain and France, in order to gain significant concessions within the EU,[28] and to retain influence within NATO,[29] struggled to maintain their supremacy in setting UN policy on Bosnia. Most of the UN's mediation and peacekeeping initiatives were instigated by these two states. Their perception of the Bosnian conflict as a civil war to be contained and resolved informed early UN decisions on Bosnia, and, as embodied by the large European contingents among the UNPROFOR II peacekeeping force, this perception was to remain the basis of official UN policy.

After initially acceding to European dominance in responding to the Yugoslav wars as a way of retreating from its 'global policeman' role, the US became involved with the activation of a UN response. Much of the disunity in the sponsoring coalition on Bosnia stemmed from disagreements between the US and the European coalition partners. The American position on Bosnia was determined by a different perception of the conflict, which saw the war in Bosnia as an international conflict, in which the sovereignty of a UN member-state was threatened by external intervention.[30]

Initially the US contemplated military intervention on behalf of the Bosnian government, but thereafter acceded to the European position of containment, relief, and negotiations, in the interests of retaining unity with Western Europe. This accession was neither consistent nor gracious, combining domestic attacks on the pusillanimity of the Europeans, with official attempts to challenge the European-formulated UN response in Bosnia. The US declined to contribute peacekeeping forces to Bosnia;[31] a fact that became a source of acrimony with the Western Europeans as the US began to advocate its policy of lifting the arms embargo on the Bosnian government and shifting the military balance in its favour using surgical airstrikes.[32] The American 'lift and strike' proposal was to become a symbol of the divisions within the Bosnia coalition, being advocated by the US but opposed by the Europeans, whose peacekeepers in Bosnia would have come under attack during the resulting escalation in the war. The Europeans, particularly the French, showed their annoyance at American reluctance to pressure the Bosnian government to accept various peace plans advocated by the UN. The dissenting American position led to splits between the European coalition partners; Britain and France expressed their irritation when German Chancellor Kohl advocated lifting the embargo on the Bosnian government at a private EU dinner on 21 June 1993 after correspondence with US President Clinton.[33]

Other dissenting members of the sponsoring coalition were the Russian Federation and Greece, largely sympathetic to the Bosnian Serb position. The Russian Federation, in particular, had vital geopolitical interests in the Bosnian conflict and the international response. Worried about the expansion of NATO influence into Eastern Europe, Russia was concerned to forestall a vigorous Western intervention in the Bosnian conflict. Consequently, Russia became closely involved in the Bosnia coalition, chiefly to guard against an assertive Western response, and placing a series of diplomatic obstacles in front of any changes to the passive UN policy in Bosnia, particularly those advocating punishing or pressuring the Serbs. The Russian leadership, determined to dampen right-wing opposition, and to appear independent of Western policy in this traditional area of Russian influence, repeatedly warned that Russia 'would not allow attempts to solve the problems in Bosnia without Russia'.[34] The Western members of the coalition, particularly sensitive to preserving the tenure of the Yeltsin regime in Russia, restrained their own initiatives to coincide with the Russian position.[35] Greece had its own geopolitical incentives to be supportive of Bosnian Serb positions in the face of Western activism. Locked in a long rivalry with Turkey, the Greeks worked hard to stay within the coalition and moderate any forceful pro-Muslim action by it. Turkey found common cause with the Muslim states in their sympathy with the largely Muslim Bosnian government, and who advocate lifting the embargo and helping Bosnia defend its sovereignty.[36] In an anomaly common in such complex and fractured coalitions, the US repeatedly found support for its policies among Islamic states with which it had hitherto experienced decades of antagonistic relations.[37]

Further complicating these clashing interests were the imperatives forced on the states by the domestic passions aroused by the war. The ferocity and visibility of the war in Bosnia stimulated a wave of international horror, and determined that much of the international response to the crisis was dictated by states responding to the demands of their publics to do something. These reactions were, however, tempered by a reluctance to become heavily involved in the conflict. Public pressure often hampered government attempts to moderate their diplomatic responses and relations with the other members of the coalition. Repeatedly states were pushed into more extreme or intransigent positions by media and domestic criticism of the governments or their coalition partners. Among American and Western European publics there was outrage at the excesses of the war and the pusillanimity of the international response. These tended to be echoed within the Islamic world, and embellished with claims that the international response was a way of ensuring the genocide of the Muslims in Europe.[38] The supporters of the Bosnian Serbs – the Russians and the Greeks – to a large extent adopted the opposite position because of the religious, historic, and ethnic ties between their populations and the Serbs. The effect of domestic pressure was therefore to exacerbate tensions within the coalition. Hence, the number of the great powers with strongly held interests in the Bosnian crisis necessitated the creation of a large sponsoring coalition for UN initiatives on Bosnia. The extent of divergence between these states' positions produced a limited and faltering response to the crisis. Much of the UN's diplomatic activity and policy responses were more attempts to preserve the fragile coalition than to address resolution possibilities within the conflict. This consideration deprived the UN response of much of its coherence and purpose.[39] These passions and interests were not sufficient to trigger a significant response from any of the states in the coalition. Proposals for a Gulf War-type operation were mooted by the Islamic states and the Non-Aligned Movement, but rejected due to the massive casualties that would be suffered by any offensive intervening force.[40] This inevitably led to states turning to the UN as a mechanism through which they could mount a response while sharing the risks and costs.

The weaknesses that these divisions within its sponsoring coalition placed in the UN mediation mission were magnified by the coalition's fundamental misunderstanding of the conflict and its required response. The misdiagnosis arose partly from the UN's unique involvement in the origins of the wars in the former Yugoslavia. Having in part prompted the conflict through recognizing the break-away republics, and watched with horror the ferocity of the wars, the UN's members saw no alternative but to attempt to adhere to the logic of this decision in their efforts to end the war. On 18 May 1992[41] Bosnia sought, and was granted, UN recognition of its sovereignty as an independent state, and membership of the organization as a sovereign state after fulfilling the Carrington Arbitration Commission's requirement of two-thirds of its voters' support for independence in a referendum. This made it incumbent on the UN to uphold the sovereign prerogatives of Bosnia: '. . . which, as a State Member of the United Nations, enjoys the rights provided for in the Charter of the United Nations'.[42] Foremost among these rights were '. . . the sovereignty, territorial integrity and political independence of the Republic of Bosnia and Herzegovina and the responsibility of the Security Council in this regard'.[43] Having tolerated the break-up of the former Yugoslavia by the consent of its populations, the UN invoked the international legal principle of *uti possedetis* in refusing to tolerate the further break-up of its constituent republics through the use of force: 'Bosnia and Herzegovina should remain a sovereign, independent, integral and multi-ethnic State in which all parts of the population could live in peace in accordance with their respective cultures and traditions.'[44] Accordingly, the UN, the ICFY co-chairmen, and the mediators '. . . deemed it necessary to reject any model based on three separate ethnic/confessionally based states'.[45] This entailed an explicit statement that the UN's '. . . primary objective remains to reverse the consequences of the use of force and to allow all persons displaced from their homes in the Republic of Bosnia and Herzegovina to return to their homes in peace'.[46] It was from these obligations that the misdiagnosis of the conflict arose: that the conflict in Bosnia was largely over issues of autonomy and self-government, rather than of ethnic assertiveness, deep fear of being 'culturally swamped', and a brutal complex of desires to live in ethnically pure states.[47]

The misdiagnosis led inevitably to the formulation of an inappropriate response. A mediation mission and a protection force were sent to reverse the results of a brutal ethnic war. The mediators were instructed to achieve 'the withdrawal of Bosnian Serb troops from territories occupied by force',[48] the reversal of '. . . the practice of "ethnic cleansing" [which] is unlawful and unacceptable, and will not be permitted to affect the outcome of the negotiations on constitutional arrangements for the Republic of Bosnia and Herzegovina',[49] and the return of 'all displaced persons . . . in peace to their former homes'.[50] The objective of the UN coalition in dispatching the mediation mission was to secure a lasting solution to the conflict based on the principles of:

> immediate and complete cessation of hostilities; withdrawal from territories seized by the use of force and 'ethnic cleansing'; reversal of the consequences of 'ethnic cleansing' and recognition of the right of all refugees to return to their homes; and respect for the sovereignty, territorial integrity and independence of the Republic of Bosnia and Herzegovina.[51]

These results were to be the outcome of 'a negotiated solution freely arrived at'.[52] With this configuration of states and instructions as its basis, the UN mediation mission was deeply vulnerable before it even neared Bosnia.

In this deeply complex civil war, the disputants' interests and objectives inevitably diverged on the way they viewed the UN interventions. The government of Bosnia, only in existence since the first free elections in Bosnia in November 1990, had watched in fear as all around it the republics of Yugoslavia imploded in bitter ethnic conflict. Pushed towards calling a referendum on independence by the disintegration rather than transformation of Yugoslavia, the government had watched the Bosnians that polled vote overwhelmingly for independence and recognition such as that given to Slovenia and Croatia.[53] Then the secessionist war that the Bosnian Serbs had threatened for so long descended on Bosnia. Deserted by the JNA, which it had hoped would protect Bosnia, the Bosnian government, with no army of its own, watched the Serbs rapidly conquer 70 per cent of Bosnian territory. As its appeals for help to defend itself brought no substantive response, the Bosnian government felt it had been betrayed by the very international community that had recognized its sovereignty. Over time, it organized an army, mainly of Muslims, and began to fight for an independent multi-ethnic Bosnia of the internationally recognized pre-war boundaries.[54] Finding its severe disadvantage relative to the Bosnian Serbs in weaponry was perpetuated by the UN arms embargo, the Bosnian government became dependent on the international community to redress the balance through its peacekeeping and mediation missions.[55] Consequently, the Bosnian government's interests were largely in accord with those of the UN mediators; indeed it found itself in a position where it had little choice but to cooperate with UN missions.

While the Bosnian Croats had territorial designs on Bosnia similar to the Serbs, they found it in their interests to cooperate with the UN mission for two reasons. The first was that, able to draw on only 18 per cent of the population, and without the help of the JNA, the Croats could not hope to advance their cause militarily, and had to rely on diplomatic means to advance their interests. The second was that the government of Croatia had, since early 1991, played a clever propaganda game, retaining the sympathy and support of the international community while pursuing ethnic territorial goals every bit as cynical as those of the Serbs.[56] Both of these imperatives dictated the policies of the Bosnian Croats. Their alliance at the war's beginning with the Bosnian government was dictated by military weakness and a desire to protect the strategically vulnerable Croatian state, with two long prongs of territory athwart Bosnia, from further encroachment by the pan-Serb state. These considerations were to prompt them to break the alliance in June 1993 and begin to fight the Bosnian government in central Bosnia, often in alliance with the Serbs. This phase of the war ended in March 1994 with the signing of the Washington agreement establishing a Muslim–Croat federation, brokered by US envoy Charles Redman. At most stages of the war, irrespective of their particular military tactics, the Croats opted to cooperate with the UN and its mediation mission as a way of diplomatically securing their interests.

It was the Bosnian Serbs whose interests were so implacably opposed to those of the mediators. Their position was based on the contention that 'as far as they are concerned the independent State of Bosnia and Herzegovina has never existed and does not exist [and] . . . that it is being forced by the international community to live within Bosnia and Herzegovina against its wishes'.[57] The Bosnian Serbs demand the same right to exercize self-determination as was extended to the former Yugoslav republics after the international community ignored their objections to Bosnia seceding from Yugoslavia. They refused to live as minorities in states ruled by other ethnic groups. Serbian President Slobodan Milosovic placed their demands in political–legal terms when he asserted that the boundaries of the republics in federal Yugoslavia were administrative, and that it was nations, rather than republics, that were sovereign.[58] They recommended partitioning Bosnia along the lines dictated by military holdings, which would have awarded the Serb state over 70 per cent of Bosnian territory. These Bosnian Serb areas, according to leaders Karadzic and Mladic, had to be linked territorially and be cleansed of communities other than Serbs.

Bosnian Serb military action took over a vast majority of Bosnian territory in the first six months of the war, and by the time the mediators presented a peace proposal to them, '. . . the reality on the ground was that Serb-held areas were already joined on the map; Serb military leaders would never sacrifice these links, which were a key element in their own plans'.[59] Any surrender of territory held was completely unacceptable to the Bosnian Serb military, led by General Mladic, who stated that the lines of conquest 'have been traced in Serbian blood and no one has the right to erase them'.[60] The Bosnian Serbs wanted eventually to unite with Serbia and the Krajina Serbs in Croatia, and wanted their holdings to be contiguous with the territories of their ethnic kin. They defended their claim to 70 per cent of Bosnian territory for 31 per cent of the pre-war Bosnian population by asserting that the Serbs in Bosnia were predominantly rural, and that the Muslims and Croats would retain the major cities and natural resources of the state.[61] These adamantly held Bosnian Serb objectives were incompatible with the solution proposed by the UN mediators. This basic aspect of the conflict dynamic, and the military preponderance of the party with these objectives, were to expose the UN mediators' fundamental weakness, that of having been given objectives that were inappropriate to the situation or their capabilities.

Mission Presence and the Military Balance

The misdiagnosis of the conflict by the UN inevitably led it to prescribe an inappropriate response. The mediators had been deprived of all flexibility to find a solution to the conflict by the sponsoring coalition's strict instructions. The UN and ICFY mediators' roles of 'clarifying the issues'[62] and acting as a 'channel of communication to clarify ideas and proposals advanced by the parties during discussions',[63] were nullified by their advocacy of definite objectives for the peace process. While the mission was welcomed by the government and acceded to by the Bosnian Croats, the legitimacy of its presence and objectives were never recognized by the Bosnian Serbs. To the Serbs, the UN mission and the ICFY's objectives threatened to take away their hard-won territorial gains, and were an attempt to once more swamp the Serb ethnic group within the Muslim Bosnian state.[64] The UN's admission and recognition of Bosnia-Herzegovina, its dedication to defend its sovereignty and unity, and its advocacy of the interests of the Bosnian government and Muslim population,[65] made it more of an arbiter[66] or a participant in the dispute than a suitable third party. The Bosnian Serb distrust of the mediators was further deepened by the adversarial way in which the UN began to characterize them. Since the first reports by the media and its own human rights rapporteurs,[67] the UN regularly expressed horror at the practice of ethnic cleansing and condemned the Bosnian Serbs as its perpetrators.[68] The Security Council repeatedly denounced the practice of ethnic cleansing and expressed concern over its use in 'the pattern of hostilities by Bosnian Serb paramilitary units'.[69] Such prejudices necessarily had an adverse effect on the negotiating process:

> The *a priori* negative characterization of one of the parties in a conflict is a sure disincentive for them even to appear at the bargaining table, and in turn can well provide the rationale for the other belligerents to refuse to participate in the process. Labelling has a powerful impact not only on the warring parties, but on the individuals and organizations designated to act as mediators.[70]

Neither was the adverse Bosnian Serb perception of the mission mitigated by a belief that the UN as a mediator could provide an outcome that was acceptable to the Serbs. To the Bosnian Serbs, the mediators were intended as executors of the great powers' plot to deprive them of their right to self-determination.[71] This harmonized with their self-image as a misunderstood, persecuted, and embattled people standing up to a hostile international community. This developed into anger and hostility towards the outside world: 'The Serbs denounced a plot of the whole world against their Nation, only guilty of continuing to assume its historic role of barrier of the Christian West against the spread of Islam'.[72] These feelings of victimization were only increased by international threats and sanctions.[73] This fundamental suspicion of and hostility towards its presence by the Bosnian Serbs became a crippling weakness to the ICFY mediation mission as it tried to negotiate the agreement of all of the parties to its peace plans.

It was the Bosnian Serbs' military preponderance at the time of the UN interventions that made it irrational for them to cooperate with negotiations that were so detrimental to their interests. The timing of UN involvement was primarily motivated by an urgent need to stop the fighting and the human rights abuses rather than by considerations of the conduciveness of the military situation to peace talks.[74] It believed that the only way of stopping the conflict and preventing its spread was to broker a comprehensive ceasefire and political agreement between the warring parties.[75] The ICFY mediators proposed an immediate 'temporary freezing of the military situation, pending agreement on return of forces to designated provinces'.[76] This, along with its other proposals, was completely at variance with the military momentum and position of the strongest party, the Bosnian Serbs. Supported and constantly resupplied from within Serbia, the Bosnian Serbs' preponderance in heavy weaponry and defiance of international threats and sanctions enabled them to hold their territorial gains with little threat of losing them to the Muslims or the Croats, until the Croatian military build-up and the sustained NATO air campaign in September 1995 altered the military balance.

Bosnian Serb military predominance translated into a hardened bargaining position and an insistence on their demands.[77] Until peacekeepers were withdrawn from vulnerable positions in mid-1995, attempts to blockade Bosnian Serb-held areas had little effect, and the first, tentative NATO airstrikes were responded to by taking peacekeepers hostage and other measures, rather than modifying the basic Bosnian Serb conditions.[78] Furthermore, the Bosnian Serbs realized that its inability to secure a settlement paralysed the UN's actions in Bosnia. It became clear that a solution would usher in not a reduction in the dangers to Bosnian Serb interests, but a more muscular international presence: all implementation plans 'signalled to the Serbs that a large NATO force would be inserted into Bosnia not if the fighting continued, but only if it stopped'.[79] The Bosnian Serbs' military preponderance, and the confidence to resist that flowed from this, exposed the weaknesses within the ICFY mediation mission that derived from its inappropriate presence and objectives. These were vulnerabilities that left the mediators prey to non-cooperation and cynical exploitation by the militarily strongest party.

Mission Design and the Belligerents' Tactics

The serious vulnerabilities of the UN mission arising from a divided coalition which misunderstood the conflict and dispatched a flawed response, put the mediators at a serious disadvantage as the talks began. The UN's advocacy of 'the imperative need to find an urgent political solution for the situation in Bosnia and Herzegovina'[80] followed closely on the outbreak of hostilities in Bosnia. The Steering Committee of the ICFY emphasized the importance of persevering with mediation when it warned of 'the dangers of escalation of the conflict if the parties turn their backs on the search for negotiated solutions'.[81] Acting on such urgent instructions, the ICFY mediators had little time to develop a formula tailored to the situation, or to wait for developments that made the conflict more conducive to a negotiated solution. The ICFY adopted a deductive approach. It attempted to deal with the problem of the strongly opposing positions of the disputants by directing its Working Groups to 'prepare the basis for a general settlement and associated measures'[82] which would then be presented to the parties who would be encouraged and pressured to sign it. The three frameworks around which the ICFY mediators worked did not manage to tie the belligerents, especially the Bosnian Serbs, to the mediation process. Attempts by the UN to pressure the Bosnian Serbs into becoming more flexible and accepting the peace plans through applying sanctions to Serbia,[83] and by issuing warnings and ultimatums, were unsuccessful.[84] The mediators were reduced to pleas reminding the parties of their previous commitments to peace: '. . . the decision to choose peace or war rests with you . . . You agreed to the principles of the International Conference adopted on 26 August. You committed yourselves that all parties should cease fighting and should engage actively in negotiations'.[85] Until the military balance changed after September 1995, the Bosnian Serbs had little rational incentive in complying with these peace plans.

By the end of 1994, the UN mediators and the ICFY had presided over the tabling of three major attempts to define a mediation and settlement framework that tried to reconcile the positions of the Bosnian parties as well as fulfilling the instructions of the UN: the Vance–Owen plan, the Serb–Croat proposal, and the Contact Group plan. The first framework advanced by mediators came in the form of a comprehensive settlement plan designed by UN envoy Vance and EU envoy Sir David Owen. In an early attempt at compromize between clashing interests, the Vance–Owen plan proposed dividing Bosnia into ten ethnically mixed cantons, each with built-in guarantees of power-sharing between all three ethnic groups and the respect of human rights. Although the plan's decentralization of the state and explicit recognition of the three ethnic groups was an acknowledgement of Serb concerns about living in a Bosnian state, the cantonization recommendation amounted to a direct rejection of the Bosnian Serb objective of ethnically partitioning Bosnia.[86] The Vance–Owen plan explicitly forbade any prospect of international personality or unification with territories or states outside of Bosnia.[87] The map drawn up by Vance and Owen proposed the reduction of Bosnian Serb-dominated[88] territory from 70 per cent to slightly over 43 per cent, and apportioning the remaining Bosnian territory between the Muslim-majority holdings and the Croat-majority holdings in proportions roughly reflecting the pre-war ethnic numbers. The Bosnian government initially rejected the plan that divided up Bosnia, but under intense international pressure and guarantees, accepted the plan. The Bosnian Croats' acceptance was more enthusiastic, because the plan offered them predominance in the stretches of central Bosnia that they had been fighting for.[89] For the Bosnian Serbs, in addition to taking over one-third of their captured territory from them, the plan proposed to deprive them of the vital northern Brcko corridor that links Serb territories in eastern and western Bosnia,[90] as well as making a linking of Serb areas together and to the Krajina and Serbia virtually impossible.[91] So inimical were the proposals of the Vance–Owen plan to the interests of the Bosnian Serbs, they were repeatedly rejected in their successive manifestations in January, April, and May 1993, by popular referendum among Bosnian Serbs.

Following the final rejection of the Vance–Owen plan, the Bosnian Serbs and Bosnian Croats advanced their own formula for peace in Bosnia. The plan proposed a confederation of three ethnically defined constituent republics, while retaining many of the constitutional principles that had been establizhed in the Vance–Owen plan.[92] While based on the positions of two of the belligerents, the plan encountered the opposition of the UN and ICFY mediators, based on their incompatibility with the mediators' own instructions. The mediators advanced several elements on behalf of the Bosnian government and Muslims that had to be included if the plan was to be successful. Their constitutional suggestions showed concern to preserve the sovereignty and integrity of the Bosnian state, while they were anxious to secure for the Muslims in the territorial divisions 'an equitable and economically viable share of territory, with guaranteed access to the Sava River and the Adriatic Sea'.[93] The international mediators remained adamant that an equitable share amounted to not less than 30 per cent of Bosnian territory for the Muslim republic. They objected to confederalism because 'it would be seen as the first step towards secession'.[94] The mediators worked intensively with Serb and Croat representatives to try to alter the plan along these lines. The Bosnian Serbs rejected all of their proposals, which they saw as ultimately incompatible with the goals of the original plan: the *de facto* partitioning of Bosnia between Croatia and Serbia. The plan was finally abandoned when 58 of the 69 deputies in the Bosnian Parliament in September 1993 voted to reject the Serb–Croat plan in line with a policy of rejecting all solutions that were incompatible with UN resolutions and principles.

The great powers mobilized to propose an alternative framework for settlement after the downfall of the Serb–Croat plan by forming a Contact Group comprised of the US, Russia, the UK, France, and Germany in London on 26 April 1994. Following the negotiation of the Muslim–Croat federation by US envoy Charles Redman in February 1994, the Contact Group advanced a fresh peace plan based on this new alignment of forces. The plan proposed dividing Bosnia between the Muslim–Croat federation with 51 per cent of the territory and the Bosnian Serbs with 49 per cent.[95] The plan explicitly prohibited the possibility of the eventual unification of the Serb territories with Serbia. The Washington agreement federating the Muslims and Croats established the basis of their commitment to the Contact Group plan. Again, it was the Bosnian Serbs who rejected the framework by the end of August 1994. Once more they objected to surrendering nearly one-third of their 70 per cent territorial holdings, particularly in the Brcko corridor and in eastern Bosnia around Jajce, Doboj, Sanski Most, and Visegrad.[96] The failure of each of the three attempts to reconcile the demands of the Bosnian disputants demonstrates the weakness of a mediation mission introduced into an inappropriate context with an unachievable mandate. This suggests that a deductive mediation design without the ability to bind the belligerents to the process and compel them towards a solution becomes vulnerable to a party that is able to resist and remain unpunished.

While the UN proposals threatened to take from the Bosnian Serbs much of which they had fought for, they were shrewd enough to realize that total withdrawal from the mediation process held the possibility of hardening the resolve of the international coalition against them. Furthermore, the Bosnian Serb leadership saw an opportunity to exploit the negotiations towards objectives not favoured by the UN, but which were advantageous to themselves. Having made and secured their military holdings by September 1993, the Bosnian Serbs became receptive to the idea of a negotiated peace based on their military gains. As they saw it, 'with control of contiguous territory making it possible to travel from Belgrade to Banja Luka and beyond into Serb-held territory in Croatia without crossing a front line, the Serbs were in a position to seek a settlement in order to get international sanctions lifted'.[97] Their serious adherence to the mediation process, however, was clearly contingent on the assumption that the peace settlement would reflect their military position and be a stage on the route to secession of the Serb areas and their integration into Greater Serbia.[98] Mediation proposals that rejected these Serb conditions were viewed as *diktats* imposed on the Serbs by the international community and deserving rejection and non-cooperation.[99] Bosnian Serb leader Karadzic repeatedly warned ICFY mediators that if their conditions were not agreed to in the negotiations, the Serbs would continue to wage war in Bosnia.[100] The Bosnian Serbs, in addition to these changes in their strategy and tactics, used their negotiating behaviour with the mediators to exacerbate the weaknesses in the mission and the divisions within its sponsoring coalition.

During the Bosnia negotiations all parties developed into a fine art the skill of using agreement, disagreement, temporizing, or tortuous haggling to manipulate the international community. It was the Bosnian Serbs, however, who continued to flirt with peace proposals as the most likely way of limiting Western military intervention and exacerbating the acrimony between the troop contributors and the advocates of stronger action.[101] The mediators came to realize that agreement on paper rarely translated to compliance in the field: 'Nor can intermediaries keep [the parties] to their word. Cease-fires are entered into in the full knowledge that they are not going to be fulfilled, and other pledges broken within hours of being made'.[102] The parties began openly admitting their intentions to enter agreements for political reasons with no intention of implementing them: 'We'll sign and then ignore the agreement. That's what everyone has done in this war so far'.[103] As a final touch, the Bosnian Serbs orchestrated their rejections of the peace plans in a way calculated to manipulate international opinion, by using referenda in their ethnically cleansed areas to overwhelmingly reject the various peace plans by 96 per cent majorities.[104] So vulnerable were the divisions and weaknesses within the UN mission, and so adept were the Bosnian Serbs at exploiting them, that the mediators found themselves being used to aggravate and worsen the original divisions within their sponsoring coalition.[105] By accordingly altering their political–military tactics, the Bosnian Serbs were able to exploit vulnerabilities in the mission's design and presence in a way that enabled them to avoid the goals towards which the mediators were instructed to work.

Links and External Support

The war in Bosnia stood alone among contemporary conflicts for the widest and most diverse range of external interests and support for the warring parties. These connections with the parties, however, failed to provide the mediators with leverage because of the international community's own deep disagreements about the war and the solution to the crisis. The variety of agendas among the various external supporters of the parties left UN mediators with very little cohesive support for their efforts. What little support materialized was faltering and ineffectual. The tightening sanctions regime applied by Security Council Resolutions 757 (1992) and 787 (1992) and the appeals and pressures of various great powers[106] finally forced Serbia to condemn Bosnian Serb intransigence and institute a blockade of military supplies to the Bosnian Serbs, monitored by the UN. States with ties to the Bosnian Serbs, such as Russia and Greece, were willing to appeal for cooperation, but adamantly opposed proposals by advocates of the Muslims to bring the Bosnian Serbs to the table with coercive action.[107] US influence over the non-Serb parties was used to engineer the Muslim–Croat alliance in March 1994. These tentative involvements by the international community, however, were insufficient to make up for the other deep weaknesses in the Bosnia negotiations.

The confidence of the Bosnian Serbs in defying the international community was in part furnished by their military preponderance and their support by sympathetic states. Their intransigence was also a result of their imperfect isolation from external support. Despite the international arms embargo around the former Yugoslavia and the tightening sanctions against Serbia and Montenegro, the Bosnian Serbs continued to receive supplies and support from various sources. Military supplies were smuggled through the porous Serbian border,[108] through Macedonia, the republic of the rump Yugoslavia with the lower international profile, from Greece through Macedonia, and through the Krajina region in Croatia. While the weapons embargo was imperfect, its existence favoured the Bosnian Serbs by perpetuating their relative preponderance in heavy weapons, which were not easy to smuggle through the embargo. Furthermore, Russian diplomatic patronage provided support for the Bosnian Serbs' intransigence and manipulation in negotiations.[109] The Bosnian Serbs' confidence in Russian and Greek sympathy, support, and protection undoubtedly buttressed their intransigence to all attempts to resolve the conflict in ways unfavourable to them. On the other hand, the Bosnian government's knowledge of American, Islamic, and general international sympathy with its cause, made it much less amenable to Bosnian Serb demands. Although international support for parties to the conflict had a negative effect on the cooperativeness of all parties, its most pronounced impact was on the Bosnian Serbs. Their sponsorship by major members of the coalition allowed them to manipulate and weaken the mediators' position, while confidently defending their own interests.

Mission Durability and Belligerent Morale and Cohesion

As a result of the deep divisions within its sponsoring coalition, the mediation mission lacked the durability, confidence, and initiative to explore other formulas for resolution. As international opinion polarized over the war, and states began to advocate the positions of different belligerents, the UN and ICFY became increasingly preoccupied with maintaining international unity at the expense of single-mindedly searching for a solution to the conflict. As a result of these pressures, the importance of the presence of UN mediators to the peace process was diminished. One of the greatest impediments to the mediators in Bosnia was the lack of cohesion in the UN behind any one preferred solution or strategy. The numerous unanimous Security Council Resolutions supporting the mediators' efforts could not hide the genuine divisions between strongly held positions both within and outside of the Security Council. These divisions were only exacerbated by each development in the fighting, as each state reappraised the status of its commitment to the initiative.[110] International disagreements over Bosnia actually pre-dated the conflict, having stemmed from the disputes over the recognition of the constituent republics of the former Yugoslavia.[111] The underlying affiliations and agendas that drove the dispute between sovereignty and self-determination endured to suffuse the positions of the UN member-states over subsequent issues in Bosnia. At one level, some states supported the various parties due to ethnic, cultural, or religious ties: the Russians and the Greeks supported the Serbs, the

Turks and Islamic countries the Muslims, and the Germans and central Europeans the Croats.

On the political level disagreements arose from different views of the war: the US saw it as a case of external aggression by a large against a small state, whereas the Europeans viewed it as a civil war driven by ethnic antagonism. Until the Bosnian Serb seizure of the Srebrenica, Zepa, and Tuzla safe havens in July 1995, the European view dictated the response: mediation, containment of the conflict, maintenance of the arms embargo, and a large peacekeeping presence. The lack of success of this policy only served to heighten the dissent and frustration of supporters of the US strategy of withdrawing the peacekeepers and lifting the embargo. The Non-Aligned Movement advocated launching a conventional multilateral intervention on behalf of the Bosnian government,[112] while the Islamic Conference Organization held the West responsible for Serb military aggression, and threatened to unilaterally break the embargo and begin supplying the Muslims with arms.[113] These deep and enduring divisions within the UN membership significantly hampered the ability of the mediators to creatively search for a solution in Bosnia.

As the UN, the ICFY, and the Contact Group had to increasingly devote their energy to preserving their own fragile unity, their directives and support for the mediators became both vaguer and weaker. Their inability to agree on the form of military action needed to give the mediators leverage or to back up their own threats and warnings[114] deprived the mediators of the crucial tool of being able to offer side-payments or threaten punishments in order to induce the parties to cooperate. The combination of the embargo and the peacekeepers placed an inertia on the mediators' position, with the peacekeeping presence giving the Bosnian Serbs and the European members of the coalition a veto over any change in international strategy to try to find a solution.[115] The lack of cohesion within the UN also meant that none of the peace plans offered was able to attract the strong international support that the mediators needed so badly due to the unacceptability of their proposals to the Bosnian Serbs.[116] Unfortunately for the mediators, this lack of cohesion was well appreciated by the Bosnian Serbs, who cleverly stalled and manipulated the negotiations in order to derive the greatest benefits from international divisions.[117] These divisions made it possible for the Bosnian Serbs to not cooperate with the mediators while escaping any serious consequences.

The Bosnian Serbs' intractability was partly inspired by their strong military position, and the high morale that flowed from this and nationalist myths. Contemptuous of the use of appeals, threats, and sanctions to pressure them into unfavourable negotiations, Bosnian Serb military commanders boasted in 1993 that they had enough martial spirit and arms stockpiles to continue the war independently for another six or seven years.[118] It was also partly inspired by their likely inability to maintain their own cohesion behind any concessions or cooperation with the mediators that was not justified by military realities. The bitterness of the Balkan conflict equated cooperation with betrayal: '. . . the expression of willingness to negotiate, the notion of compromise, and the very idea of dialogue were often taken as treason'.[119] The Bosnian Serb leadership was itself beset by serious factionalism, a factor that led to its paranoia, militarism, and uncompromising positions during negotiations.[120] Any concessions, particularly over the surrender of captured territory, were vociferously opposed by hardline politicians, local Serb warlords, and the Bosnian Serb military led by General Mladic.[121] The Bosnian Serb cadre and supporters were so internally divided that orders from the leadership were often ignored, without having 'any consistent and tangible impact on the ground'.[122] These severe divisions among the Bosnian Serbs led to a paranoid leadership making use of the 'parliament' at Pale and referenda to make important decisions regarding the peace talks. These factors of cohesion and morale made it even more irrational for the Bosnian Serbs to cooperate with the mediators.

The Holbrooke mediation mission that finally secured peace in Bosnia through brokering the Dayton Peace Accord was free of the weaknesses that ultimately frustrated the mediation missions in which the UN was involved. The Holbrooke mission was sponsored by a single great power, capitalized on significant Bosnian Serb military reversals, and followed an impressively devastating demonstration of military potency by the mission's sponsoring agent, the US. The fundamental weaknesses and deep confusion and paralysis of UN attempts to end the conflict stemmed from the obsession with consensual action between its fundamentally disagreeing member-states. These diverging positions arose from a number of impulses: different perceptions of the conflict; internal demands from public opinion; perceived responsibilities; and a variety of historical, ethnic, or religious ties. The obsession with preserving consensus among such a large and discordant group perpetuated the UN's misdiagnosis of the conflict and prescription of an inappropriate response. The conflict dynamic in Bosnia proved particularly resilient against such a vulnerable mediation mission. This was largely attributable to the Bosnian Serbs' military predominance and continued external support, which led to their confident obduracy. While within sight of military victory, it was irrational for them to accept proposals inimical to their position made by a divided mission lacking any significant leverage. The Bosnian Serbs demonstrated masterfully how components of a robust civil war conflict dynamic are able to exploit vulnerabilities in a UN mission's inappropriate objectives, presence, and design, to aggravate the divisions within its supporting coalition in such a way as to frustrate the mission.

EL SALVADOR: A TIMELY SUCCESS

In the early aftermath of the Cold War, the UN played a major role in mediating an end to the civil war in El Salvador. Since 1980, the Salvadoran government had been locked in a brutal struggle against a front of left-wing insurgents, the *Frente Faribundo Marti para la Liberacion Nacional* (FMLN). In October 1980, against a background of increasing civil violence and unrest, the FMLN formed, under Cuban sponsorship, from five groups rebelling against the right-wing military dictatorship of José Napoleon Duarte.[123] This resistance had its roots in the considerable opposition among intellectuals, trade unions, and the church to the wealth disparities and the power of the military in Salvadoran society. Drawing on this protest, FMLN propaganda proclaimed itself as the vanguard of the opposition, committed to 'the unification and leadership of the oppressed against the imperialist North Americans and the millionaire oligarches . . . combined with their followers and defenders'.[124] After the failure of its 'final offensive' in January 1981 to spark a general insurrection in the cities and topple the government, its 6000-strong army retreated to the countryside to wage a Castro-ite guerrilla campaign supported by Soviet bloc, Cuban and Nicaraguan aid. It gained support among sections of the Salvadoran peasantry, and carved 'liberated zones', over which it resisted government attempts to regain control, and where it gained quasi-sovereignty as a shadow government providing rudimentary public services, order, and commodities. The government, however, maintained a high level of support among the populations of the larger cities. It began, with large amounts of US aid, a counter-insurgency campaign against the rebels. The Salvadoran armed forces swelled to 55 000, trained and equipped by the US. Over the years of civil war, the enormous state expenditure on the armed forces, plus the FMLN's tactics of economic sabotage, particularly of the electricity grid, other infrastructure, and oligarchic-capitalist interests, were to slowly drain the country of its wealth and population.[125] Nearly a decade of armed struggle did not bring either side victory. Meanwhile, the civil war had settled into a brutal stalemate, the horrors of which echoed around the globe, between the FMLN, the counter-insurgent Salvadoran army, and the sinister death squads.

Responding to growing calls to end the horror, the UN mediation effort followed a number of regional peace initiatives which, although unsuccessful, began to build a platform for eventual talks.[126] Following calls from the regional actors for direct UN involvement,[127] the Security Council directed the Secretary-General to apply his good offices to attempt to terminate the war in El Salvador.[128] Direct mediation by the Secretary-General and his Special Representative, Alvaro de Soto, began in January 1990. Over the next two years, the UN negotiators led the Salvadoran government of Alfredo Christiani and the FMLN to an agreement, signed in Mexico City on 16 January 1992. It committed the government to significant constitutional and socio-economic changes and reduction and purging of the armed forces in return for the FMLN's ceasefire, disarmament, demobilization, and participation in the democratic process. By applying the analytical framework to the UN mediation mission in El Salvador, this section will explore the extent to which weaknesses were absent from the UN mission, and to what extent this ultimately influenced the success of the mediation.

Objectives

The UN mission sent to mediate an end to the Salvadoran civil war was given specific instructions on the type of resolution it was to secure. These instructions were based largely on the desire of the concerned member-states to end the civil war. The majority of the resulting coalition had a relatively high stake in ending the war. Regional states were concerned and frustrated by the continuing threat that wars in El Salvador, Nicaragua, and Guatemala posed to the internal stability of their own states, and the repellent effect that this instability had on investment and development in the region.[129] Many also resented the continuing external involvement in the affairs of Latin America. The Contadora process, advocating peace, an end to external intervention, and the economic benefits of stability and cooperation, began to assemble the eventual sponsoring coalition within the UN for a solution in El Salvador.[130] The election of Arias in Costa Rica and Cerezo in Guatemala, and their participation in the Esquipulas group added more regional members to the coalition.[131] As they became more engaged in improving their bilateral relations, the superpowers joined the coalition, keen to remove Cold War thorns such as their proxy war in El Salvador from the continued growth of their cooperation. The US, following the embarrassment of the Iran–Contra scandal,[132] was keen to transform its relations with Central America into an overt involvement dedicated to cooperation and prosperity. The superpowers' commitment to the UN sponsoring coalition became complete in August 1991, when Secretary of State Baker and Foreign Minister Besmertnykh urged the Secretary-General to become personally involved in mediating the Salvadoran conflict.[133] Britain, France, Spain, and Germany, responding to popular concern over the wars in Central America, completed a comprehensive UN coalition exhibiting a high level of agreement in resolving the civil war in El Salvador.

The UN's instructions to its mediators were given relevance by a reasonably accurate diagnosis of the conflict dynamic and the wishes of the belligerents. Its concern to resolve the civil war in a way that upheld the sovereignty and territorial integrity of one of its member-states, largely coincided with the interests of both belligerents in taking power of the whole state rather than partitioning it between them. The UN and the combatants also coincided in the view that it was vital to put an end to external involvements in the Salvadoran civil war. A solution to the conflict that allowed the people of El Salvador to adjudicate between the contending claims was a desirable outcome for a UN initiative, as well as for the government and the FMLN, both of which were confident of prevailing in a fair election contest. The objectives of the UN mission thus showed a high level of member-state agreement, as well as reflecting an accurate diagnosis of the civil war. It set out to terminate the hostilities and develop a formula for peacefully adjudicating the contending claims, distributing the disputed commodities, and establishing a single, legitimate, sovereign Salvadoran government.[134]

The interests of the incumbent Salvadoran government largely reflected its decade-long successful democratization away from a military dictatorship, as well as its overwhelming desire to rid itself of the crippling civil war. The ARENA government of Alfredo Christiani had watched the end of the Cold War and the peaceful democratization of Eastern Europe with interest, and was determined to put an end to the subversive Soviet, Cuban, and Nicaraguan intervention in El Salvador.[135] It was also concerned about the decade-long outflow of wealth and people, fleeing the Salvadoran civil war, while its association with the death squads, whose atrocities had echoed around the world, were a continuing international embarrassment. The government of El Salvador was confident of its popular endorsement; in successive national elections, it had beaten contenders from the left, despite FMLN boycotts and disruptions.[136] In all of these electoral contests, it had invited the participation of the FMLN, on the condition that it laid down its arms.[137] At no time did the FMLN participate. The Salvadoran government's central objective was to end the civil war. Its major demand was that the FMLN cease its insurgency, and beyond that, surrender its arms and military structure in order to ensure that it could not restart its struggle at a later stage.[138] José Napoleon Duarte's 1984 election victory and Alfredo Christiani's 1986 election victory were both won overwhelmingly on pledges to seek an end to the civil war.[139] Based on this mandate, the Christiani government was prepared, and indeed had tried, to offer the FMLN acceptance back into civil society if it laid down its arms.

The objectives of the FMLN were determined by both its political goals and its military fortunes. As a Marxist insurgent movement, the FMLN was dedicated to overthrowing the Salvadoran government and seizing power in order to address 'the structural causes of war':[140] primarily the concentration of wealth, influence, and property in the hands of a small elite. As its military position and external sponsorship changed, the FMLN pragmatically altered its demands from complete revolutionary overthrow to the transformation of El Salvador into a more just society through the democratic process. Specifically, it demanded admittance into a power-sharing government in order to oversee this evolution while ensuring the security of the movement and its followers.[141] Immediately prior to UN involvement, the FMLN dropped its insistence on power-sharing and acknowledged the centrality of the electoral process to the resolution of the conflict.[142] The FMLN was confident that it would form the government chosen by such an election, and that this would be a transitional stage on the path to socialism.[143] These peaceful methods, however, needed to offer the movement a significant chance of securing these goals, a level playing field on which to compete for power. For the FMLN, a prominent condition for such a level playing field was the end of US influence in El Salvador, in a way 'that national sovereignty [would] be restored and that . . . relations with the US be reoriented on the basis of the unconditional respect of the right of self-determination and independence'.[144] The FMLN's commitment to peaceful methods, however, was greatly tempered by its concern for the security of the organization and the safety of its followers from the revenge of opponents within the government, armed forces, and Salvadoran society. Central to the objectives of the FMLN was the reform of the Salvadoran armed forces and other paramilitary elements such as the death squads, which it identified as posing the greatest threat to its post-bellum security: 'What use is there in talking about democratisation, cease-fires, political participation when the government continues waging a dirty war with its death squads against unarmed civilians?'[145] Close links between the government, the ruling ARENA party, the army, and the death squads, prompted FMLN fears that its political candidates would be murdered and its followers intimidated.[146] The FMLN therefore insisted on a reduction and restructuring of the security forces to ensure its safety. So much importance did it place on this that the armed forces issue became central to the mediation and a major impediment to an agreement.[147]

There was essential synchronicity between the objectives of the UN mediators and those of the belligerents in El Salvador. Each of the three was devoted to ultimately stopping the war and establishing a mechanism for the fair and legitimate resolution of the conflict. Any differences were in form and succession rather than substance: while the UN's and the incumbents' first priority was to end the war, the FMLN was determined to preserve its military potential for as long as possible during the mediation process. It remained for the UN mediators to adapt to these minor differences and concentrate their efforts on creatively devising a formula that would eventually reconcile the demands of the Salvadoran government and the FMLN into an agreed process for reconciling their competing claims. Despite these differences, both belligerents saw the UN intervention as an opportunity to advance their demands. Their acceptance of the mediators' objectives, then, showed the accuracy with which the UN had diagnosed the conflict and prescribed a response, as well as translating ultimately into a strong base from which the mediators could work. From this fundamental advantage, the UN mediators were able to overcome the parties' opposing approaches by devising a formula to address the concerns of both simultaneously, thereby tying them to the mediation process.

Mission Presence and the Military Balance

A consequence of the accord between the objectives of the UN mediators, and the interests of the belligerents, was that the incumbent government and the FMLN saw the UN intervention as both acceptable and desirable. By the time of the UN initiative, both sides had independently realized that their continued use of violence was not going to progress their interests any further. Concurrently, both had become convinced that these interests would be advanced by cooperation with the peace process. Because of this universal recognition of the desirability of the UN presence, the UN was able to secure the participation of both parties in the negotiations, and then to use its position to steer them towards a resolution of the conflict.

The negotiations were built on the solid foundations of recognition: the belligerents recognized each other's importance and legitimacy in the peace process and the vital role played by the UN mediators. The UN saw both parties as necessary participants in the peace process, because there could be no resolution without the agreement of both, and either party had an endless ability to disrupt a process from which it was excluded.[148] The Security Council and General Assembly repeatedly called on the government and the FMLN to cooperate with the mediation process,[149] and the mediators held preliminary secret talks with the FMLN prior to the start of the mediation initiative. In return, both belligerents saw the importance of the UN mediation mission. The government had, by the time of UN involvement, realized that it would be unable to govern El Salvador without first coming to terms with the FMLN, which it was unable to defeat, and which could play a disruptive role indefinitely. The FMLN recognized that in order to advance its objectives, it would first have to find an agreement with the government, which it had failed to overthrow. Both belligerents separately urged a UN role in the mediation process.[150] An important component of the UN's indispensability to the peace process was its perceived impartiality. Because of Latin America's history of interventions, other potential mediators, from the superpowers, regional states, and the OAS, were seen by one or both sides as irreversibly biased.[151] The FMLN in particular was insistent on heavy UN involvement in mediation and verification.[152] Both parties trusted the UN to draw up proposals for dealing with the most contentious issues: the armed forces, police, and socio-economic modifications. The heavy involvement of the UN was used by both sides to monitor each other's fidelity to the mediation process, and as a safeguard against bad faith.[153] In May 1991, the UN established the United Nations Observer Mission in El Salvador (ONUSAL) to verify the agreements already reached between the parties, and monitor the human rights and security situation in support of further negotiations.[154] The mediators also used ONUSAL verification as one of the methods of tying the disputants to the mediation process; this mechanism was duly built into the Caracas framework for mediation.[155] The value of the UN mediation to both belligerents was built on the UN's correct assessment of the conflict and formulation of a response. This accuracy was to be used in the design of the mediation initiative, to draw the sometimes hesitant and suspicious belligerents to a negotiated agreement.

More than any other factor, it was a stalemated military balance that led to their welcoming of the UN mediation initiative. The fatigue and stalled military momentum of the government and the FMLN by the late 1980s had made them amenable to resolution proposals by the early 1990s. The civil war in El Salvador had settled into the recognizable pattern of a stalemated insurgency: the FMLN insurgents had proved unable to defeat or topple the government, while the government was unable to flush out and defeat the guerrilla forces. The incumbent government, even with vast US support in materiel and training, and with a 9:1 ratio of troops over FMLN guerrillas, had been unable to defeat the FMLN, which was steadily bleeding the country dry. While government troops could maintain relative calm in the urban centres, the ARENA government was aware that the FMLN would always retain the tactical initiative. Its impotence against impressive surprise offensives such as that in 1989 which struck at the heart of San Salvador, had begun to bring home to the government just how far it was from military victory.

Similarly, the FMLN had no hope of militarily defeating the government's large, American-trained and -supplied army. It had also become well aware that the Castro-ite model of popular revolution had failed, and that the guerrillas had been unable to spark a popular uprising.[156] Prospects of such an uprising receded further and further as the government strove to address the socio-economic inequalities that had started the uprising.[157] The government's steady self-legitimization through popular elections and peaceful transfers of power, and its crackdown on death-squad activity further deprived the FMLN of support.[158] By 1989, then, both the government and the FMLN had realized that not only were they not winning the war, but that with each wartime month that passed, they were losing the popular support that the government would need to retain power, and that the FMLN would need to complete the democratic transformation of El Salvador. They saw that Salvadorans, dying, emigrating, and getting poorer from the war, desperately wanted peace, and that popular support would accrue to any party advocating, pursuing, and delivering peace.[159] In response to this popular feeling, the government had begun its democratization and clampdown on the death squads in the mid-1980s. The FMLN had also begun to respond to the popular will. Beginning in 1987, the FMLN leadership made the decision to 'humanize' the civil war and seek talks with the government and thereby seize power democratically.[160] So the stalemated military balance between the government and the FMLN dictated the extent to which both needed to commit to peace talks, and why both looked so favourably on the UN mediation initiative.

Mission Design and Belligerents' Tactics

The UN, having correctly diagnosed the Salvadoran civil war, and chosen an apt moment to intervene, believed that mediation was the appropriate form of mission to send to try and begin to resolve the long and bitter stalemate between the belligerents. Both the Security Council and the General Assembly had overwhelmingly advocated a mediated and peaceful solution to the conflict since the early 1980s.[161] Secretary-General Perez de Cuellar had a close interest in the conflict, maintaining close contacts with the regional governments and other actors such as the OAS. As his term of office drew to a close in 1991, he staked his reputation on mediating an end to the war in El Salvador. It remained for UN mediators to secure the commitment of the government and the FMLN to the mediation process as the way of resolving the conflict. While both parties saw a need to end the civil war, their military, political, social, and economic demands differed considerably. Furthermore, they differed considerably over the process of the negotiations: while the government demanded the FMLN stop fighting and disarm before any political reforms were discussed, the FMLN remained determined to preserve its military potential until the necessary guarantees were in place to enable it to reintegrate into civilian society in full legality and safety.[162] Faced with these differences, the UN mediators had to find a mediation design that reconciled the parties' divergent demands while promising both the opportunity to secure their objectives.

Once the government and the FMLN had accepted the mediation mission, the problem for the UN mediators was to reconcile the FMLN's desire to preserve its military capacity until its political, economic, and security demands had been met, with the government's refusal to begin serious negotiations before the FMLN had stopped fighting and disarmed. The mediators held a series of secret meetings with the FMLN and the government in early 1990, from which they produced a framework for negotiation which creatively addressed the concerns of both parties.[163] The Geneva framework and the subsequent Caracas Agenda compressed the political talks and the ceasefire issue into a two-stage process: the first resolving the issues of the armed forces, human rights guarantees, the judicial system, elections, constitutional, economic and social reforms, and UN verification; the second creating security guarantees for the reincorporation of the FMLN into Salvadoran society.[164] These schedules also established a defined timetable incorporating a date and duration for a ceasefire.[165] The timetable for negotiations made creative use of deadlines to hasten agreement and minimize obduracy 'by forcing the negotiating parties to confront potential blame for failed negotiations'.[166] In both parties' sensitivity to the opinion of the electorate, the UN had a substantial source of leverage. Such blame was seen by both parties as damaging to their election prospects. The mediation framework selected was largely deductive, seeking to build broad agreement on the important issues and then discussing outstanding items while steadily establishing the conditions for a ceasefire and demobilization of both sides. The compromise between the FMLN's insistence on political settlement first and the government's insistence on ceasefire first was that while the political agreements would be negotiated before the ceasefire, talks on the implementation of these agreements would follow the ceasefire.[167] The Geneva Agreement also tied both parties to the mediation process, containing the undertaking of both not to abandon negotiations unilaterally.[168] In this way, the UN mediators, using an appropriate mediation formula, were able to secure the commitment of the government and the FMLN to the mediation mechanism to a level consistent with their own commitments and convictions.

The prestige, diplomatic expertise, and personality of Secretary-General Perez de Cuellar played a large role in the success of the mediation design adopted by the UN to negotiate a solution to the conflict. As his tenure as Secretary-General drew to a close, Perez de Cuellar became passionately committed to ending the Salvadoran civil war as a prestigious way to conclude his distinguished career. He became the prime mover and initiator of UN action during the mediation, working to secure resources, attention, and member-state support for the negotiations. The mediation process showed marked acceleration and yielded greater results when the parties met face-to-face under the direct mediation of Perez de Cuellar or de Soto.[169] His mediating style was also particularly well-suited to the needs of the Salvadoran belligerents. Predominantly quiet and retiring, Perez de Cuellar's reputation for confidentiality and integrity had become well known. Vowing to reach a negotiated solution before surrendering office at the end of 1991, Perez de Cuellar bent all of his skills towards mediating agreement. This culminated in a dramatic climax after midnight, 31 December 1991, at UN headquarters, when the clock was stopped on Perez de Cuellar's official retirement while the FMLN, the Salvadoran government, and the Secretary-General thrashed out the remaining obstacles to a solution.

The effectiveness with which the UN mission was able to advance its mediation framework was in large part due to the pliability of the conflict dynamic, a consequence of the willingness of both the government and the FMLN to choose to abandon their war and explore a peaceful settlement. Even before the UN intervention, the government was committed to ending the brutal insurgent war that was continuing within its borders. Previously it had tried to end the war through prevailing in its counter-insurgency, but had realized that this method would not, and could not, end the war. The Christiani government, and the other political parties, had come to realize that a form of negotiated solution was the only viable method of ending the FMLN's guerrilla war and the Cuban–Nicaraguan subversion. It had also determined that negotiations were the only method of re-establishing a functioning civil society, and bringing not only the leftist rebels, but also the death-squad violence under control. At the point of UN intervention, the FMLN had, due to various military, strategic, and international factors, decided to eventually abandon war in favour of finding a peaceful way to secure its objectives. It did not, however, modify its objectives of attaining political power, effecting socio-economic change in El Salvador, and ensuring the safety of its cadres and supporters. The FMLN, therefore, entered mediation under UN auspices believing and assuring its rank and file that the peace talks were another route to victory over the government.[170] Convinced that the military path to imposing a unilateral solution had closed, the FMLN '. . . primarily viewed [a negotiated] settlement as its last, best hope for achieving fundamental societal and political reforms'.[171] The FMLN was thus committed to peace talks, while preserving its military capability based on its belief in the 'correlation of forces' and its desire to ensure its safety from the armed forces and the death squads.[172]

While both the government and the FMLN were committed to exploring the peace option, neither of them was prepared immediately to change its strategy and tactics to renounce war completely. This was partly because of a desire to see how they, especially the FMLN, could exploit the process, and partly through the process of bargaining and the need to negotiate from strength. Initially, the FMLN's reluctance to abandon its military capability until after a peace agreement was signed, and its use of insurgent violence to bolster its position during the negotiations, aroused the suspicion and anger of the government, and impeded the progress of the negotiations. The FMLN's decision to negotiate did not mean it was ready to surrender its military capacity immediately. True to its revolutionary ideology, the FMLN believed that success depended on a favourable correlation of forces, and was prepared to complement its negotiations with military actions designed to enhance its political leverage.[173] Throughout the negotiations the FMLN established a tradition of staging incisive military attacks against government targets on the eve of negotiating rounds in order to demonstrate its continuing potency. Its particularly successful 1989 general offensive gave the FMLN the confidence to fully participate in negotiations, having demonstrated its disruptive power, and its ability to trade a demonstrated military potential for significant concessions.[174]

Neither did the government sufficiently trust the FMLN to forgo all of its counter-insurgency activities. These continued right up until the peace agreement was signed. Furthermore, on several occasions, the government threatened to withdraw from the talks in protest over their lack of progress.[175] The mediators' use of a negotiating framework and timetables, however, began to tie the government and the FMLN ever deeper into serious negotiations. On 14 November 1991, the FMLN announced an indefinite ceasefire, and entered the final round of negotiations to end the civil war. Its growing commitment to negotiating a satisfactory peace agreement entailed a parallel growth in its co-operativeness and veracity in its negotiating behaviour, and a growing co-operativeness by the government. By the time of the final New York round of negotiations, both the government and the FMLN had sent their highest-level representatives to negotiate the agreement. Thus the mission design adopted by the UN mediators was able to capitalize on the pliability of the conflict dynamic and the willingness of the belligerents to consider peace, to tie those former enemies into a process aimed at resolving the bases of their decade-long war.

Links and External Support

The civil war in El Salvador had become, by the early 1980s, a proxy war between the superpowers, each supporting one of the belligerents. Each side's dependence on this external assistance furnished the mediators with potent sources of leverage, depending on the co-operativeness of the superpowers. Each superpower had, by the time of the mediation initiative, considerably more interest in ending the war than in continuing to unilaterally support its client. The UN mediators found both superpowers willing to use their leverage to support them and encourage flexibility in the belligerents. The US, with the heaviest involvement in the conflict, having supported the government with $4 billion in aid over the eleven-year conflict, exercised the greatest influence on both parties' willingness to compromise. It creatively manipulated its aid levels in response to the parties' military and negotiating behaviour. The Bush administration apportioned $85 million in aid to the Salvadoran government for fiscal year 1991, but withheld half of the funds, which were to be released only under certain conditions. The US made clear that this potential aid was to be used as an incentive for the FMLN and the government to negotiate.[176] The aid was released following increased FMLN military activity and uncooperativeness in the negotiations in early 1991. The FMLN soon realized that US support of the government could be interdicted by its own co-operativeness in the peace process, thereby increasing its own relative strength and influence in the negotiations. The US, as a close supporter of the government, was also able to furnish the FMLN with guarantees of ensuring government compliance with any agreements.[177]

The UN mediators also made use of the support of other actors that were prepared to use their influence with the parties towards an agreement. In August 1991, Perez de Cuellar requested that the US and the Soviet Union write a joint letter urging concessions from the parties, a move which was to prove successful in breaking a deadlock.[178] Another *ad hoc* group of interested states, calling itself the Four Friends of the Secretary-General, composed of Mexico, Venezuela, Colombia, and Spain, formed to complement the mediators' efforts and urge both sides to come to an agreement as quickly as possible. Vital external communication between the FMLN, the UN, and the US was handled through the parties' connections with the

Four Friends.[179] The mediators also used the support of the general membership of the UN as a form of leverage on the parties to reach an agreement by using UN headquarters in New York as the site for a crucial round of negotiations in September 1991. The combination of the interest and support of the entire international community, and the personal mediation of Perez de Cuellar worked to produce a timely agreement and created an impetus for the successful conclusion of the mediation effort. International support thus became crucial to the success of the UN mediators.

The leverage that these links gave the UN mediators over the belligerents was furnished by the great dependence both belligerents had on outside support, and their fear of losing that support. US aid was vital to the government, not only to enable it to defend itself against the insurrection, but to help it save the state from financial collapse. The steady decline in the levels of aid, as the US government struggled to come to terms with its deficit, as well as the prospect of a unilateral stoppage of aid if it was uncooperative with the UN mediators, was seen as potentially catastrophic to the government's political, economic, and military position. The FMLN's military position was also threatened by its growing isolation from the international sponsors upon which it had formerly depended so heavily. For most of the war it had made use of the assistance of the Soviet Union, Cuba, and Nicaragua, all of whom saw supporting the FMLN as advancing their objectives of spreading revolution through Latin America and tying the US to a costly obligation to support the embattled Salvadoran regime. The end of the Cold War and Soviet new thinking in foreign policy began a process of receding Soviet interest and assistance to former clients in the developing world. Support declined for Cuba and Nicaragua, and ultimately dried up for the FMLN from all three sources. The Bush administration applied heavy pressure to the Soviet Union to stop all aid to the FMLN.[180] Regional states, particularly Costa Rica, Guatemala, Honduras, and Nicaragua, combined to condemn FMLN uncooperativeness, thereby intensifying its isolation at crucial impasses in the negotiations.[181] The Four Friends of the Secretary-General at the July 1991 Iberoamerican Summit in Guadalajara sent a strong warning to Cuba to support the negotiations and stop aiding the FMLN.[182] Finally, the electoral defeat of the Sandanistas in Nicaragua in February 1990 completed the process of isolation of the FMLN that contributed to its co-operation with the mediation process. The leverage granted the mediators by the belligerents' heavy dependence on external sponsors, and the willingness of the states with those links to manipulate them on behalf of the UN, thus translated into a potent source of influence to complement the pliability of the conflict dynamic, through which the UN was able to advance its mediation framework.

Mission Durability and Belligerent Morale and Cohesion

The durability of the UN mediation mission to El Salvador was a contributing factor to the success of the mission. It enabled the mediators to proceed creatively but firmly with their mediation framework, progressively tying the belligerents to their commitments and inducing them to make concessions towards the eventual agreement. It allowed the mediators to make confident use of their leverage over the belligerents to overcome moments of non-cooperation. The durability of the mediation mission derived largely from the agreement within its sponsoring coalition, and the willingness of the members of that coalition to give meaningful support to the mission. While the Reagan administration expressed some opposition to international intervention within its hemisphere, the Bush administration accepted the UN as the most acceptable mediator and possibly the only actor capable of finding agreement between the parties and thereby removing a thorn from relations with the Soviet Union. Security Council support for the mediators was unanimous, cohesive, and constant.[183] The parties' awareness of strong international support for the mediation process played an important role in their co-operation with and confidence in the negotiations.

Morale levels in the government and FMLN forces appear to have played a minor role in each side's calculations to explore peaceful methods of advancing their interests. Recruitment levels to both the government's armed forces and the FMLN did not drop appreciably in the years leading up to the peace agreement.[184] Neither did the factionalized nature of both sides significantly hinder the progress of the peace talks. While the government armed forces were firmly under civilian direction, and responded to central control, there were worries that the extremist death squads might use terrorism to disrupt the peace process.[185] Determined government action was able to restrain much of the activity of the death squads, while the subsequent COPAZ (*Comision Nacional para la Consolidacion de la Paz*) mechanism established by the peace agreement was to facilitate the investigation and prosecution of death-squad activities.[186] The FMLN, as a loose umbrella organization of five groups, had the potential to be plagued by factionalism as it began to negotiate. However, its cohesion was largely maintained through the groups' high level of ideological homogeneity, and the FMLN's adoption of democratic centralism as a method of making and enforcing decisions.[187] Factional discontent was further forestalled during negotiations by including the leaders of the most influential groups in the negotiating team: Villalobos of the ERP, Schafik Handal of the PCES, Cienfuegos of FARN, and Martinez of the PRTC.[188] Nevertheless, internal criticism still occurred over what some factions saw as premature concessions on human rights and the armed forces questions, and repeatedly forced the FMLN negotiators to temporarily adopt intransigent positions.[189] Generally, FMLN negotiators and leaders managed to carry the bulk of their membership and support with them towards the peace agreement, a vital factor in the final agreement and the successful conclusion of the peace process.

The Salvadoran peace agreement emerged as the most successful mediated by the UN after the Cold War in terms of success, longevity, and implementability. In direct contrast to the ICFY mission, the successful Salvadoran mission showed a marked absence of the weaknesses nominated by the framework. It also operated in an extremely pliable conflict dynamic, whose belligerents were willing to consider a peaceful settlement, and who were able to be influenced to co-operate with the mediation process. It appears that the lack of weaknesses in the mission continued as the mediation process progressed. The robustness of the mission's origins, in a cohesive sponsoring coalition, was mirrored in accurate diagnosis, a good mediation design, and useful sources of leverage. It was also fortunate in being dispatched to resolve an extremely pliable conflict dynamic. The pliability of the conflict dynamic arose from both belligerents simultaneously recognizing that they were unlikely to advance their objectives through further war, and that a peaceful alternative should be tried. Both were reinforced in these views by rapidly retracting commitments from their former sponsors. Into this conducive environment, the UN sent an appropriate mission type, with an influential mediation design. Far from being unwanted or exploitable, the mediation mission was seen by the belligerents as an opportunity to advance their interests, and consequently both adjusted their strategies to renounce war to embrace a negotiated, eventually electoral, solution. The peace agreement led to a successful peace process; a general election was held in March 1994, which the FMLN contended as part of an opposition coalition. ARENA won the elections, but there was no return to warfare by the demobilized FMLN.

CONCLUSION

The comparison of the unsuccessful UN mediation efforts in Bosnia with their successful counterparts in El Salvador shows how structural weaknesses caused the failure of the Bosnian missions. The coincidence of interests in the UN coalition that dispatched the mediation missions proved to be crucial. In Bosnia, the divisions among the international community were in many ways more complex than the divisions among the belligerents. This factionalism made a misdiagnosis of the conflict, and the formulation of an infeasible response, more likely, as extraneous factors rather than genuine observation informed judgements. By failing to understand not only the bases, but also the balance, of the conflict dynamic in instructing the mediators, the sponsoring coalition made the mission unacceptable to the strongest belligerent, crippling the mediators from the outset. While the goals of the mission were endorsed by the weaker parties, what they proposed to negotiate was seen as completely incompatible with their interests by the Bosnian Serbs. In the El Salvador coalition, not only an extraordinary agreement on the need for peace, but the tangible momentum of international pressure for peace in the region that had built up, provided a solid foundation, free of any weaknesses, for the mediators. This was coupled with a reasonably accurate understanding of the conflict and the requirements for a solution, probably a result of the years of trying to find solutions to the war. The selection of an apposite response – a high-profile UN mediation mission with appropriate instructions – was interpreted by the belligerents as an opportunity, not a threat. In El Salvador, the appropriateness of the response resulted not in the aggravation of weaknesses by the conflict dynamic, but of a reinforcement of its desirability by the conflict dynamic and the interests of its participants.

The strengths or weaknesses imparted on the mediation missions through their UN coalitions' objectives were translated into the corresponding acceptability or unacceptability of the mission in the conflict dynamic. In Bosnia, two of the belligerents saw the UN mission as an opportunity to secure interests that they were unable to secure militarily. However, the enormous preponderance of the Bosnian Serbs in the military balance dictated their calculations that the proposals of the UN mediators would deprive them of much of what they had gained militarily with no compensation, and were inimical to their interests. The sympathy of the UN proposals with the interests of their opponents, and the growing international hostility to the Serbs, influenced Bosnian Serb characterizations of the UN mission as another antagonist in the conflict, to be frustrated and manipulated. In El Salvador, the belligerents saw the UN mediators as an important opportunity to secure their interests, an opportunity that had eluded them during a decade of war. The UN was the mediator of choice for the parties in El Salvador, being seen as more impartial than the other mediators available. It was clear that the Salvadoran belligerents' receptivity to the peace process was based heavily on their stalemated military position, and the influence of this on their calculations concerning the UN mission. The military balance in Bosnia and El Salvador determined whether the UN mission's presence became a weakness or a mechanism of acceptance: the militarily preponderant Bosnian Serbs were prepared to negotiate, but only in order to secure their military gains via a peace agreement, whereas the militarily frustrated Salvadoran belligerents saw mediation as an opportunity. The acceptability of a UN mediation mission, therefore, is determined by the accuracy of the UN's reading of the conflict dynamic and its military balance, and its ability to use this understanding to dictate a feasible response.

The prospect of success of the mediation design was shown to be heavily determined by the existence of weaknesses in the objectives and the mission presence. In both Bosnia and El Salvador, the UN mediators used deductive mediation frameworks to try to establish broad agreement before moving the belligerents to consensus on more particular issues. In Bosnia, the mediators were hampered by the weaknesses in the mandate they had been given; however creative they tried to be in fashioning mediation formulas, they were in the end frustrated by the basic incompatibility of their instructions with the interests of the Bosnian Serbs. In El Salvador, the deductive mediation design worked, because the absence of weaknesses in the sponsoring coalition and its instructions freed the mediators to be creative in maintaining the momentum of the negotiations towards agreement. The effect of the existence of these prior weaknesses on the viability of the deductive mediation design was demonstrated by the difference between the Bosnian Serbs' and the Salvadoran belligerents' modification of their tactics to address the peace process. The Bosnian Serbs, convinced of the antagonism of the international community and its mediators, adjusted their tactics to best frustrate and exploit the mediation missions' vulnerabilities for their own interests. In El Salvador, the parties, increasingly focusing on the results of the peace process, and worried about the effects of their actions on their electoral popularity, found themselves steadily altering their tactics to pursue their interests through the peace talks.

Manipulation of the belligerents' dependence on external support through links to UN members also appeared to affect their co-operation or their manipulation of the missions' weaknesses. In Bosnia, the mediators lacked any such means of leverage to compel the unco-operative Bosnian Serbs to comply with their mediation designs. This was because the Bosnian Serbs were to some extent self-reliant for their military preponderance, and also because those states with influential links to the Bosnian Serbs were unwilling to manipulate these links to compel them to co-operate with anything against their interests. In El Salvador, the cohesive international momentum for peace in Central America was reflected in the willingness of member-states with links to the belligerents to do all in their power to support the UN mediation. At certain points this proved crucial, with the extremely externally dependent parties being persuaded to reverse momentary lapses in their co-operativeness by member-states willing to manipulate levels of external assistance. These factors also informed the durability of the missions. In Bosnia, an awareness of the bitter divisions within their sponsoring coalition made the mediators tentative and their mediation proposals short-lived. The obviousness of the international disagreements, on the other hand, encouraged Bosnian Serb obduracy and manipulativeness during the negotiations. The El Salvador mediators were confident of the cohesive backing of the UN's powerful members, a factor that gave them the assurance and authority to compel the at times reluctant belligerents to a solution. The comparison of the Bosnia and El Salvador mediation missions, then, shows us that while strong mediation design, leverage, and durability are important to the mission's successful mediation of an agreement, it is the status of the mission's base within the UN that is crucial. A divided and distracted sponsoring coalition is likely to misdiagnose the conflict and prescribe an inapt response. If the resulting mission objectives and presence are incompatible with any aspects of the conflict dynamic, these basic weaknesses are likely to frustrate the mission.

3 Peacekeeping

With a peacekeeping mission, the UN enters the civil war conflict environment. But despite their helmets, side arms, and APCs, the peacekeepers' function remains more diplomatic than military. Their purpose is to work with the belligerents, rather than to compel them using offensive military action. This basic fact, as in mediation missions, means that the existence of underlying structural weaknesses can jeopardize the mission's ultimate success. Such weaknesses can be even more problematical when directly exposed to the conflict dynamic, and their consequent vulnerability to more complex forms of exploitation and aggravation by the less co-operative belligerents. This chapter searches for the presence of these weaknesses and the effects of their exposure to a civil war dynamic in a failed peacekeeping mission. It then tests a successful mission for the absence of these weaknesses or the mission's escape from the effects of the conflict dynamic.

Peacekeeping has conventionally been conceived as 'the prevention, containment, moderation and termination of hostilities between or within states, through the medium of peaceful third party intervention organised and directed internationally, using multinational forces of soldiers, police and civilians to restore and maintain peace'.[1] The task of peacekeeping in civil wars is more difficult and complex than that of separating national armies; to secure a permanent end to the conflict, they often have to deal with collapsed political, administrative, security, economic, and infrastructure systems. To respond to these demands, the UN often needs to dispatch multi-component peacekeeping operations, charged with a combination of the following tasks: ceasefire monitoring and pacification; protecting aid flows; disarmament, demobilization and reintegration of former belligerents; de-mining; repatriation of refugees; rehabilitation of the security and juridical apparatus; ensuring the respect of human rights; monitoring elections; building popular political participation; and rebuilding war-damaged infrastructure. To add to the difficulty of these tasks, peacekeeping forces are charged with implementing these immensely complex mandates in a more difficult civil war environment. They must operate among a frightened and demoralized population; in a volatile conflict zone; over damaged infrastructure; and interact with untrustworthy belligerents.

A peacekeeping mission is not intended to compel co-operation from these untrustworthy belligerents. Its very presence in the conflict to some extent is evidence of the sponsoring coalition's rejection of the costly and difficult option of a forceful intervention in the conflict. Furthermore, peacekeepers 'are almost by definition outgunned by the disputants they are sent to monitor, [and] any recourse to force must be calibrated to localise and defuse, rather than escalate, violence'.[2] The function played by the peacekeepers is one of neutralizing the aspects of the conflict dynamic that perpetuate the cycle of hostilities in order to allow a particular arbitration or resolution mechanism to apportion the disputed commodities or interests at the base of the conflict. Often the peacekeepers are intended as a component of the UN's mechanism for replacing war with a peaceful method of addressing the bases of the conflict by 'overcom[ing] a coordination problem between two adversaries: the peacekeeper seeks to ensure that both parties to a conflict understand the agreed-upon rules of the game and that compliance with or deviation from these rules is made transparent'.[3] Peacekeeping, like mediation, therefore, must also rely on the consensual co-operation of the belligerents; its attempts to displace the war interaction among the disputants cannot rely on its own ability to coerce. The peacekeeping mission, in a similar way to other UN missions, must therefore rely on favourable calculations by the belligerents as to the value of the peacekeeping force for advancing its interests.

To the belligerents, a large armed force entering their conflict environment will impact heavily on their calculations. Foremost among these calculations will be how the peacekeeping force, and the mandate it has been set, will impact on their position. Being locked in a struggle for power and survival, the belligerent calculations will be first and foremost self-regarding, being primarily interested in the opportunities offered or the dangers posed to their interests and survival by the presence of the peacekeeping force. The first assessment they make is probably about the impact of the peacekeepers and their mandate on the belligerent's chances of survival: 'Any agreement must eliminate the insecurity of all significant local factions . . . members of all factions must be assured of their safety regardless of who wins the political contest. If any of the competing groups . . . faces physical elimination, it will obviously prolong the bloody struggle rather than meekly accept its doomed fate.'[4] The other necessary assessment is one that determines a belligerent's co-operativeness with the peacekeeping force; it is a calculation of whether its interests will be better advanced through the peaceful means proposed by the peacekeepers and the UN. Such calculations will also inform assessments of the acceptability of the mission's presence: if the mission is not seen as advancing its interests, a party is likely to see it as an impediment to its further successes. However, peacekeeping forces can also be used effectively by a non-cooperating party to advance its military objectives. The exploitation of a mission plagued by weaknesses by the belligerents is an ever-present danger, and 'peacekeepers are likely to be viewed instrumentally rather than as actors whose independence should be respected'.[5]

The singular impact that peacekeepers have on disputants' perceptions in civil wars makes them particularly vulnerable to any weaknesses which they may carry in their dispatch or mandates. These added vulnerabilities are not compensated for by any unique powers of compulsion: peacekeepers are largely dependent on the same leverage mechanisms as are mediators. For these reasons, the analytical framework will be used to search the record of the spectacular failure of the UNOSOM II mission for these weaknesses, their attack from within the Somali conflict dynamic, and the responsibility of this interaction for the failure and withdrawal of the mission. It then asks the same questions of the successful ONUMOZ mission to Mozambique: did it carry these weaknesses and were they accentuated by the civil war, and if not, does this help explain the mission's success?

HANDLING SCORPIONS IN SOMALIA

By late 1992, Somalia had descended into the chaos that Boutros-Ghali had warned of in *Agenda for Peace*: brutal clan warfare had destroyed all central governing authority, mortgaging Somalia's future to a vicious cycle of hunger, insecurity, and lawlessness.[6] The Somali civil war had begun when the coalition to overthrow dictator Mohammed Siad Barre dissolved into anarchy as the clans[7] fell on each other in a ferocious struggle to inherit the reins of state.[8] The war polarized between two factions of the Hawiye clan's United Somali Congress: the Abgal sub-clan of Ali Mahdi Mohammed, installed as interim President; and the Habr Gedir sub-clan of Mohammed Farah Aideed, which formed the United Somali Congress-Somali National Alliance (USC-SNA) to challenge Ali Mahdi's claim to the presidency. Banditry proliferated in a countryside awash with weapons left over from the Cold War, resulting in a murderous anarchy fuelled by clan opportunism, brigandry, and qat, an indigenous narcotic plant.[9] All of the clans initially sought to use the anarchy in Somalia for their own ends. The main contenders to power hoped to prevail over the others, and emerge out of the anarchy to seize the advantages that would accrue to any clan that ruled Somalia, as Siad Barre's Maheran clan had done throughout his dictatorship. Just as important to the clans was to deny this ascendancy to any of their rival clans.[10]

Under pressure to end the anarchy and brutal warfare between the USC-SNA and the other clans, the UN sent UNOSOM II to Somalia in May 1993, charged with pacification, protecting aid flows, disarming the militias, repatriating refugees, and promoting reconciliation. Within six months the force was embattled in Mogadishu, and the focus of bitter recriminations and sagging commitment in New York. Soon after, UNOSOM II entered the vocabulary of debate as a metaphor for the crisis in UN peacekeeping. By March 1995, the force had withdrawn, having spent $3 billion and thousands of lives over nearly two years, leaving Somalia in much the same state of anarchy as it had found it. Such a spectacular failure was the result of glaring weaknesses in the mission and a determined and virulent attack on these from within the conflict dynamic. An analysis of the progress of UNOSOM II allows the observation of how an extremely resistant conflict dynamic was able to act on the weaknesses within a UN mission in such a way as to allow a collection of ragged militias to repel the intervention of the most powerful UN peacekeeping mission ever mounted.

Objectives

The most fundamental weaknesses within the UNOSOM II mission were located within its sponsoring coalition and its formulation of a response to the Somali crisis. As evidence of the humanitarian tragedy accumulated, the organization became increasingly embarrassed by its initial withdrawal from Somalia in January 1991, and the lack of impact of its first UNOSOM operation on the crisis. By August 1992, the UN reported that over 300 000 Somalis had died as a direct result of the civil war and famine. Press photographs of emaciated and dying women and children mobilized enormous public empathy, especially in Western and Islamic societies. Much of the pressure to 'do something' was directed at the Bush administration in the US, which had coined the 'new world order' rhetoric in the aftermath of the successes of the Gulf War and operation to protect the Kurds in northern Iraq.[11] The US responded, beginning aid drops in August 1992 and mobilizing the UNITAF operation in December 1992. Nevertheless, pressure continued to mount on the UN to respond. The EU called on the UN to act in August 1992, Secretary-General Boutros-Ghali publicly castigated the Security Council for its preoccupation with the 'rich man's war' in Bosnia while ignoring Somalia, and UN Special Representative to Somalia Mohammed Sahnoun resigned over the poverty of the UN response. By early 1993, the new Clinton administration in the US was applying pressure on the organization for a UN operation to relieve the UNITAF force.[12] Thereafter it was the US, keenly supported by Boutros-Ghali, that initiated action for a UN force, and proposed the composition, structure, capabilities, and responsibilities of the operation. Finally, the pressures caused a sponsoring coalition to form around the US to send a more UNITAF-like

UN force into Somalia. The US was supported by the Western Europeans, particularly Italy, the former colonial power, the moderate Islamic world, Saudi Arabia, Turkey, Pakistan, the OIC, and the League of Arab States, and concerned regional states, Ethiopia, Kenya, and Djibouti. At the time of its formation, no clear divergences of interest within this coalition existed over Somalia, or the need for the UN to respond to the crisis.

The weaknesses were to derive from the coalition's response to the public and diplomatic pressure to act, which hurried it into mistakes in understanding and responding to the conflict that were to prove disastrous for UNOSOM II. The intense pressure on the member-states of the coalition rushed them into formulating a response before they had an understanding of the conflict in Somalia. The coalition worked on a conception of the conflict that visualized an anarchic situation driven by banditry, rather than as a dynamic struggle by clans competing for political power and using the anarchy as a significant part of their strategies.[13] Compounding this misunderstanding, the coalition was pressured into an over-reaction to the crisis, dispatching a large, heavily armed force to deal with the lawless situation, and then charging it with a mandate to rebuild a functioning polity from these conditions of chaos.

The coalition overestimated the abilities of a peacekeeping operation – even the most powerful ever launched – in entrusting it with building political reconciliation from anarchy in the face of local opposition. The objectives it set UNOSOM II were to secure aid flows, promote internal stabilization, and to impose order and political reintegration. Rather than just facilitating aid delivery, UNOSOM II was required to terminate the war and resurrect the collapsed state. The mission's mandate included the tasks of: 'Assisting . . . in the ongoing political process in Somalia, which should culminate in the installation of a democratically elected government,'[14] which could ultimately maintain order and rebuild the country.[15] The UN was aware that the conflict could potentially threaten regional security,[16] and so placed the pacification and termination of the fighting as its first priority. UNOSOM II was inserted into Somalia to help implement the framework[17] of the March 1993 Addis Ababa Agreement, wherein the factions agreed to a peace process in which a ceasefire and disarmament would precede a transitional period of reconstruction and reconciliation, and the setting up of a Transitional National Council (TNC) to administer Somalia until elections could take place.[18] The ceasefire was also seen as essential to the delivery of aid and the protection of the aid agencies.[19] UNOSOM II's primary task, then, was 'to assume responsibility for the consolidation, expansion and maintenance of a secure environment throughout Somalia,'[20] in order for the successful subsequent implementation of the 'other aspects of UNOSOM [II]'s mandate, be they political, civil, humanitarian, rehabilitation or reconstruction'.[21] As it tried to implement this mandate of incredible complexity and difficulty in the midst of the Somali conflict, UNOSOM II was to find itself plagued by a basic weakness: being charged with a near impossible task in an environment with which it was not equipped to deal.

The UN coalition had misunderstood the medieval nature of the Somali power struggle. So glaring was its miscasting of the response to this crisis that the objectives it set were fundamentally inimical to the most powerful belligerents. The war between the USC-SNA and the Ali Mahdi alliance was 'a raw power struggle, devoid of ideological or ethnic motivation, with both . . . claiming to be the rightful successor to ousted President Mohammed Siad Barre'.[22] The struggle for control of the state, the gatekeeper of security, wealth, cultural survival and prestige, had generated an escalating sub-clan security dilemma: 'As the conflict continues, subclan loyalty – even sub-clan security – is increasingly at stake, with the fear that the future [seizure of power by the rival sub-clan] may bring murderous retaliation against the losers.'[23] The June 1991 Djibouti Accords had given the USC faction under Ali Mahdi a comparative advantage by installing him as interim President of Somalia, as a measure towards ending the war and finally deposing of Siad Barre forces.[24] A number of the clans clustered around the interim presidency, which began to advocate ending the war and re-establishing mechanisms of authority and control, partly as a method of legitimizing the Abgal sub-clan's authority.[25] These motives were supported by the international community's attempts to calm the fighting and alleviate the famine. The USC-SNA, wanting supreme power for itself, was bitterly opposed to the instalment of Ali Mahdi as interim President, and viewed the struggle for power in zero-sum terms.[26]

The USC-SNA's objectives centred on the seizure of power and preventing Ali Mahdi from consolidating power. Among the Somali clans, the USC-SNA held the political–military advantage. Aideed, benefiting from his military background,[27] armed and trained his 500-strong clan-based militia to a higher standard than the other forces.[28] He was also politically adept at mobilizing the Somali people, being able to identify with and personify the wider Somali identity,[29] and use emotive appeals to nationalism, anti-imperialism, and threats of external danger to mobilize and control the fissiparous, independently armed clans and allies of the USC-SNA.[30] Cognizant of the 30 per cent literacy of Somalis, and the strong oral tradition of Somali society, he was able to use the Radio Mogadishu station, captured by the USC-SNA, as his primary means of disseminating propaganda and tactically mobilizing the clans.[31] The USC-SNA was using its military strength to benefit from the anarchy in Somalia; by fostering the warfare, banditry and starvation, it would destroy the political base of its Ali Mahdi opponents, and seize power from amongst the confusion. It adopted the basic strategy of military destabilization: 'Aideed . . . did not create domestic anarchy in Somalia absent-mindedly. The insecurity of the Somali population was [his] very objective, the basis of [his] power and revenues.'[32]

Within the first few months of its deployment, the USC-SNA 'decided that the UN, in its efforts to restore representative government . . . represented some kind of threat . . . and decided to . . . obstruct in every way the mandate that [UNOSOM II was] carrying out'.[33] UNOSOM II's presence and objectives were a serious danger: 'Simply by being . . . the dominant military force in the country, UNOSOM reduced the influence of those political leaders, General Aideed eminent among them, who had hitherto disposed of substantial forces. While UNOSOM remained in place, guns would no longer trump all other sources of influence.'[34] The USC-SNA's propaganda alleged that UNOSOM II had a secret agenda of operating as an invasion force to turn Somalia into a UN protectorate.[35] The USC-SNA was also opposed to UNOSOM II's protection of humanitarian relief. In that famine-stricken environment, food had become a valuable commodity,[36] and the control of food and its distribution was an important political–military instrument.[37] Before the arrival of UNOSOM II, Aideed had repeatedly asserted that the USC-SNA could distribute aid.[38] This was rejected by the Security Council, and the introduction of UNOSOM II to control aid distribution deprived the USC-SNA of a powerful military tool, threatening to marginalize it as a force in the struggle for power in Somalia. So not only had UNOSOM II been given an impossible mandate; it had incurred the resistance of the most powerful faction of an extremely resistant conflict dynamic.

Mission Presence and the Military Balance

Not surprising, by embodying the ill-conceived response of the UN coalition, UNOSOM II's presence was unwelcome by some aspects of the conflict dynamic in Somalia. Those elements that benefited from stability and the alleviation of the humanitarian disaster welcomed the intervention. Indeed, the Ali Mahdi alliance requested an international monitoring of the peace process, asserting that 'a ceasefire agreement without international monitoring and supervision would not hold'.[39] However, the USC-SNA voiced opposition to any international presence, with Aideed reiterating 'the reservation of his faction to the stationing of a peacekeeping force in

Mogadishu or to any identifiable UN military presence'.[40] In negotiations between March and August 1992, Aideed had rejected UN monitoring of the ceasefire between the USC-SNA and the Ali-Mahdi alliance, at first insisting on neutral monitors from the Hawiye clan,[41] but finally agreeing to a small force,[42] unarmed and wearing UN insignia clearly.[43] Further commitment was not forthcoming: 'The agreement of "the parties" could not be obtained for the deployment of UN forces . . . when agreement was obtained, it was violated; and the small unit whose deployment in Mogadishu was agreed was not large enough to control the increasingly violent and lawless situation in that city.'[44] The intervention of the muscular UNOSOM II force, against the wishes of some of the parties, led to a 'widespread perception among Somalis that the UN [had] decided to abandon its policy of cooperation and [was] planning to "invade" the country'.[45] Aideed's propaganda stirred up popular antipathy against Boutros-Ghali,[46] capitalizing on his former position as the Foreign Minister of Egypt, a former Siad Barre supporter.

As the war polarized between the USC-SNA and the Ali Mahdi alliance, which by this stage consisted of twelve of the fourteen major Somali factions calling itself 'Manifesto',[47] and as its relations with the USC-SNA became more and more conflictual, UNOSOM II inevitably started to identify with, and receive encouragement from, the anti-USC-SNA Manifesto alliance.[48] The contacts between some UNOSOM II contingents, particularly the Italians and the Belgians, and the Somali factions, began to develop into ties of patronage and political support in Mogadishu and Kismayu.[49] Many clan leaders saw UNOSOM II, not as an impartial peace broker, but as another armed group to be incorporated into the calculus of interclan relationships.[50] When UNOSOM II responded forcefully to attacks against it to try to reassert its authority, it provoked a general anti-foreigner response and a heightened hostility to the UN.[51] As UNOSOM II came under increased attacks and was forced into a defensive posture, it became increasingly irrelevant to the pacification and relief effort. As hostilities continued and armed banditry increased, USC-SNA hostility made 'movement for Somali commercial traffic, UNOSOM personnel and international humanitarian relief supplies increasingly dangerous'.[52] With its impartiality irrevocably compromised, UNOSOM II became part of the conflict it was expected to terminate. From that time, peacekeeping and techniques of working co-operatively with the parties to resolve the conflict ceased to be options available to the force and its weaknesses became open to attack or exploitation by the belligerents.

The complex and escalating military situation in Somalia confronted UNOSOM II with a conflict dynamic that was extremely resistant to pacification, let alone the conflict resolution and peacebuilding activities the force had been set. It intervened in a civil war in which the major belligerents were well-armed and committed to war, in which the fighting had not stabilized, between parties whose military calculus had not yet begun to be affected by a protracted campaign. The USC-SNA was progressing in the military struggle for power by taking advantage of the anarchy. It had begun to expand its objectives towards the seizure of power by eventually achieving the ability to take control of the state and impose its own order on the chaos.[53] It was inevitable that it would view a large UNOSOM II force, charged with pacifying the situation and alleviating the humanitarian crisis, as inimical to its objectives and at variance with its military impetus. It began to characterize UNOSOM II as an enemy to be defeated. The inappropriateness of a muscular UN intervention was acknowledged by staff and diplomats at UN headquarters,[54] but the UN was pressured by the need to relieve the UNITAF force and by humanitarian organizations and public opinion demanding that it assume responsibility for alleviating the crisis in Somalia.[55] As a result, UNOSOM II was faced with a situation in which it had little chance of fulfilling a conventional peacekeeping role, and in which it was mentally and doctrinally unprepared to undertake a war-fighting mission. The ascendant position of the USC-SNA in the military balance made it rational for it not to cooperate with the mandate of UNOSOM II, which was so opposed to its strategic interests.

Mission Design and Belligerents' Tactics

The UNOSOM II mission's most visible weakness, and that which the USC-SNA directly attacked, was that the mission design it was assigned was in no way capable of achieving its unrealistic mandate, yet increased opposition to it by virtue of its aggressive force posture. This was recognized in time by the UN Secretariat, but over-ridden by the member-states of the coalition, eager to respond to allay domestic political pressures to do something about the crisis. In early 1993, the Secretary-General and the UN Department of Peacekeeping Operations were not convinced that a peacekeeping response was appropriate without significant consent or a viable ceasefire in place.[56] Within the Security Council, the US had begun to insist that the UN relieve the burden and expense of the overwhelmingly American-run UNITAF operation. The relevant Departments within the UN contended that until UNITAF disarmed the Somali militias and established a peace process, a peacekeeping force would be inappropriate.[57] Bowing to American pressure, the Security Council finally over-rode

Secretariat opposition and endorsed the dispatch of UNOSOM II. The heavily-armed, 30 800-strong UNOSOM II force was finally deployed on the basis of the vague and precarious Addis Ababa Agreement to a ceasefire and an international monitoring mechanism.[58] From the beginning there was confusion about the roles and methods of the force. When finally deployed, UNOSOM II was the culmination of escalating commitments and force levels, as each additional task was thought to hold the key to the pacification and rehabilitation of Somalia. The factions' resistance to UNOSOM II resulted in 'growing impatience'[59] over 'the lawlessness and lack of security that prevail throughout Somalia'.[60] The Security Council 'doubted whether the methods employed by the UN to date could bring the situation under control. Strong support was expressed for [the] view that the time had come when it was necessary to move into Chapter VII of the Charter of the UN.'[61]

The UN coalition had become convinced that the USC-SNA was the most problematic faction and 'the single biggest obstacle to peace' in Somalia.[62] It made repeated attempts to gain Aideed's consent to the deployment of a peacekeeping force, but was continually thwarted by his manoeuvring.[63] Frustrated in its attempts to secure the USC-SNA's co-operation with the resolution process, and following its attacks against UNOSOM II, the UN decided that Aideed needed to be removed from the equation; 'to eliminate [Aideed's] means for doing those kinds of acts and frankly get him under arrest . . . the intimidation and the terrorism won't stop until he is arrested'.[64] Aideed and the USC-SNA were criminalized and blamed for the failure of the peace process and the continuing crisis in Somalia. According to the Special Representative of the Secretary-General: '[Aideed] bears a large portion of the responsibility for the thousands and thousands of deaths by civil strife and starvation that occurred in the years before, which caused the UN to come to the rescue of the Somalis.'[65] Following this logic, and feeling 'that the situation in Somalia [had] deteriorated beyond the point at which it [was] susceptible to peacekeeping treatment,'[66] the Security Council authorized UNOSOM II to take 'appropriate action against any faction that violates or threatens to violate the cessation of hostilities'.[67] The Security Council mandated the 'use of force . . . to ensure, on a lasting basis, that the current violence against the international relief effort was brought to an end . . . this action would help de facto to bring about a ceasefire between warring factions and that this would be a positive factor in the context of national reconciliation'.[68]

The Security Council had quite consciously decided to embark on its first experiment in peace-enforcement, a concept which it had approved along with the other components of *Agenda for Peace* nine months previously.[69]

UNOSOM II's approach differed radically from that of traditional peacekeeping operations. In determining to over-ride consent and impose peace and stability, the force became an arbiter rather than a facilitator; a military rather than a diplomatic instrument. Heavily armed to enforce UN directives, UNOSOM II became a military threat to the belligerents, rather than an impartial guarantor and buffer. In embracing enforcement, the UN had adopted an approach for which it had no doctrine; the ensuing confusion and mistakes were to lead to serious acrimony between force contingents[70] and within the UN. To make UNOSOM II's task even more difficult, the Security Council had entrusted a vast nation-building assignment to the peacekeepers, in a situation where there was no viable peace agreement and no peace to keep. By being directed to attack the USC-SNA and exclude it from the peace process, UNOSOM II had been made an automatic target of military attack, but not supplied with the doctrine to protect this gaping vulnerability.

Despite being better armed than any previous UN peacekeeping force, UNOSOM II was doctrinally ill-equipped to deal with USC-SNA attacks. The weakness that it was given by its sponsoring coalition's over-reaction was that it became a peacekeeping force that was viewed as an enemy army. As it switched to enforcement and pacification, it was confronted by one of the toughest military problems: dealing with an urban insurgency in a Third World city.[71] UNOSOM II's personnel were faced with tens of thousands of potential belligerents, heavily armed,[72] largely unresponsive to any higher or central command, and extremely familiar with Mogadishu's warren of narrow, winding streets and mud houses. For its pacification task, it was inappropriately equipped: its high-calibre weaponry could not be used without significant collateral damage and civilian casualties in such a heavily populated area, and it was not initially issued with riot control gear.[73] UNOSOM II was a foreign force, which made it insensitive to the requirements of the Somali population, and vulnerable to charges of imperialism. The USC-SNA's propaganda made full use of this, and its use of rioting civilians as shields, which attracted fire from UNOSOM II troops,[74] widened the popular resentment and resistance to UNOSOM II and its mandate. The mission was hampered by a lack of quality intelligence: much of its human intelligence proved inaccurate or was deliberately misleading; and the American signals intelligence technologies were often inappropriate for the low-tech militias and the maze-like nature of Mogadishu.[75] Finally, doctrinal shortcomings compounded all of UNOSOM II's difficulties; a subsequent UN inquiry found that a lack of co-ordination between its political and military components produced the inopportune uses of military force, and that a lack of seasoned peacekeeping experience within UNOSOM II's command structure led to often heavy-handed and incompetent actions, particularly in the areas of weapons cantonment and inspections.[76] All of these weaknesses made UNOSOM II extremely vulnerable to manipulation and attack from within the conflict dynamic, of which it was to become a part.

The Manifesto factions attempted to exploit UNOSOM II by factoring it into their alliance and trying to exploit its presence to further their own interests in the struggle. These clans made use of the weaknesses in UNOSOM II's mandate by playing on the overawed peacekeepers' need for co-operative parties to help implement their vast mandate. Their increasing connections with the force were to compromise its impartiality, thereby further motivating and inviting attack by the USC-SNA. The USC-SNA, threatened by the peace process advanced by UNOSOM II, was unprepared to allow it to implement its mandate free from interference: 'the objective conflict between the [USC-SNA's] interests and UNOSOM's mandate' led Aideed to calculate that 'by demonstrating his ability to turn Mogadishu into a zone of grave insecurity, he could force UNOSOM to alter its programs so that they were compatible with his bid to play a, and probably the, leading political role in a reconstituted Somalia'.[77] Aideed exploited the factionalism within the force by treating different UNOSOM II contingents in different ways. He hoped to destroy its cohesion, by splitting first the American and then the Muslim contingents from the force.[78] Ultimately, however, the USC-SNA's objectives became to repel the invading force, and it adjusted its tactics accordingly. It 'declared that . . . peacekeeping patrols would no longer be tolerated in the streets of Mogadishu,'[79] and warned that weapons inspections and cantonments 'must not be performed and that, if they were, it would lead to "war"'.[80] When UNOSOM II began to carry out its mandate faithfully, the USC-SNA launched a 'calculated, premeditated series of major ceasefire violations meant to challenge and intimidate UNOSOM II,'[81] and to 'increase the costs of the UN operation particularly for certain key national contingents as to trigger the operation's termination'.[82]

The USC-SNA drew UNOSOM II into the conflict dynamic, a situation which so accentuated the mission's inherent weaknesses that it resulted in its frustration and withdrawal. After a USC-SNA attack left 23 Pakistani peacekeepers dead, the Security Council expanded UNOSOM II's mandate 'to take all necessary measures against all those responsible for . . . armed attacks . . . including against those responsible for publicly inciting such attacks, to establish the effective authority of UNOSOM II throughout Somalia'.[83] UNOSOM II turned on the USC-SNA, demonizing the movement as the prime cause of the anarchy in Somalia, and issuing a

$25 000 bounty on Aideed. Thereafter UNOSOM II launched a series of attacks against USC-SNA equipment, ordnance and its radio station, as well as beginning a highly publicized manhunt for Aideed, judged responsible for the attacks against UNOSOM II.[84] The attacks escalated in scale as the US Rangers repeatedly failed to capture Aideed. More disastrously, with expanding levels of collateral damage against Somali civilians,[85] hospitals, and even UN personnel by mistake,[86] UNOSOM II began to incur the hostility of Somalis and international opposition.

The USC-SNA's attacks on UNOSOM II, and the ill-conceived peace-enforcement response, successfully reimposed the conditions of instability that were so favourable to the USC-SNA.[87] The hostilities between UNOSOM II and the USC-SNA escalated over the next months, and culminated in a fifteen-hour battle in the Bakhara Market in Mogadishu on 3–4 October, which left twelve US Rangers dead, seventy injured, and one captured, and thousands of Somalis dead and injured. The Security Council responded by suspending the arrest and enforcement tasks of UNOSOM II.[88] This resolution was the beginning of a retreat leading to the failure and withdrawal of UNOSOM II in March 1995. The ramifications of the UN's first attempt at peace enforcement are still being felt. Much of the resulting criticism was directed at the poverty of the peace-enforcement concept, and the inappropriateness of the American approach to peacekeeping, which relied too strongly on overwhelming force and firepower.[89] Analysis has shown, however, that the causes lay in the inherent weaknesses in the mission, and their attack by an extremely resilient conflict dynamic.

Links and External Support

The UNOSOM II mission did not possess adequate military abilities to protect its mission weaknesses from direct attack. Neither was it able to protect its vulnerabilities by calling on member-states to use their links with the combatants to modify their behaviour. The UN's response was prompted by humanitarian motives rather than any member-states' previous involvements in the civil war. Much of the international support for the UN's efforts came from regional organizations: the League of Arab States, the Organization of African Unity, the Islamic Conference Organization, the Standing Committee of the Countries of the Horn, and the Non-Aligned Movement all lent their assistance to the mediation efforts of the UN.[90] Apart from these inter-governmental organizations, little international pressure was applied to the parties on behalf of the UN, in large measure because of the lack of significant contacts between the parties and third-party states. The largely media-generated international commitment to alleviate the humanitarian crisis crumbled as soon as UNOSOM II ran into trouble, as the UN saw 'unmistakable signs of fatigue among the international community as it continues to be called upon to extend such assistance through the UN. This was reflected in the increasing delays in obtaining personnel from member-states and even longer delays in obtaining their financial contributions'.[91] As early as October 1993, the US had pledged to reduce and withdraw its contingent, as had Italy; France, Belgium, Sweden, and Norway withdrew their troops soon after. Appeals from the UN to Western countries for more troops for Somalia were firmly rejected, resulting in a growing proportion of UNOSOM II being furnished by poorly equipped troops from Third World states: Egypt, Pakistan, India, Bangladesh, Malaysia, and the United Arab Emirates.[92]

Neither did any fear of losing external support moderate the Somali clans' ability or will to continue the war. At the beginning of the civil war, the UN had imposed an arms embargo around Somalia in an attempt to isolate all of the warring factions.[93] Reports suggested that the embargo was not airtight, and that arms continued to trickle into Somalia from the region,[94] from Iran,[95] and from South Africa.[96] None of the parties had any significant support from an international sponsor; the Somali conflict seemed isolated more by a lack of strategic interest in a region of declining importance than by the UN-imposed embargo. This had little impact, however, because of the general self-sufficiency of the Somali factions. The USC-SNA and its rivals were amply supplied by enormous caches of weapons and materiel that had been pumped into Somalia by the competing superpowers during the Cold War. Their looting of international relief operations supplied them with food and medical supplies, a factor that only increased their determination to exercise ultimate control over the relief effort. Furthermore, especially for the USC-SNA, the anti-foreigner thrust of its propaganda made its self-reliance and isolation a point of pride and a source of strength. As a result, UNOSOM II derived little benefit from the international isolation of the USC-SNA.

Mission Durability and Belligerent Morale and Cohesion

Based on a hurried reaction to humanitarian pressures, the UNOSOM II operation showed no durability in the face of determined attacks against its weaknesses. Its fragile political base was the first aspect of the mission that splintered once it began to be attacked in Mogadishu and criticized by the world's media. UN member-states had been at first content to ignore the Somali civil war until the situation attracted appeals for help from international humanitarian agencies and criticism from the Secretary-General.

During UNOSOM II's deployment, the Security Council made its ephemeral commitment to the Operation clear by reminding 'all parties in Somalia . . . that continued UN involvement in Somalia depends on their active cooperation and tangible progress towards political settlement'.[97] Once UNOSOM II came under attack, began to suffer casualties, and started to respond forcefully, often against rioting civilians, the UN coalition fell into acrimonious debate about the direction of the operation, and the desirability of using force for a humanitarian purpose. Many of the coalition members and troop contributors reassessed their commitment to the operation, and, calculating the political and ethical costs to be too high, began to withdraw their contingents.[98] As a result, the cohesion within the force itself dissolved: 'Owing perhaps to the particularly complex and dangerous conditions under which UNOSOM found itself operating, the actions of some contingent commanders had the effect of weakening the integrity of UNOSOM's military command structure.'[99] The loss of cohesion resulted in a lack of concerted direction,[100] and degenerated into recriminations between contingents.[101] Faced with crumbling support for the UNOSOM II operation, the UN issued a warning to the Somali parties that 'Unless they show evidence almost immediately of significant movement towards reconciliation and the formation of a broad-based government, the Security Council will have no alternative but to bring [UNOSOM II's] presence in Somalia to an end.'[102] No such agreement was forthcoming, and UNOSOM II was withdrawn in March 1995.

Motivated by ancient clan rivalries and only loosely controlled by their leaders, the Somali factions were little affected by morale considerations in their decision to continue fighting. It is unlikely the clan leaders could have stopped the fighting even if they had wanted to. The huge Cold War weapons stockpiles had been widely distributed during the civil war; these armed elements were only loosely controlled by the factions through propaganda, shifting alliances, and vague ties of clan and sub-clan relationships. This meant that often '[t]he central figures of the USC were powerless to control the very people they had supplied with weapons'.[103] There was also a large number of armed bandit gangs controlled by no faction.[104] This situation was encouraged and exploited by the USC-SNA for its own political–military purposes. Its vague mechanisms of command were radio propaganda and clan ties. This anarchical situation made it extremely difficult for the UNOSOM II force to establish the conventional peacekeeping requirement of local consent. The lack of any cohesive command structure among the belligerents meant that faction leaders could not realistically be held accountable for the actions of the armed elements. Agreements negotiated with the parties' leaderships became meaningless on the ground, where 'Even when they . . . agreed, [the parties'] subsequent cooperation with UNOSOM [was] at best spasmodic, [because], by their own admission, they [did] not exercise authority over all the armed elements in the areas which they claim[ed] to control.'[105]

The demise of UNOSOM II offers important insights into the sources of the misdiagnosis of the civil war and the results of pressure on coalition members to respond. UNOSOM II's mandate was the result of an over-estimation among the coalition members of the abilities of UN peacekeeping forces, combined with a desire to experiment with the new concept of peace-enforcement. Encouraged by the success of the Gulf War and the UNITAF experiment, the UN coalition decided to pledge the difficult project of nation-building in an anarchic society to a massive, heavily armed force. In doing so, they placed a central weakness in the mission, by charging it with an unrealistic mandate. This was added to by giving the mission authorization to forcefully override any resistance to its task, adding the weaknesses of being seen as a threat that needed to be attacked, to the impossibility of its mandate. The UNOSOM II mission, and its weaknesses, encountered an extremely robust conflict dynamic, generated by clans which were benefiting from the anarchy in Somalia, and were unprepared to tolerate a large, potent international armed force imposing peace, distributing relief, and introducing an alien system of political reintegration. Their attack on the mission's weaknesses brought about the frustration of the mission's mandate, the fracturing of its sponsoring coalition and the force, and finally its defeat and withdrawal.

PURCHASING PEACE IN MOZAMBIQUE

The UN was obliged to oversee an end to the war in Mozambique, a member-state that had been reduced to the poorest in the world by a brutal civil war instigated and fomented by neighbouring states. Since 1976, the Marxist Mozambican government, established from the former Frelimo national liberation movement, had been fighting the anti-communist Resistencia Nacional Mocambicana (Renamo) insurgency, formed from disaffected groups opposed to Frelimo's Marxism. Renamo was entirely a creation of external states, being created and funded first by the Rhodesian Central Intelligence Organization, and then directed after 1980 by South African Military Intelligence.[106] Both Rhodesia and South Africa used Renamo as a destabilization tool against the frontline States – Mozambique, Zimbabwe, and Zambia – which were supporting the Zimbabwean and South African liberation movements against white minority rule.[107] Based and supplied in the remote Gongorosa mountains, Renamo developed into an almost completely military organization, rigidly controlled by its flamboyant leader, Afonso Dhlakama, but dependent on its external sponsors for direction and supply.[108] The organization made no attempt to explain its political programme, mobilize supporters, or provide services to the population in the areas it controlled.[109] Renamo's military strategy was to isolate the government in Maputo, and destabilize it using economic sabotage. Tactically, Renamo's 20 000-strong army, organized into 200–300-strong battalions, attacked transport corridors, pipelines, electrical grids, health centres, schools, government offices, and development projects, and made no attempt to create and defend a 'liberated zone' like other insurgencies.[110] Renamo also utilized a scorched earth policy,[111] as well as widespread genocide, rape, and terror against the population, for recruitment and control.[112] The increasingly beleaguered government, watching the country descend into famine and chaos, was desperate to rid itself of the insurgency which was destroying all of its attempts to build Mozambican society and prosperity. By the end of the 1980s, Renamo's campaign had not toppled the government, but had turned Mozambique into the poorest state on earth, caused 1 million deaths, and created 4.5 million refugees. The war in Mozambique had become a running sore that needed to be resolved.

After sustained negotiations, Renamo and the Mozambican government signed a peace agreement in Rome in August 1992, requesting a UN peacekeeping force to oversee the settlement.[113] In December 1992 the Security Council unanimously approved the creation of ONUMOZ, a 7500-strong peacekeeping force to monitor the government–Renamo ceasefire, organize elections, disarm and demobilize the two sides, create a new, unified army, and guard the transport corridors through Mozambique to its landlocked neighbours.[114] All involved in the Mozambican peace process were aware of the recent failure of a similar operation in Angola. However, by October 1994, multiparty elections were held and won by the incumbent government. ONUMOZ withdrew in December having registered a much-needed success among the peacekeeping failures of 1994. Yet the developing success of the operation was jeopardized by avoidable hitches in the mounting and running of the operation. These hitches were evidence of organizational weaknesses within the ONUMOZ mission. How then did it succeed in resolving this most brutal of civil wars?

Objectives

The weaknesses that resulted in the problems in the ONUMOZ mission originated within its sponsoring coalition, but in an attenuated form. While no significant divergences of interests existed within the coalition over Mozambique and the diagnosis of and response to the conflict were reasonably accurate, these factors were not able to avert the churlishness with which the members of the coalition prevaricated over and tried to minimize their contributions to the response. None of the major members of the Mozambique coalition had any compelling interest in the conflict over which to disagree. During the civil war, neither superpower had adjudged the conflict important enough to consider sponsoring either side heavily. The Frelimo government received small-scale arms transfers from the Soviet bloc and China.[115] Renamo had been unable to gain Western states' sponsorship, even during the heyday of the Reagan doctrine, despite the advocacy of its cause by conservative groups and senators in the US.[116] Mozambique's neighbours had more compelling interests in the conflict, but these were all in accordance with ending the festering war that was costing them so much. Zimbabwe, Botswana, and Malawi all suffered from disruptions in the traffic on the transport corridors through Mozambique that connected them to the Indian Ocean. Zimbabwe in particular wanted to end its long and costly defence of these corridors. The combination of this defence and lost revenue from Renamo's attacks on the corridors was estimated to have cost Zimbabwe $350 million per year.[117]

The UN coalition had the luxury of having an accurate diagnosis and an appropriate response provided to them within the Rome Agreement. These were unmodified by diverging member-state interests. The agreement, negotiated by a number of non-state representatives and the Italian government, appreciated the externally driven nature of the conflict, and the modifications to the parties' positions by the changes in these external circumstances. The provisions of the agreement had been developed to satisfy the belligerents' interests, and had accurately determined the need for a large, impartial, and authoritative peacekeeping force to oversee their implementation. By essentially acceding to the requests of the Rome Agreement, the UN coalition was able to dispatch an appropriate response.

While the UN mission was appropriate, it was weakened by the apathy of the sponsoring coalition. While there was a general unity of position among ONUMOZ's sponsoring coalition, there was also a general agreement on the non-compelling nature of the requirements in Mozambique. To some extent, the response in Mozambique was prompted by humanitarian concerns over the conflict. Yet the Mozambican civil war had not grabbed international headlines sufficiently to prompt concern or outrage among the Western publics that would have motivated their governments to act decisively to end the conflict. The dissociation of major powers from the conflict left the field open for a minor power such as Italy, to take the lead within the UN in initiating and sustaining UN initiatives in support of the resolution of the Mozambican civil war. There were also general regional stabilization interests in ending the war. The resolution of the conflict in Mozambique was seen to offer a positive impulse to the other more compelling facets of the southern African peace process: the dismantling of *apartheid* in South Africa, the independence of Namibia, and the attempts to resolve the Angolan civil war. Within the region, the main participants in the South African Codesa talks were keen to dissociate themselves from the legacies of their struggle in the region. Rather than representing any compelling strategic concern in its own right, however, the resolution of the Mozambican civil war was seen as a side game to the more important regional peace processes. This generally relaxed attitude towards responding to the Mozambican civil war was to result in severe weaknesses appearing in ONUMOZ's mounting and deployment.

The mandate given to the ONUMOZ force by the UN coalition was to implement the peace and rehabilitation settlement contained in the Rome Agreement.[118] As had been set out in the Rome Agreement, the Security Council expressed its desire to see an end to the insurgency, and a process of peace, democracy, and national unity take place.[119] It supported the provision of immediate aid to distressed areas, the disarmament of the marauding armies, and the reconstruction of damaged infrastructure.[120] It attached a 'vital importance' to the holding of free elections as a mechanism of legitimation, reintegration, and democratization.[121] The Security Council recognized that all of these tasks needed to be based on a stable and enduring ceasefire, urging the parties to 'respect scrupulously the ceasefire . . . a necessary condition for the fulfilment by the Operation of its mandate'.[122] The mandate given to the ONUMOZ force by the UN coalition, then, was largely determined by the objectives of the Rome Agreement. Fortuitously for the mission, these objectives had previously been agreed to and signed by both parties to the civil war.

Mozambique's Frelimo government had found it difficult at first to come to terms psychologically with Renamo's insurgency, choosing to view it as an externally sponsored intervention rather than a genuine internal challenge arising from dissatisfaction with Frelimo rule.[123] Eventually, it found it impossible not to take Renamo seriously, as the insurgents systematically destroyed every attempt to build Mozambique into a prosperous socialist state, while plundering and traumatizing the country and its population. Over the decades of war, the government had been forced into a massive internal war effort; and while it was dependent on foreign aid for 70 per cent of its income, it watched Mozambicans' average national income plummet to $80, the lowest in the world. Yet despite spending 45 per cent of its budget on fighting the guerrillas, it was unable to prevail militarily.[124] The regional partners it found to provide external assistance for its counter-insurgency and protection of the transport corridors had become increasingly impatient with the war and its strain on their own resources. Its attempts to come to terms with the South African government and thereby address the insurgency's external roots through the 1984 Nkomati Accord had failed, due to bad faith by the South Africans. By the late 1980s, Frelimo changed tack. In November 1990 it introduced a new constitution that signalled an end to one-party rule, proposing multiparty elections, freedom of the press, the legal right to strike, and opening the way to abolishing collectivized agricultural production.[125] Where it had previously refused to negotiate with Renamo, it began exploratory talks with the rebels, under the prompting of its international aid donors. As the peace momentum increased in Southern Africa, the government began to see the possibility of genuinely ending the war. With the signing of the Rome Agreement and the arrival of the peacekeepers, the government's objectives were twofold. Most pressing was to end the destructive insurgency, and to begin to rebuild the shattered country. For the government, the ending of the insurgency was intimately linked to access to the foreign aid that was needed to begin rebuilding. Frelimo's other objective was more partisan: throughout the discussion of the 1990 constitution, the secret talks with Renamo, and then the Rome Agreement negotiations, it had resisted Renamo's pressure for a power-sharing government in favour of multiparty elections.[126] In the Rome Agreement, it had secured the opportunity to compete with Renamo in free elections. So the government saw its objectives embodied in the Rome agreement, and ONUMOZ as the guarantor of that agreement.

As domestic and international changes deprived it of a *raison d'être* and emphasized the poverty of its ideological base, Renamo was forced to moderate its objectives. Its 1981 Manifesto's vague political goals, advocating anti-communism, democratic elections, social reforms, and a mixed economy, were an attempt to gain domestic political legitimacy and broader international support for a movement supported and directed by South Africa.[127] The negativity of its political stance was reflected in its use of terrorism to gain supporters and 'paralyse the country through destruction of the communication and transportation infrastructure and elimination or mutilation of Frelimo leaders'.[128] It was deprived of its justification for continuing the war by the government's liberalizing reforms, admitting that 'Frelimo has started using all our lines – democracy, freedom of speech, freedom of worship.'[129] Its unsavoury tactics, connections with South Africa, and ideological poverty were threatening to marginalize it. As Frelimo instituted its own programme of perestroika, Renamo realized it was unprepared to compete in the pluralist system it had long advocated.[130] By 1989, it had changed its demands to power-sharing with a guarantee of major portfolios, irrespective of the outcome of elections, and a chance to debate the 1990 liberal constitution adopted by Frelimo.[131]

Renamo was also a money-making enterprise. In the poorest state in the world, crippled by civil war and drought, the 'plundering and attacking of settlements and convoys [became] designed as much for replenishment of supplies and generation of booty as a reward for [Renamo's] combatants as for economic disruption for political ends'.[132] Renamo leaders saw that they would have to end the war to stop and reverse the process of its marginalization, but were reluctant to lose its wealth-creating potential. Consequently, the Rome Agreement 'guarantee[d] the distribution to all parties competing in the elections . . . of subsidies and logistic support for the election campaign apportioned on the basis of the number of each party's candidates'.[133] By the time the ONUMOZ force deployed, this provision translated into a blatant demand for financial incentives from the international community for its co-operation with the peace process.[134] Renamo also sought a settlement that would guarantee the security of the movement, after it had abandoned the war and begun to reintegrate into Mozambican society. It duly insisted on the inclusion of security provisions and international observation of the peace process in the Rome Agreement. Renamo's concerns were therefore not so much about its own destruction, as about the prospects of its marginalization and impoverishment. The Rome Peace Agreement process and the peacekeepers offered it a chance to avoid both of these calamities by offering it access to the Mozambican political system and the international donor community.

Mission Presence and the Military Balance

Having signed a peace agreement that they each saw as offering them a positive chance to advance their interests, both the government and Renamo saw a UN peacekeeping presence as an acceptable, and necessary aspect of the peace process. They saw the peacekeepers as a guarantee, providing security during the ceasefire and demobilization, and access to international funds. Their acceptance of ONUMOZ was determined by the appropriateness of the solution called for in the Rome Agreement.[135] Its presence was vital to all stages of the peace process: monitoring the ceasefire, conducting troop concentrations and disarmament,[136] and chairing the Cessation of Armed Conflict Mechanism (CAC), Ceasefire Commission (CCF) and the Committee for the Reintegration of Demobilized Personnel (CORE).[137]

ONUMOZ's protection of the transport corridors[138] was needed to stabilize the region while the peace process developed within Mozambique.[139] Such a delicate process between two mistrustful and bitter enemies needed a 'stabilizing factor' to prevent a return to the war.[140]

All of those involved in the peace process were aware of the lessons of Angola, where Unita, unhappy with the peace process and not adequately monitored and demobilized by the UNAVEM II peacekeeping force, had suddenly returned the country to a catastrophic civil war. Mindful of that failure, the UN was determined to provide a comprehensive armed presence in Mozambique.[141] It was so instrumental to the process that Renamo saw its 'presence in certain Renamo areas as a guarantee that another party could not take advantage of the demobilisation of Renamo forces'.[142] ONUMOZ also held access to the donor community for both parties. The government saw it as vital to be seen to be co-operating with the peacekeepers in order to secure the goodwill and aid of the international community, while the Special Representative of the Secretary-General made several specific requests to international donors on behalf of Renamo for more funds.[143] For its part, ONUMOZ did little to jeopardize the parties' positive image of it, taking pains to be equally rigorous in investigating both sides' ceasefire violations and complaints.[144] It maintained this impartiality by complying strictly with the conditions of the Rome Agreement and rejecting the appeals of either party to alter its provisions, stressing 'the unacceptability of attempts to gain more time or further concessions, or to attach new conditions to the peace process'.[145] The UN's image as an honest broker, carefully nurtured by both the Security Council and ONUMOZ, thereby served to establish the parties' perceptions that the operation was necessary to their protection and the progress of the peace process.

The acceptability of the peacekeeping mission and the peace agreement was based on both belligerents' willingness to abandon a struggle that had lost its rationale. The deep weaknesses that were to emerge in the mission design of ONUMOZ were not exposed and accentuated by either belligerent in such a way as to frustrate the mission's purpose. The eventual irrelevance of these weaknesses to the mission's overall progress was determined by the essential pliability of the conflict dynamic. By the mid-1980s, both Renamo and Frelimo had recognized that neither had the ability to win the war outright, but that their opponents had an indefinite ability to deny them victory.[146] The government, long confined in its jurisdiction to the coastal cities by the effectiveness of the Renamo campaign, was well aware that it was impossible for it to prevail militarily over the rebels. This calculation, and its desire to free up the 45 per cent of its budget it was spending on the war for other purposes, made the government only too willing to abandon the war and explore any peaceful methods of ending the destruction.[147] While Renamo was essentially a military organization, its signature of the Rome Agreement, and its ultimate co-operation with ONUMOZ was based on its realistic appraisal of its military situation. It calculated that a favourable peace agreement would allow it to escape a stalemated civil war and achieve its modified objectives through negotiation and political reintegration. Both the government and Renamo realized that the war was destroying Mozambique and alienating the majority of the population as it became increasingly difficult to mobilize supporters or raise recruits for the war effort.[148] As Frelimo began to introduce democratic reforms and Renamo realized that to counteract its marginalization it would eventually have to compete in free elections, both parties recognized the loss of popular support that continued warfare would entail. Renamo thus calculated that persevering with its military campaign would further marginalize the movement, while agreeing to and advocating peace would generate support among a war-weary populace. The eagerness of both sides to end the war and take advantage of the peace process granted the peacekeeping mission an extremely pliable conflict dynamic with which to work. As weaknesses emerged in the conflict dynamic, this pliability was to prove extremely lucky for the UN mission.

Mission Design and Belligerents' Tactics

The strong basis of the peacekeeping mission in the unity of its sponsoring coalition and the appropriateness of its presence was jeopardized by the tardiness of its deployment. Having agreed to provide the peace process with peacekeepers, the UN's member-states' lack of interest in the conflict, and consequent parsimony in contributing troops and resources, made it extremely difficult for the Department of Peacekeeping Operations to assemble a force of the necessary size for the mission.[149] The Security Council unanimously approved the creation of a 7500-strong peacekeeping force in December 1992.[150] The Rome Agreement specifically requested a prompt deployment of peacekeepers in order to secure a viable peace process, asking the UN mission 'to start its functions of verifying and monitoring the ceasefire on the day of entry into force of the General Peace Agreement'.[151] Yet the UN was not able to fully assemble and deploy ONUMOZ until April 1993. These delays were partly due to overstretch of UN resources, but was mainly due to the extreme reluctance of those member-states approached by the UN Secretariat to volunteer resources and troops.[152] Compounding ONUMOZ's sluggish arrival was its failure to negotiate a Status of Forces Agreement until May 1993.[153]

These weaknesses in the deployment and design of the mission could have proved disastrous for its ability to advance the peace process, by allowing a belligerent that had been disposed to non-cooperation to take advantage of the absence of the Peace Agreement's insurance mechanism to advance its own interests. There were early signs that these weaknesses were indeed being exposed and exploited. Both sides took advantage of the slow arrival of the peacekeepers to seize territory before the peace process could begin.[154] These developments heightened the tension between the parties, and several breaches of the ceasefire occurred. Furthermore, Renamo refused to begin demobilizing until ONUMOZ was fully deployed and operational.[155] Luckily for the UN, however, neither of the belligerents judged it to be within its interests to take further advantage of the slow deployment of the peacekeepers, or to break the Rome Agreement and return to war. Once ONUMOZ was fully operational, it renegotiated a revised timetable and an effective agreement for the movement of troops to counter ceasefire violations[156] with the co-operative belligerents.[157] The parties' compliance was further ensured through their participation in the Supervisory and Monitoring Commission (CSC), a dispute resolution and co-ordinating body overseeing the settlement process.[158] ONUMOZ succeeded in tying both parties, through a number of agreements, bodies, and timetables, to a unidirectional process of de-escalation of the conflict. It was able to secure Renamo's compliance with the enormously difficult task of disarmament and demobilization by linking financial assistance to its co-operativeness,[159] and by channelling its access to humanitarian relief and other reintegration aids through ONUMOZ-monitored assembly areas.[160] The receptiveness of both belligerents to the peace process, and the pliability of the conflict dynamic, allowed the UN to escape the potentially disastrous weaknesses that could have plagued ONUMOZ because of its slow deployment.

Special Representative of the Secretary-General to Mozambique Aldo Ajello made clear the importance of co-operation of both sides; that the UN could not 'promote and establish peace without the cooperation of the parties [and that] the political will of the parties to achieve a peaceful settlement must be demonstrated not only with public statements but with concrete action'.[161] Both belligerents were prepared, in order to secure the advantages of the peace process, to radically change their tactics and abandon the use of war to pursue their interests through co-operation with ONUMOZ. Initially, both Renamo and the government continued to manoeuvre to increase the size of the territory they controlled in the early aftermath of ONUMOZ's deployment.[162] Rather than an attempt to manipulate the peacekeepers, however, it became clear that these manoeuvres were merely attempts to enhance their bargaining positions. Within a short time, ONUMOZ was able to secure their co-operation, using the CAC and CCF mechanisms, and by including the representatives of both belligerents on the CSC. Furthermore, UN representatives specifically negotiated between the parties an agreement on troop movements and their oversight by peacekeepers.[163]

Renamo held initial doubts about the wisdom of co-operating with a UN peacekeeping force. At the outset of the ONUMOZ deployment, Renamo remained suspicious of a foreign military presence, and displayed an initial 'reluctance to allow timely investigation of alleged ceasefire violations and insistence on keeping certain areas under its control'.[164] Renamo further refused to co-operate until ONUMOZ was substantially deployed and operational.[165] Once it deployed, ONUMOZ tailored several specific measures to satisfying its concerns, in addition to including it in the CAC, CCF, and CSC mechanisms. ONUMOZ provided a verification mechanism to oversee the withdrawal of pro-Frelimo Zimbabwean troops from Mozambican soil,[166] while ensuring its security from attack by government troops during the ceasefire and demobilization process, and during its move into offices in Maputo. Finally, Special Representative Ajello specifically provided the Renamo leadership with access to an international conference of donor countries organized by Italy to finance the activities of the Mozambican political parties. These mechanisms were enough to secure Renamo's change in tactics from warfare to demobilization and co-operation. In agreeing to the peacekeeping mechanism, it undertook to 'refrain from armed combat and instead to conduct its political struggle in conformity with the laws in force, within the framework of the existing state institutions and in accordance with the conditions and guarantees established in the General Peace Agreement'.[167] It thus acceded to the peacekeepers and their conflict resolution mechanisms which were to guarantee a fast, balanced and irreversible process of implementation of the ceasefire, and the separation, concentration, and demobilization of forces. At the end of the disarmament process, Renamo's declaration of the numbers of troops and weapons that had failed to comply with the disarmament schedule testified to its good faith and behaviour change.[168]

Links and External Support

Former sponsors of the Mozambican government and Renamo, as well as other influential states, were supportive of the UN efforts to maintain their co-operation with the peace process. South Africa, which had for so long supplied and directed Renamo, was instrumental in delivering Renamo to

Rome during the mediation of the agreement.[169] During the peace process, both the South African government and the ANC maintained pressure on Renamo to co-operate with the UN.[170] Regional and African leaders meeting in Harare in October 1994 warned both sides that they were prepared to intervene in Mozambique if either party defaulted on the peace process and returned to war after the elections.[171] An influential non-governmental supporter of ONUMOZ was Lonhro Corporation President Tiny Rowland, who maintained constant pressure on Renamo first to enter and agree to the peace process, and then to comply fully with its provisions.[172] In support of ONUMOZ's efforts to tie the parties to the peace process and the outcome of the elections, the US and Portugal jointly conducted all-party talks in the lead up to the elections and persuaded them to agree to a power-sharing transitional administration in the aftermath of the elections.[173] Finally, many states were supportive of the UN's efforts to raise money for the parties through the Trust Fund and the Donor's Conference, used by ONUMOZ to maintain Renamo's co-operation with the operation.[174]

Both parties were motivated to co-operate with the peace process by their actual or impending desertion by much-needed external sponsors. While the government had been unable to gain major military assistance for its war with Renamo, it was highly dependent on overseas sources of aid, which comprised 70 per cent of its income. By the late 1980s, these donors were explicitly demanding that it enter formal negotiations with Renamo in order to forestall further destruction and impoverishment of Mozambique.[175] Furthermore, its one consistent military supporter, Zimbabwe, had notified the government of its desire to withdraw its troops from the transport corridors and the war, which was costing it $350 million per year.[176] Similarly, a factor in Renamo's military calculus to abandon the war was its desertion by most of its major external sponsors. As a creation of external interests, Renamo remained throughout its existence heavily dependent on the training, support, and direction of first Rhodesia and then South Africa.[177] Renamo also gained support from embittered Portuguese ex-colonists, and its anti-communist orientation gained it the support of religious fundamentalist groups in the US.[178] By the end of the 1980s, reports of its waging of a systematic war of terror, rape, and genocide against civilians,[179] began to dry up its support. The Southern African peace dynamic[180] began to isolate Renamo militarily and diplomatically. South Africa's new de Klerk government, keen to protect its own delicate reform process from external destabilization, halted all official assistance to Renamo. It also committed the government to preventing the aid intended for Renamo from right-wing South African and Portuguese groups and from groups within the South African Defence Forces from reaching the movement.[181] The threat or actuality of the loss of the external assistance on which they had formerly relied played a role in the military calculations of both parties to abandon the war and pursue a peaceful settlement. The drying up of external support delivered pliable belligerents, unwilling to take advantage of the weaknesses of ONUMOZ's sluggish deployment to frustrate the mission.

Mission Durability and Belligerent Morale and Cohesion

The ONUMOZ operation was not so much hindered by its sponsoring coalition's lack of cohesion as by its lack of interest. The overstretch of UN peacekeeping and security machinery at the time of the mounting of the ONUMOZ operation meant that the Security Council members' attention was diverted to higher-profile operations and more pressing security concerns. The UN struck difficulties in mounting the operation when willing troop contributors at first were difficult to find, and then were tardy in dispatching those contingents they had pledged to take part in ONUMOZ.[182] Throughout the operation the Security Council was obsessed by limiting the duration of the peace process and cutting its operational costs, repeatedly 'Stressing the necessity . . . to continue to monitor expenditures carefully during this period of increasing demands on peacekeeping resources.'[183] Once ONUMOZ deployed, however, it was able to recover from the setbacks of its late arrival, largely because of its durability and confidence supplied by the unified support of its sponsoring coalition. This allowed ONUMOZ, and its Special Representative, to be inventive in renegotiating the peace process timetable, mediating an agreement on the movement of troops, and an agreement on power-sharing after the elections.

An aspect of the government's eagerness to join the peace process was its concern over the loss of morale among its supporters and its loss of control over sections of the army, which had begun large-scale banditry and looting of the people it was intended to be protecting. Furthermore, the government was aware that its need to constantly recruit new soldiers was causing widescale discontent in the countryside, which was ironically translating into support for Renamo in some areas.[184] The decision of Renamo's leadership to co-operate with the peace process was jeopardized to some extent by its lack over control over its cadres. Renamo began and remained a decentralized movement, dependent on external direction rather than its central leadership for strategic direction.[185] Renamo leader Dhlakhama remained unsure of his position and unable to assert strong control over the movement. His initial inability to tie all of the Renamo factions to the peace process was evident in the continued Renamo attacks on the transport corridors.[186] ONUMOZ was aware of this difficulty as it deployed,[187] and was careful to link material and humanitarian incentives to all ranks during the ceasefire and disarmament process to ensure general Renamo compliance with the peace process. Also, its comprehensive troop levels and patrolling procedures were able to control low-level defiance of the ceasefire by small factions and bandits.[188] In this way, Renamo's lack of cohesion was overcome and not permitted to be an obstacle to the peace process, while the state of the government's military forces served to enhance its attachment to the process.

The ONUMOZ mission provides an intriguing case of a UN mission that displayed weaknesses in design, but managed to secure its objectives because the extremely pliable conflict dynamic with which it had to work did not act on these weaknesses in such a way as to frustrate its objectives. This suggests that weaknesses deriving from the parsimony of member-states are less serious than those deriving from diverging interests in the coalition and a misunderstanding of the conflict and the response required. While both belligerents in Mozambique were prepared to co-operate with the peacekeepers despite their slow arrival, it is not likely that they would have been so compliant had the peacekeepers represented a response based on a complete misunderstanding of the conflict. Had ONUMOZ been weakened by being inappropriate, and threatened the interests of either party, it is likely that that party would indeed have taken advantage of its tardy arrival to break the Rome Agreement and restart the war. ONUMOZ's successful demobilizing of the Renamo insurgency, and then oversight of the elections attests to the bypassing of its weaknesses by a pliable conflict dynamic, and also of the durability and creativity given to the mission by its unified support and the appropriateness of its response.

CONCLUSION

The observation of the progress of UNOSOM II and ONUMOZ allows a comparison between a failed, and a successful peacekeeping mission. It is a comparison with some intriguing variations on the presence and relationship of mission weaknesses and factors in the conflict dynamic, and their effect on outcomes. Both missions exhibited weaknesses; however, the difference in the outcomes of these missions came as a result not only of the differences in size and scale of the weaknesses, but in the capacity and the willingness of actors within the conflict dynamics to expose and aggravate them sufficiently to frustrate the missions. Both missions began with a unity of interests within their sponsoring coalitions, but there the similarities ended. The coalition that formed over Somalia lacked the insights delivered by a peace agreement or even extensive peace talks, and did not have the time to pursue a greater understanding of the conflict. Its response was rushed and ill-conceived: an over-ambitious mandate based on a under-estimation of the conflict dynamic. The ONUMOZ coalition was able to rely on the luxury of the Rome Agreement, which accurately defined the conflict and recommended an appropriate UN response. The difference between the adequacies of these two responses becomes clear when each is compared against the objectives that drove the respective conflict dynamics: UNOSOM II's represented a threat to the interests of the most powerful party to the conflict, while ONUMOZ's were complementary with the Mozambican belligerents'. This was the basis of UNOSOM II's accumulating weaknesses and misguided reactions to resistance, while the appropriateness of ONUMOZ's response enabled it to secure its objectives despite the weaknesses that appeared in its mission design.

UNOSOM II's presence was feared and resented by those clans whose interests its mandate threatened. These were the clans that were ascendant in the military balance, and keen to protect the anarchy upon which their ascendancy depended from the UN's conflict- and hunger-alleviating presence. By contrast, the appropriateness of ONUMOZ to the Mozambican peace process ensured that as it deployed it was welcomed by belligerents within a conflict dynamic that was ripe for resolution. Both missions suffered from vulnerabilities in their mission designs. Serious weaknesses in UNOSOM II's mission design were directly exploited and attacked, and led ultimately to the mission's failure. But what may have developed into a crippling vulnerability for ONUMOZ – its slow deployment during a vital phase of the peace process – was eventually able to be managed by an adept peacekeeping mission. It is at this point that the effect of the varying levels of robustness of the conflict dynamics on the missions' outcomes become clearest. So powerful was the Somali conflict dynamic that even the Manifesto factions that supported the UN presence tried to manipulate it for their own advancement, while those which opposed its presence did not hesitate to attack and expel it. By contrast, the Mozambican combatants, while initially prepared to exploit ONUMOZ's slow arrival for their own ends, eventually succumbed to their eagerness to end the war, changing their tactics to abandon the war and co-operate with the peace-keepers despite their late arrival. This reveals a vital insight into UN missions and their weaknesses: a necessary condition for the weaknesses to frustrate their missions is their exposure to conflict dynamics that are able and disposed to capitalize on these vulnerabilities.

The external links of the Somali and Mozambican belligerents emerged as a strong determining difference between the pliability of the conflict dynamics. In Somalia, the clans had no pressing need for external arms and resources, a fact that made them not only immune to the effects of the UN blockade, but proudly self-reliant and determined in their struggle for power. In Mozambique, the parties' fear of losing the external support on which they depended contributed to their desire for peace. The differing levels of mission durability between UNOSOM II and ONUMOZ had an effect on the missions' abilities to overcome their weaknesses. UNOSOM II splintered at the diplomatic and operational levels soon after the first concerted attacks, and was thereafter unable to recover from its self-defence posture to salvage its mandate. When disadvantaged by its late arrival, ONUMOZ was able to draw on the courage and inventiveness that flowed from its unified sponsoring coalition, and its confidence of its value to the peace process, to rectify its weaknesses by creatively renegotiating the timetable of the peace process and some of its provisions and mechanisms. The different effects of aggravated as opposed to dormant weaknesses on the missions' success levels is obvious: while UNOSOM II staged a nervous evacuation from Mogadishu, leaving behind much the same conflict it had entered, ONUMOZ left a Mozambique free from war for the first time in almost two decades.

4 Election Monitoring

Election monitoring is one of the UN's peace-building activities in which the mission actually comes into contact with the conflict dynamic. Elections often symbolize the end of a civil war: 'UN monitored elections should be regarded as a watershed event in a nation's emergence from civil insurrection . . . following commitments by rebel groups to participate peacefully in a political process.'[1] Yet while elections usually only occur after some advancement of the peace process, this does not necessarily mean that all the belligerents have irrevocably abandoned the conflict dynamic. For elections to succeed in ending the civil war, former belligerents must both participate co-operatively and abide by the result. Furthermore, the nature of democratic elections makes them viable only in certain conditions. For these reasons, there is great potential for weaknesses to appear in UN election monitoring missions, and for a nascent conflict dynamic to act on these weaknesses to frustrate the whole process. This chapter applies the analytical framework to a failed and a partially successful election monitoring mission to search for the responsibility of common weaknesses and their vulnerability to the conflict dynamic for the missions' different levels of failure.

Election monitoring is the oversight of an election or plebiscite by an invited, international presence, in order to ensure the free and democratic conduct of the election process. The UN sees election monitoring as an essential part of its post-conflict peace-building, in which the organization takes 'action to identify and support structures which will tend to strengthen and solidify peace in order to avoid a relapse into conflict'.[2] UN assistance in the holding of elections is an increasingly common post-Cold War activity, as a desire to end civil conflicts combines with a 'groundswell of popular support for greater participation in political processes . . . [b]roader individual involvement and greater government accountability'.[3] Elections are seen as a mechanism of conflict resolution and 'a broadened concept of peacekeeping: peacekeepers become the guarantors not only of peace but of democratisation'.[4] Peacekeepers have evolved from serving as protectors of the peace to 'functioning as a guarantor of democratic rights'.[5] Equating democracy with peace and stability has acquired greater currency after the Cold War,[6] and the UN attempts to cap its conflict termination efforts with a democracy-securing election.[7] Elections held after civil wars are a 'procedural solution', which 'are neutral in appearance, for the conciliator is not opting for one type of outcome but merely for one way in which an outcome can be reached, substituting a peaceful for a violent means of conducting conflict'.[8] The UN, through trying to implement an election, makes an attempt at 'changing the values and goals of the actors [and in this way] dealing with the underlying causes of the conflict'.[9]

Elections, therefore, become a method of ensuring internal resolution of the conflict and external stability. The viability of the democratization depends on the fairness and authenticity of the elections. In the suspicious aftermath of a civil war, fair elections require neutral observers to ensure that pluralism, universal suffrage, a high level of participation, and a lack of intimidation prevails.[10] The presence of UN election monitors is designed to alleviate the distrust on all sides: '[t]hey serve the government by helping to keep the opposition in the race, a prerequisite for a legitimate process, and they serve the opposition by ensuring that the election will either be fair or else be denounced as fraudulent'.[11] The observers can help correct specific shortcomings or irregularities.[12] When the UN combines observation with peacekeeping, it also provides security for the process and its participants against disaffected groups who try to disrupt the process violently.[13] The monitors are also instrumental to the electorate's participation by reassuring 'a sceptical population regarding the secrecy of the ballot, the efficacy of the process, and the safety of the voters'.[14]

For belligerents which have formerly been at war, participation in an election can be a daunting experience. Both incumbents and insurgents have to accept that by participating in elections, they surrender their ability to militarily seize power, and submit to the electorate's choice. In agreeing to participate in a genuinely democratic election, they will have no guarantee that they will take power: '[t]he results of democratic elections cannot be predicted from the rules under which they are conducted. If they could, they would not be democratic'.[15] As the disputants surrender their military means of seizing power and protecting themselves, they become vulnerable to being taken advantage of by their former opponents, and vice versa. International observers are their best guarantee, and UN election monitors often are crucial to the parties' agreement to submit to the resolution process. If they have determined to abandon the war and pursue their interests peacefully, participating in democratic, internationally observed elections can carry benefits. It can be a means of securing political power legitimately and peacefully. Even if they lose the elections, the belligerents can still secure tangible benefits. The growing international belief in the legitimacy of popularly elected governments reflects on the participants in the electoral process; formerly warring disputants can gain both international and domestic legitimacy by submitting to the popular will.[16] Elections further legitimate the system of government and all of the participants in the political community,[17] making that state more eligible in the increasing competition for aid and investment.[18] For belligerents attempting to renounce warfare and move into the political system, elections are a method of securing a legal basis for themselves and their goals, magnifying their influence in the governance of the state, and providing an accepted legislative voice for their supporters.[19]

Democratic elections are often unfamiliar propositions in states that have been locked in civil wars. Their very nature makes their success dependent on the full co-operation of the relevant parties. Often the prospect of participation in an election, and having to rely on their popularity rather than their military ability to secure power, is an unknown behaviour for former belligerents. These factors make the presence of inadequacies or weaknesses in UN election monitoring missions all too common, and all too likely to frustrate the mission when confronted with a robust conflict dynamic. These weaknesses are likely to be similar to those which can exist in mediation and peacekeeping missions. They will therefore be searched for using the analytical framework to determine the extent to which they were responsible for the failure of the UNAVEM II monitors in Angola. The same framework will be used to determine whether the partial failure of the UNTAC mission is able to be explained by these mission weaknesses and their aggravation by the Cambodian conflict dynamic.

THE ANGOLAN ELECTIONS: WAR BY OTHER MEANS

The Angolan civil war had long occupied a prominent position in international relations, as a flashpoint in the relations between the superpowers, one of the detonators of the second Cold War,[20] and one of the nodes of the volatile southern African security complex. Since gaining independence from Portugal in 1975, Angola had been riven by a destructive civil war between the Marxist MPLA[21] government and the *Uniao Nacional para a Independencia Total de Angola* (Unita) insurgent movement. The MPLA and Unita emerged as the two strongest national liberation movements after the Portuguese withdrawal in 1975.[22] The Portuguese had negotiated the Alvor Agreement between the MPLA, Unita, and the FNLA in which all three groups would co-operate with the Portuguese in a transitional administration until elections could be held on 11 November 1975. Before elections could be held, however, fighting broke out between the movements, and the Soviet-backed MPLA was able to seize control of most of Angola. Unita retreated to the central highlands around Huambo, where it set up a provisional government and began to wage insurgent war against the government. From this territory, it was able to generate funds for its war by exploiting the diamond mines and hunting elephants for ivory. While its regular army waged a conventional war for position in the south-east, Unita's 35 000-strong guerrilla army carried out economic attacks to destabilize the government in the rest of Angola.[23] Unita soon gained support from South Africa, which invaded Angola in support of Unita first in September 1975, and then a number of times through the 1980s. The government, hard pressed to stop the SADF invasions, appealed for, and was granted, assistance from around 20 000 Cuban troops. By the early 1980s, Angola had blown into a fully-fledged proxy war, as the US rescinded the Clark Amendment and began to openly support Unita's war effort,[24] through the provision of weapons,[25] aid, and military intelligence from the Defence Intelligence Agency.[26] South Africa provided vital logistical and materiel assistance, as well as deploying its own troops, artillery, and airforce to fight alongside Unita.[27] The war in Angola had become not only a brutal conflict, but a permanent source of tension between the superpowers, South Africa, and Cuba.

The late 1980s had seen progress in a long process of international disentanglement from Angola and Namibia,[28] and the beginnings of negotiations between the Angolan government and Unita. These culminated in the signing in Portugal of the May 1991 *Accordos da Paz*, mediated by the US, the Soviet Union, and Portugal, in which both sides agreed to stop fighting, disarm and form a new combined army, and contest general elections by November 1992. Following a request by the Angolan government and within the peace accords for UN verification of the peace process,[29] the Security Council acquiesced by expanding and updating the UN Angola Verification Mission (UNAVEM), already deployed to verify the Cuban withdrawal, to become UNAVEM II,[30] which was duly mandated to observe the elections.[31] The elections, held in September 1992, and won by the incumbent government, were rejected on the basis of fraud and intimidation by Unita, which resumed its insurgency to great effect, rapidly seizing 70 per cent of Angola and beginning the most brutal phase of Angola's 31-year civil war. This section will apply the analytical framework to the UNAVEM II mission to investigate how weaknesses within the mission were utilized by Unita to withdraw from the peace process and resume the war.

Objectives

The sponsoring coalition behind UNAVEM II registered significant agreement on the need to resolve the Angolan conflict. Having already achieved a withdrawal of Cuba from Angola and South Africa from Namibia, however, its interest in southern Africa was beginning to wane. As one of the biggest causes of tension during the second Cold War, the Angolan civil war became an issue of prime concern for resolution as relations between the superpowers thawed. After the withdrawal of Soviet troops from Afghanistan, the withdrawal of Cuban troops from Angola became an important step towards closer superpower relations.[32] The wider international community was keen to further develop the southern African peace dynamic – the end of *apartheid* in South Africa, the independence of Namibia, and peace in Angola and Mozambique – and thereby eliminate an enduring source of tension and instability in international affairs. The interlinking of these conflicts caused the advancement of peace in one to impact positively on the others.[33] Angola's oil and diamond reserves also offered a rich resource base to potential trading partners.[34] Maintaining the momentum of the peace dynamic after the successful Namibia operation, the US, the Soviet Union, and Portugal mediated a peace agreement between the government and Unita, which requested UN oversight of the peace process. Support for the update of UNAVEM to fulfil this request formed around the three mediating states. Zaïre, South Africa, Côte d'Ivoire, Cape Verde, and Ghana took an interest in the process, as did Western European states and Canada, which eventually sent independent observers to verify the elections. Having secured the withdrawal of Cuban troops and the independence of Namibia in 1989, the UN found itself obliged to contribute to the completion of the peace process in Angola. After these operations, however, the attention of the UN and its members had begun to be diverted by other concerns. UNAVEM II was thus a product of coinciding, but vague interests among its sponsoring coalition, which was keen to conclude as cheaply as possible a peace process from which its attention had moved on.[35]

Yet the real weakness in the UNAVEM II mission derived from a faulty mandate which was based on a flawed peace agreement. Based on the provisions of the *Accordos da Paz*, UNAVEM II's objective was to ensure that the Angolan elections resolved the bases of the civil war and achieved 'the full implementation of the Peace Accords for Angola'.[36] Ideally, the UN hoped to leave Angola a reunified, territorially integrated state, with a functioning democratic political process and an accepted government beginning the process of reconstruction.[37] It expressed support for the objectives of the Peace Accords in resolving the conflict,[38] and their use of elections rather than violence to settle the war.[39] As a method of adjudicating over the disputed location of power over the Angolan state, the UN committed itself to the result of the elections,[40] to the irreversibility of the process,[41] and to their use as an example for resolving other similar conflicts.[42] It wished to see not only the end of the war, but a centralization and unification of the Angolan state, with 'the extension of the Central Administration to those areas of Angola that are presently beyond the range of its authority'.[43] It believed that the establishment of durable peace and stability in Angola would have a positive impact on the delicate processes of resolution in South Africa and Mozambique that were hoped to bring stability and peace to southern Africa.[44]

Yet the diagnosis of the conflict by the mediators, and then the UN coalition which endorsed the Peace Agreement, was seriously flawed in that it believed that the organization of observed elections would resolve the civil war. The war was much more than a dispute over popularity. The conflict dynamic was based on ethnic chauvinism, competing claims of legitimacy, traded accusations of being puppets of foreign intervention, and considerable personal antipathies. The *Accordos da Paz*, having structured the electoral process as a one-off, 'winner-take-all' contest, and by ignoring questions of representation, national reconciliation, or minority guarantees for the post-election period, in effect left the shape of the future Angolan state to be decided by the winner of the elections.[45] Elections became a test of the MPLA's and Unita's claims to have the support of the majority of Angolans, rather than the collection of Cuban- or *apartheid*-backed foreign mercenaries and thugs.[46] Unita's signature of the Peace Agreement was based on its certainty of election victory, to the extent that leader Jonas Savimbi declared at election rallies that the only way Unita could lose was by rigging the elections.[47] The weakness in the diagnosis of the conflict, which was passed into the provisions of the Peace Agreement, was that it was unlikely that the loser of the elections, especially if it was Unita, would respect the results or the peace process.

This weakness was passed directly from the Peace Agreement into UNAVEM II's monitoring task by requiring that 'genuine . . . national reconciliation . . . cannot be achieved without the full participation of UNITA, the second largest party . . . whose legitimate concerns must be addressed'.[48] Both the MPLA's and Unita's participation were needed to give the elections internal legitimacy, to allow them, as two of the three major post-colonial groups, to represent their supporters in the elections and the ensuing political system. International legitimacy also required participation by Unita, especially in states such as the US, where Unita was seen as the legitimate democratic opposition to the Marxist MPLA government.[49] The desire to establish a functioning democracy meant that the *Accordos da Paz* emphasized that not only Unita, but '[a]ll political parties and interested persons will have the opportunity to organise and to participate in the elections process on an equal footing, regardless of their political positions'.[50] UNAVEM II was dependent, in order to complete the tasks it had been set, on the loser of the elections agreeing to be bound by their results. Unfortunately little about the peace process suggested that the party that lost the elections would be prepared to accept the loss of political power.

To differing degrees, neither the government nor Unita appeared totally committed to abandoning war for democratic peace. The government had long resisted power-sharing or democratic elections.[51] Responding to the peace dynamic and the ending of the Cold War, however, the Angolan government pragmatically discarded its Marxist ideology in December 1990, in favour of democratic socialism and economic reforms. Its final acceptance of multiparty elections as the culmination of the peace process were a part of its objectives to finally rid Angola of the Unita insurgency and normalize relations with its two great power tormentors: the US and South Africa. The peace agreement promised it these objectives, but it is unclear how comfortable the MPLA would have been with a Savimbi government.[52] Unita's objective in the peace process was to seize power over the Angolan state. It had advocated national reconciliation, power-sharing,[53] and elections[54] for years, believing that inevitable electoral victory over the vastly unpopular MPLA government[55] would secure what it had been fighting for since 1975. Elections would have the added advantage of giving its accession to power the international and domestic legitimacy that it had long craved.[56] The *Accordos da Paz* had secured for Unita what it had been fighting for: the holding of free and fair elections advocated, but never held, under the 1975 Alvor Agreement with Portugal.[57] Unita was convinced that elections would give it total power and enable it to finally dispose of the MPLA. Democratic coexistence and loyal opposition were concepts that did not fit either side's zero-sum perception of their struggle: the ethnic basis of the conflict,[58] the urban–rural rivalry,[59] and the intensity of the personal hostility between Unita's leadership and the government,[60] meant that power was seen as the exclusive preserve of the victor, and a means of protection from the rival group.[61] It appears then that in the run-up to the elections, neither side was completely committed to respecting the results of the elections in a way that was crucial to the success of UNAVEM II's mission.

Mission Presence and the Military Balance

While both parties accepted the UNAVEM II presence in the peace process, it was confined to such a restricted role that it was unable to play a significant moderating role in the zero-sum electoral struggle that ensued.

The parties made certain that the responsibility for the implementation of the *Accordos da Paz* and the administration of the elections remained in their hands. They invited the UN 'to send monitors to support the Angolan parties'[62] to execute the Accords. Both parties agreed to a UN presence, but only on the condition that it played a detached, strictly observer role:

> These verification teams would work closely with, but remain separate from, the monitoring groups composed of the representatives of the two parties. They would observe closely the manner in which those groups were carrying out their functions in order to verify that the joint monitoring machinery was working effectively.[63]

The UN's participation in the Political–Military Integration Commission (CCPM) established in the *Accordos da Paz* was restricted to 'the capacity of an invited guest'.[64] Thus, although 'UNAVEM electoral observers . . . would monitor and evaluate the operations and impartiality of the electoral authorities at all levels,'[65] the UN had no substantive control over the conduct of the process, since it was subordinate to the likely transgressors. To compound this powerlessness, the UN team was much too small for an election of that size: 400 observers were required to observe the polling of 4.83 million voters at 6 000 polling stations in a state the size of Western Europe.[66] Thus the lack of a significant or effectual observer presence only served to compound the weaknesses within the flawed concept of the Angolan elections.

Neither side had completely accepted the 'second best' strategy of shared power, because their military fortunes had not declined far enough to force them to abandon the military option and opt genuinely for elections. Both sides tried to prevail in the immediate aftermath of the withdrawal of Cuban and South African troops, but failed to deal each other the knock-out blow.[67] Although by 1990 the war had stalemated, and neither side had the ability to militarily prevail over the other, both still possessed the resources and personnel to struggle on.[68] The length of the insurgency and the bitterness of the war had left the MPLA and Unita convinced of their military potency. This was demonstrated by the incomplete willingness of both sides, but particularly Unita, to surrender their weapons faithfully to the scheduled disarmament and demobilization process. When Unita agreed to elections as a method of retaining international support and legitimacy, and as a way of seizing uncontested power, it preserved its discipline, military structure, and weapons. The fact that neither the government nor the insurgents in Angola had been significantly disadvantaged by the military balance made neither willing to completely commit themselves to elections and peaceful coexistence.

Mission Design and Belligerents' Tactics

UNAVEM II was unable to prevent the weaknesses in its mission concept from being exploited by the belligerents because of further inadequacies in its mission design. The restrictions on its role in the peace process and its abilities to steward the progress of the peace process in effect surrendered any role it might have played in stopping the breakdown of the elections. In agreeing to monitor the elections, the UN gave its tacit support[69] to the structure and organization of the electoral process outlined in the *Accordos da Paz*, and the highly restrictive role they assigned to the UN mission.[70] The UN therefore committed itself to 'entrusting the main tasks to the parties themselves, [so that] the arrangements proposed would have the advantage of reducing the costs to the international community at a time when there is an ever-growing demand for funds for peacekeeping'.[71] As a result, the election mechanism 'depended critically on the parties' good will, rather than on a stringent inspection regime'.[72] The peace process and elections were to be administered by the government of Angola and the government-Unita controlled mechanisms of the CCPM, and the CMVF (Joint Verification and Monitoring Commission), to which UNAVEM II would report any violations or irregularities.[73] The administration of the ceasefire and demobilization was left to the parties, the CCPM, and the CCFA (Commission for the Formation of the Armed Forces).[74] The belligerents consistently failed to disarm, blocked the functioning of the CCPM and CMVF,[75] while UNAVEM II could only observe, patrol, and report on their progress,[76] and the UN was left to urge cooperation, restraint, and tolerance.[77] The peace process made no provision for the welfare or reintegration of the demobilized soldiers, and had no mechanism for inducing the parties to demobilize genuinely. While over 80 per cent of the government's troops demobilized, Unita disarmed less than 10 per cent of its troops, and then remobilized large numbers of them in its own territory.[78] It also refused access to its areas to government administration, electoral registration, and peacekeepers and monitors.[79] In the run-up to the polling and in the aftermath of the polls, Unita turned against UNAVEM II and Special Representative Anstee, with its radio station *Vorgan* 'impugning the integrity and impartiality' of the mission.[80] The continuing military potential of the opponents and their unallayed suspicions of each other and the process prevented the conduct of the elections in a neutral environment, and ultimately doomed the results,[81] despite calls from the UN to accept the results,[82] and warnings of isolation if Unita returned to war.[83]

UNAVEM II's lack of authority and the thinness of its presence became cumulative weaknesses that spread to other parts of the mission, as UNAVEM II proved unable to take any meaningful actions to correct breaches in the peace process or even rely on itself for protection. The *Accordos da Paz* declared that '[t]he security of the monitoring groups and all UN personnel shall be the responsibility of the party that controls the zone where they are present'.[84] UNAVEM II noted the problems with the disarmament and demobilization process,[85] the difficulties with the extension of government administration into Unita-controlled areas,[86] the registration of voters, and criticized the partiality of, and lack of access to the government-controlled media.[87] None of these complaints had any impact on the peace process, and the UN was too concerned about 'Angola being a sovereign independent country, [making] the organization and supervision of all tasks under the Accords . . . the responsibility of the Angolan parties themselves'[88] to agitate for a greater influence on the process. Its last-minute attempt to ultimately affect the peace process by attesting to the integrity of the elections was to prove ineffectual in stopping Unita from rejecting the election results. UNAVEM II carried out its own quick count of the results,[89] and when these tallied with the results, declared the results and the elections 'to have been generally free and fair,' after it had investigated Unita's allegations of fraud.[90] This had little impact on Unita's decision or ability to resume the war.

For Unita, elections were not a method of adjudication so much as the continuation of its struggle for power by other means. The government's commitment to the elections and the peace process was more genuine. This was shown during the peace talks by its proposal of a three-year transition period between the agreement and elections to allow a proper environment to be prepared for the conduct of elections. Unita pressed for elections to be held within twelve months of the signing of the Accords so that it could capitalize on its military and political advances and the support – forced or voluntary – of the areas it controlled.[91] With misgivings about such a short pre-election period, the American, Soviet, and Portuguese mediators negotiated a compromise period of eighteen months.[92] During the run-up to the elections, the government further demonstrated its good faith by demobilizing 80 per cent of its army, an act of trust that made it all the more vulnerable to Unita's resumption of the struggle.

By contrast, Unita believed that so certain was its victory and so great was its support, that the elections were a formality and any result except a Unita victory was fraudulent and inadmissible.[93] It formed a political party after the signing of the *Accordos da Paz* in May 1991, and Savimbi began an energetic and populist campaign advocating an end to foreign presences and often playing on ethnic rivalries.[94] Its campaign and approach to the elections reflected 'a reliance on conflict rather than conciliation and compromise as the form of political discourse'.[95] Unita had no intention of surrendering its military potency during the election run-up; responsible for its own demobilization, FALA (Unita's military wing) made sure that 'a much lower proportion of ex-FALA troops were demobilised and even then they did not leave their assembly areas. Almost all seem[ed] since to have been remobilised,'[96] and that its forces remained highly disciplined and equipped.[97] With these resources in place, Savimbi was able after the elections to denounce the National Electoral Council as 'an MPLA puppet,'[98] to complain of 'widespread, massive and systematic irregularities and fraud,'[99] and resume Unita's insurgency, seizing its areas of support and 70 per cent of Angolan territory rapidly and brutally.[100] Unita did not modify its tactics to embrace peace and democratic elections very much at all. Its avoidance of demobilization allowed it to preserve the potential to exploit the vulnerabilities of the peace process in case the unthinkable happened – the MPLA proved more popular than Unita.

Links and External Support

The lack of international interest in the Angolan peace process and a general unwillingness to become closely involved by former sponsors of the war compounded the powerlessness of UNAVEM II over the conduct and viability of the elections. By 1992, the international community seemed to be weary of the Angolan conflict, and had regarded the withdrawal of Cuban troops and the independence of Namibia to be a considerable success and a milestone in stabilizing southern Africa and increasing international co-operation. The successful implementation of the Namibia settlement removed most of the international confrontation from the region, and the powers diverted their attention to other regional conflicts that were hindering their co-operation or threatening stability. In the implementation phase of the *Accordos da Paz*, therefore, 'the international community showed a surprising complacency towards Angola which implied a belief that the hard work had been done actually reaching the agreement one year earlier'.[101] Such pressure that was exerted by states with former links to the belligerents was unable to apply any compelling leverage. Both South Africa and the Russian Federation maintained contact with their former clients, urging their co-operation with the election process.[102] African states, including Côte d'Ivoire, Botswana, Burundi, Cameroon, Cape Verde, the Central African Republic, Chad, Congo, Gabon, Guinea-Bissau, Mali, Mozambique, Nigeria, Rwanda, São Tomé and Principe, Zambia and Zimbabwe, long concerned that the Angolan civil war had come to symbolize foreign intervention in Africa, collectively and individually applied pressure on the parties to settle the conflict peacefully.[103] The US used its contacts with Unita, and its economic links with the government, to maintain a constant insistence on the aptness of elections for resolving the conflict, reacting angrily but impotently after Unita rejected the election results.[104] The lack of compelling interest in the peace process made these efforts sporadic and ineffectual, and did little to compensate for the existing weaknesses in the Agreements and the UNAVEM II mission.

The inability of these measures to secure Unita's respect for the peace process and the election results was in part undermined by the movement's confidence in its continuing support from external sources. As the Cold War ended, the US and the Soviet Union, in addition to working together, with Portugal, to mediate an end to the Angolan civil war, agreed on the 'zero-zero' option: to stop supplying their respective clients with lethal material once a ceasefire was reached.[105] The US, however, continued its support for Unita, to decreasing levels, until well into the peace process. The Reagan administration, as part of its 'rollback' policy, obtained a repeal of the Clark Amendment in 1985, and supplied Unita with up to $20 million of military equipment in the later 1980s.[106] Elements within the South African military also continued to supply Unita with military equipment and expertise, well after official South African support for Unita had ended.[107] This American support, along with support from South Africa and Zaïre, had a negative effect on Unita's co-operativeness, by convincing it of the strength of its position to seize power in Angola, with or without the elections. Either these suppliers were unprepared to exercise influence over Unita on behalf of the UN, or those willing to pressure Unita were losing leverage over the group through cutting back their aid.[108] Neither did the decreasing levels of external support drastically affect Unita's military calculus: its military leaders boasted its arms stockpiles could sustain a military campaign for at least two years,[109] while its export of timber and diamonds enabled it to fund other covert sources of supply.[110] Unita's insulation from the effects of external isolation thus emboldened its exploitation of the weaknesses in the peace process and UNAVEM II mission and enabled it to return to war after an unsatisfactory election result.

Mission Durability and Belligerents' Morale and Cohesion

Deprived of adequate resourcing or a significant role in implementing the peace agreement, UNAVEM II possessed little durability to allow it to try to salvage the election results. The inadequacy of its resourcing and support was reflected in the Security Council's obsession with minimizing the costs of the operation,[111] and its eventual dispatch of a skeleton observation component for UNAVEM II.[112] The Security Council remained determined to minimize the costs of the operation, providing UNAVEM II with one-quarter of the budget of the UNTAG operation in Namibia to monitor an electorate ten times as large.[113] Unita's rejection of what UNAVEM II had determined to be a 'free and fair election,'[114] however, brought belated cohesion and interest among the sponsoring coalition. The prospect of all it had worked for being undone galvanized 'the full and unequivocal support of the Security Council for the efforts of [the] Special Representative and UNAVEM II . . . in . . . the implementation of the Peace Accords'.[115] It assembled an *ad hoc* Commission, of representatives from Cape Verde, Morocco, the Russian Federation, and the US, which travelled to Angola in support of UNAVEM II to try to persuade Unita to respect the election results and remain in the peace process. This cohesion and interest came too late and were unsuccessful; Unita had tested its electoral strength and once this had been found to be inadequate, it easily returned to its insurgency.

Unita's ability and confidence to avoid disarmament and reject the election results were furnished by its disciplined cohesion and morale based on Savimbi's personality cult.[116] By the time of the elections, Unita had developed into one of the most cohesive insurgent movements with which the UN had to deal. Its strict hierarchy and control are based on the personal power of Savimbi and the filling of key positions with his family members.[117] This control had been intensified by power struggles and purges within Unita in the late 1980s.[118] This central discipline made Unita even less psychologically prepared for genuine democratic participation. Savimbi's exclusive contact with sycophants and his accustomization to automatic obedience convinced him of his universal popularity and made him certain that Unita could only lose the elections through fraud.[119] Unita's rigid discipline enabled it to maintain a potent military force during the conduct of the elections, and to make rapid military gains once it had rejected the election results. In these ways, Unita's strong internal cohesion allowed it to take advantage of the weaknesses of a failing peace process and reject an outcome that it saw as inimical to its interests.

Unita's rejection of the election results and return to war allowed it to quickly seize over 70 per cent of Angolan territory. The subsequent resumption of the civil war ushered in a phase of brutality unprecedented in all of Angola's internal turmoils since 1962, and through all of its foreign interventions. This is significant to the explanation of the failure of the peace process. The great powers' mediation of the *Accordos da Paz*, and their endorsement of its processes through mandating UNAVEM II to help implement them, reflected their belief that it was the external interventions that were driving the Angolan civil war. By leaving the implementation of the agreement to the belligerents themselves and assigning a token UN force a restricted role, the powers were in effect claiming that because the problem of competing external interventions had been solved, the resolution of the Angolan civil war was only a formality. The reflection of this belief became the deepest source of weaknesses in the UNAVEM II mission. Its reliance on the willingness of the government and Unita to renounce their war became a glaring vulnerability when confronted with an extremely robust conflict dynamic. Neither party was prepared to uncritically discard its military potential and embrace the elections process if this yielded anything but uncontested power. UNAVEM II's restricted role and token presence were unable to even slightly impact on these perceptions and their manipulation of the peace process. International pressure came too little too late, and left the UN with a continuing headache of trying to mediate an end to a vicious civil war by two even more distrustful belligerents.

CORRALLING THE KHMER ROUGE IN CAMBODIA

By the end of the 1980s, Cambodia had acquired a reputation internationally as a charnel house, tortured by the competing interventions of cynical great powers and neighbours, and by the activities of genocidal domestic factions. Drawn into the Vietnam war, it became target to a massive American bombing campaign. The resulting anarchy allowed the seizure of power by the Khmer Rouge. Its attempts to create an egalitarian, agrarian society between 1975 and 1978 led to the deaths of over 1 million Cambodians, or one-seventh of the population, from torture, murder, and starvation, and the departure of 500 000 refugees. Vietnam, backed by the Soviet Union, invaded Cambodia in late 1978, and installed a regime replacing the Khmer Rouge. The Khmer Rouge retreated into the jungles of western Cambodia, from where it waged a guerrilla war, supported by China. Two other groups, the Khmer People's National Liberation Front (KPNLF), and the Front for an Independent, Neutral, Peaceful and Cooperative Cambodia (Funcinpec), supported by a collection of Western and ASEAN powers, were also engaged in fighting the Vietnamese-backed regime. ASEAN diplomacy was able to forge the KPNLF and Funcinpec into an alliance with the Khmer Rouge, the Coalition Government of Democratic Kampuchea (CGDK), under the auspices of which the three movements were able to share, on a rotating basis, the seat of Cambodia at the UN.

None of the parties in this complex civil war was able to prevail over the others, and the Cambodian people continued to suffer from the brutal stalemate. As the great-power rivalries around Cambodia dissipated, the UN played a leading role in mediating an end to the war in Cambodia. These talks resulted in the Paris Agreements of 23 October 1991, where all four Cambodian disputants agreed to a comprehensive peace process, in which Cambodia would be run by a UN transitional administration (UNTAC), in consultation with a Supreme National Council (SNC) comprising representatives of all four parties. During this time, under the direction of an UNTAC peacekeeping force, all parties would be disarmed and demobilized, mine clearance would be started, refugees repatriated, and free multiparty elections would be held. The UNTAC Force was inserted into Cambodia in March 1992 to oversee the implementation of the Paris Agreements. Within months, the peace process was in serious danger of breaking down. After imperfectly complying with Phase I of the peace process,[120] the ceasefire, the Khmer Rouge formally withdrew from Phase II, the disarmament and demobilization stage, in June 1992. The UN decided to persevere with the elections despite Khmer Rouge non-cooperation. The elections were held successfully in May 1993, and resulted in the formation of a domestically and internationally endorsed power-sharing government. The continuing of the Khmer Rouge insurgency, however, suggests weaknesses in the peace process that led to the elections. In another variation on the action of a resistant conflict dynamic on mission weaknesses, the experience of the UNTAC mission shows that despite deep weaknesses that the conflict dynamic was able to exploit, the durability and strong design of the UNTAC mission enabled it to resist complete frustration and salvage much of its mandate.

Objectives

The weaknesses in the UNTAC mission derived, paradoxically, from the extraordinary coincidence of interests within the sponsoring coalition on the need to terminate the civil war in Cambodia. The civil war in Cambodia had long been the site of great power rivalries and proxy conflict. A geopolitical struggle in Indochina between Vietnam, China, and the ASEAN countries had overlapped with an ideological rivalry primarily between China and the Soviet Union, and to a lesser extent between Vietnam and the Soviet Union and the West. As the Cold War ended and East Asian economic growth soared, the great power rivalries in which Cambodia had been entangled began to thaw. The Soviet Union, keen to strengthen relations with China, the West, and Asia, advocated resolving the Cambodian civil war to remove it as an impediment to closer relations.[121] Responding to Soviet pressure, as well as its own intervention fatigue, Vietnam in 1989 unilaterally withdrew its troops from the civil war in Cambodia which had cost it so much, domestically and internationally. By this time, China had gained numerous diplomatic and geopolitical benefits from its support of the Khmer Rouge against the Vietnamese-backed regime. Following the Vietnamese withdrawal, and revelations of Khmer Rouge genocide, however, China became aware that the costs of association with the Khmer Rouge were mounting, as was international pressure to participate in ending the civil war. The ASEAN states, along with regional powers such as Australia, Japan, and India, began to campaign for an end to conflict and instability in the region, agreeing with Thailand's Prime Minister Chatichai, who advocated turning Indochina 'from a battlefield into a marketplace'.[122] France, the former colonial power, and Britain added their interest to the coalition wanting to resolve the civil war, as a way to end their sponsorship of the non-Communist resistance.[123] All of these interests agreed on the need to end the civil war, and coalesced around the Security Council's Permanent Five Contact Group, first activated to find a solution to the Iran–Iraq war, but increasingly concerned with the Cambodian civil war. France, as a representative of the Security Council Permanent Five, and Indonesia, as a representative of ASEAN, became Co-Chairmen of the Paris Conference group, a large and cohesive international coalition seeking to end the civil war in Cambodia.

It was this extraordinary coincidence of interests among the UN's and the region's great powers which heightened the sponsoring coalition's state-centrism. The coalition members' state-centrism first led them to misdiagnose the Cambodian civil war. Because China, the Soviet Union, the ASEAN states, Britain, France, and the US had been to different extents involved in sponsoring the conflict in Cambodia, they overestimated their role in perpetuating the war. In assuming that their agreement to end their support for the warring parties would end the war, they misdiagnosed the strength of the indigenous dynamic driving the Cambodian civil war. This misdiagnosis led them to misprescribe a solution to the conflict. The confidence that their agreement gave these states led them to overestimate their influence on the disputants in authoritatively securing the Paris Peace Agreements, and then overseeing their implementation. During the mediation process, the coalition had formulated the framework for the Paris Agreements, and then relied on considerable diplomatic pressure to secure the parties' agreement to it, especially over the Khmer Rouge's opposition.[124] The UN coalition expected this forced agreement to be inviolable and not open to any interpretation. The weakness that this placed at the heart of the UNTAC mission was that it configured UNTAC in a way that anticipated it dealing with parties that were co-operative and compliant with the peace process. This weakness was to become apparent as soon as UNTAC deployed into a resistant conflict dynamic, and encountered a Khmer Rouge that never intended to comply with a peace agreement that it had been pressured into signing.

As laid out in the Paris Agreements, the UN's ultimate objective in Cambodia was to end the civil war and install a stable, legitimate, and internationally recognized government in place of the four contending claims that had existed since 1978.[125] The sponsoring coalition was '*convinced* that free and fair elections [were] essential to produce a just and durable settlement to the Cambodia conflict, thereby contributing to regional and international peace and security'.[126] It was determined that 'the Cambodian people may have an opportunity to choose freely their own government'.[127] All of the other provisions in the Paris Agreements were designed to 'create a neutral environment in which free and fair elections could take place'.[128] Primary among the provisions of the Paris Agreements enabling the holding of elections was '[t]he regroupment, cantonment, disarming and demobilisation of the military forces of the Cambodian parties'.[129] While UNTAC's election component was separate from the military component, the dependence of the successful conduct of elections on the factions' demobilization necessitated a close relationship between UNTAC's components. The electoral component was charged with a number of tasks while the military component demobilized the parties. These included the establishment, in consultation with the SNC, of a system of democratic electoral laws and administrative measures, the design and implementation of a voter education programme, the registration of eligible voters and political parties, the oversight of free access to the media, and a fair campaign. During the elections, UNTAC was charged with conducting the polling and counting, ensuring its freedom from irregularities, and announcing and validating the results.[130] The UN coalition stated its support for the process and the efforts of the electoral component, stating before the elections its 'determination to endorse the results of the election for the constituent assembly provided that the UN certifie[d] it free and fair'.[131]

Unfortunately, this vast mandate was appropriate only to the more compliant factions in the conflict dynamic. The Vietnamese-installed regime, calling itself the State of Cambodia (SoC), had, after initial resistance, decided to genuinely accept the Paris Agreements. This resulted from its belief that it would win the UN-administered elections in Cambodia because of popular opposition to the resistance in general and the Khmer Rouge in particular, and because of its ability to use the resources and coercive power of the state to its advantage while co-operating with UNTAC.[132] It saw the UN-sponsored peace process as a way of ending its international isolation, symbolized by its inability to take the Cambodian seat at the UN, and accessing international aid for the rebuilding of Cambodia. The non-Communist resistance, the royalist Funcinpec and the democratic KPNLF, welcomed the peace process and the elections as ways of ending their long years in exile and the jungles.[133] It was the Khmer Rouge which never intended to comply with its forced acquiescence to the Paris Agreements. It had signed the agreements having resolved to manipulate them in its favour once they began to be implemented. Elections and the reliance on the popular choice of the people to apportion political power were anathema to the Khmer Rouge, which had long relied on military conquest and brutal coercion as its sole means of exercising political influence. Furthermore, years of struggle for power had convinced the Khmer Rouge that it operated in an anarchic environment 'in which guarantees were usually underwritten by force and were at best a vehicle for discussion when the factors of power projection altered'.[134] It was convinced that the transitional arrangements in the peace process – the erosion of the control of the SoC by the UNTAC transitional authority, the formation of the SNC in which the Khmer Rouge could dominate the other resistance factions, and the disarmament of the other factions – would provide it with the opportunity to infiltrate the structures of power to a point from which it could launch its military seizure of power.[135]

The success of this strategy was contingent on the Khmer Rouge's ability to withhold its co-operation from key components of the peace process: demobilization and electoral registration. It tried to use its refusal to disarm after June 1992 to modify the agreement on the transitional administration of Cambodia, advocating the replacement of the SNC with quadripartite control of key fields of administration,[136] a measure which would allow it to infiltrate the government's core.[137] Pol Pot calculated that any elected government, 'whatever its composition . . . [would] be a collection of unmixables . . . [and that] the Khmer Rouge [would] triumph from this disarray by maintaining their political discipline, preserving the strongest military force and appealing to Khmer chauvinism'.[138] He is reported also to have ordered the delay of elections until the Khmer Rouge forces controlled enough of Cambodia to be able to intimidate voters to elect it to power.[139] The Khmer Rouge's authoritarian hold over its cadre and 'supporters', the source of its political discipline and military dominance, was threatened by demobilization and exposure to UNTAC election registration and voter education programmes. Of all the Khmer Rouge's multiplicity of objectives and strategies for the peace process, none was based on the process it had agreed to in the Paris Agreement. The mandate of UNTAC, to implement these Agreements, thus contained a serious weakness, in that it relied on the co-operation of a faction that had never intended to honour commitments into which it had been pressured by the international community.

Mission Presence and the Military Balance

The Khmer Rouge had calculated that it would be able to manipulate UNTAC along with its exploitation of the peace process to increase its own influence. It did not count on the conviction among UNTAC's leaders that given the volatility and complexity of the Cambodian civil war, it was imperative to adhere closely to the Paris Agreement to preserve their impartiality and the support of the sponsoring coalition.[140] Once the Khmer Rouge realized that UNTAC intended to implement the Paris Agreements to the letter, the mission became a threat. This was because the maintenance of its military organization and potential were essential to its strategy for subverting the peace process. Integral to its military discipline was its ability to remain the sole source of influence, ideological indoctrination, and authoritarian terror over its cadre and the population in its 'liberated zones'.[141] Both UNTAC's military and electoral components threatened to erode this Khmer Rouge advantage. The disarmament and demobilization of its forces by the UNTAC military component would destroy the sole basis of its power, while the exposure of its soldiers and 'supporters' to the electoral enrolment and democracy education teams would destroy its disciplined control. By 10 June 1992, the Secretary-General's Special Representative in Cambodia had received a letter from Khmer Rouge General Nuon Bunno stating that it 'was not in a position to allow UNTAC forces proceed with their deployments' in Khmer Rouge areas.[142] Thus while the other factions welcomed UNTAC's arrival in line with their acceptance of its objectives, the Khmer Rouge saw its presence and determination to implement the Paris Agreements as a threat to its interests.

The Khmer Rouge's determination to resist UNTAC's influence on its cadre and supporters was based partly on its confidence in its strong military position. By the time UNTAC deployed to oversee the implementation of the Paris Agreements, the Khmer Rouge had established an unassailable military potential. The Cambodian civil war had settled into a stalemated cycle of wet- and dry-season offensives which neither side was capable of winning outright. In the meantime, however, the Khmer Rouge had consolidated a tightly disciplined guerrilla army, well-supplied from hidden caches of weapons, and timber and gem smuggling. It had also established its safety from attacks on its bases in the Cardamom mountains and across the Thai border, with the covert co-operation of the Thai generals. From this position, the Khmer Rouge was secure in its potential to disrupt any form of settlement or administration with which it disagreed for a long time in the future. The Vietnamese occupation of Cambodia provided the Khmer Rouge with a rationale for fighting, a morale-sustaining threat, and international legitimacy as a resistance group.[143] The loss of this rationale following the Vietnamese withdrawal in 1989 had necessitated token Khmer Rouge co-operation at the Paris Peace talks. But this was only for the sake of appearances. After the failure of the Khmer Rouge attempt at a military solution when the Vietnamese withdrew by the end of 1989,[144] it retreated to guerrilla warfare once more to wait until the objectives conditions were propitious for the military seizure of power. It was determined to maintain its military potential and political discipline until UNTAC's departure, whereupon it could launch an attack on the new government. This military strength of the Khmer Rouge made the other factions committed to the peace process, partly in the hope that it would end the Khmer Rouge threat.[145] Unfortunately, it was the Khmer Rouge's military strength, and its determination to resist any attempts to erode this strength, that gave the conflict dynamic its robustness in acting on the weaknesses within UNTAC.

Mission Design and Belligerents' Tactics

The UNTAC mission, despite these weaknesses that existed in its mandate and presence, was able to salvage much of the peace process due to a strong mission design. The high level of agreement and diplomatic support within the UN for the operation meant that UNTAC was extremely well-resourced, being at the time of its deployment the biggest UN mission ever mounted. A tardy deployment, due to organizational sluggishness, did place an initial weakness within the mission design. Upon the signature of the Paris Agreement, the Security Council sent the UN Advance Mission in Cambodia (UNAMIC) to plan the UNTAC mission. UNTAC was not subsequently fully deployed until March 1992, five months after the parties had signed the agreement. This time lag became a weakness in the UN mission that the parties were willing to exploit for their own advantage, re-evaluating the agreement in light of territorial gains they had made.[146] Violations of the Phase I ceasefire provisions became commonplace, especially by SoC and Khmer Rouge forces.[147] However, it was weaknesses within the mission objectives, deriving from its forced signature of the Paris Agreements, that the Khmer Rouge took advantage of in withdrawing from Phase II of the peace process, the disarmament and demobilization stage.

The UNTAC mission's reliance on 'the full cooperation of all parties concerned, and their implementation in good faith of the obligations they have undertaken in the comprehensive settlement agreement',[148] was a fundamental vulnerability for the mission. The Phase II disarmament and demobilization of the factions was needed to 'stabilise the security situation . . . so as to reinforce the objectives of the comprehensive political settlement and minimise the risks of a return to warfare'.[149] The Khmer Rouge's withdrawal from Phase II seriously compromised 'the ability of UNTAC to adhere to the timetable set by the Security Council'.[150] The other Cambodian factions began to canton and disarm their forces, but UNTAC soon realized that the Khmer Rouge's failure to disarm at a proportional rate would soon place them at a severe military disadvantage to a fully operational Khmer Rouge.[151] It duly stopped the disarmament process, 'because of the need to ensure that [the disarmament] process [was] undertaken in such a way as to maintain the military balance between the four parties'.[152] This was a serious setback for the prospects for the election: '[the Khmer Rouge's] refusal to participate in the second phase of the ceasefire . . . [and] the continuing existence of large and sometimes undisciplined armies, as well as attempts by some of them to improve their positions on the ground . . . had an adverse effect on the security situation in the country'.[153] The Khmer Rouge's refusal to co-operate thereby made the task of the UNTAC election monitors infinitely more difficult: 'The election will take place while a substantial part of the forces of the Cambodian parties remain under arms . . . [which] will add to UNTAC's difficulties both in organising the election and in ensuring, as best it can, the security of candidates, voters and electoral officials through the electoral process'.[154]

The weaknesses within the UNTAC mission had been exposed and utilized by the Khmer Rouge. Having been confronted with the mission's vulnerabilities, the UN sponsoring coalition within the Security Council made an important decision. It resolved to try to salvage a significant part of the mandate by making adjustments to the mission design, because '[n]ot to proceed would mean ceding to unacceptable threats and giving the right of veto over the peace process to an armed group that has rejected its commitment under the Paris Agreements'.[155] It directed UNTAC, despite Khmer Rouge non-cooperation, to carry out the election process 'in accordance with the timetable laid down in the implementation plan'.[156] It did not make the mistake it made in Somalia, however, and directly attack the Khmer Rouge. Its reaction was to attempt to use pressure and persuasion to induce the group to rejoin the peace process. At first UNTAC took 'a number of steps designed to meet the concerns of the [Khmer Rouge]'.[157] The Khmer Rouge acknowledged UNTAC's efforts,[158] but continued to reject appeals[159] for co-operation.[160] UNTAC made 'every effort . . . to . . . persuade [the Khmer Rouge] to join Phase II and to cooperate with UNTAC and the other three parties',[161] and for the remainder of its deployment maintained contact with the Khmer Rouge, informing it of developments within the Mixed Military Working Group, the SNC, and of the results of its investigations of ceasefire violations.[162] The Khmer Rouge position was rejected by the UN as inconsistent with the Paris Agreements,[163] while the Security Council[164] imposed a fuel embargo and logging and gemstone moratorium on Khmer Rouge areas.[165] Meanwhile, the UN decided to press ahead with the elections, bypassing Phase II, and warning that the Khmer Rouge risked 'international and internal isolation if it is seen to have attempted to disrupt the Cambodian elections'.[166]

The mission was able to carry out these new instructions, and compensate for its mission weaknesses, because of its strong mission design and leadership. Following the abandonment of Phase II, UNTAC was redeployed to 'correspond to the borders of the Cambodian provinces . . . [to] conform with the deployment of electoral teams and shorten the time taken to respond to potential threats to them'.[167] The military component of UNTAC took care to monitor the borders of Khmer Rouge territory, effectively sealing it off from the rest of Cambodia, and thereby allowing the electoral component to carry out its tasks in relative safety.[168] Its concept of self-defence was strengthened to include 'defence of the process[es] which [are] fundamental [to] the Paris Agreements' in order to operate in an environment in which the belligerents had not been disarmed.[169] Much of the resulting success in partially implementing the Paris Agreements was due to UNTAC's skill in coping with Khmer Rouge opposition while firmly stewarding the rest of the process to its conclusion. Its consultation with all parties, and its extensive use of human intelligence, allowed it to respond effectively to Khmer Rouge actions against the peace process.[170] The UN made a decision that it would not attempt to challenge the Khmer Rouge's non-cooperation and try to register and poll the population in the Khmer Rouge-held areas.[171] Nevertheless, it instructed UNTAC to endeavour to 'create and maintain a neutral political environment conducive to the holding of free and fair elections' in the remainder of Cambodia.[172]

Concentrating on the non-Khmer Rouge areas, the UNTAC electoral component was able to register 4.6 million Cambodians to vote, over 96 per cent of the eligible voting population. As the elections drew close, and the international media predicted a disaster precipitated by 'inevitable'

Khmer Rouge attacks on the election process,[173] UNTAC's military and electoral components worked out an ingenious strategy to protect them from Khmer Rouge disruption and intimidation. Using the six-day election period to the full, UNTAC concentrated the bulk of its security forces and electoral personnel on polling in the low-risk areas at the start of the elections. This method ensured that 84 per cent of the vote had been cast by day three of the elections. Following this, all of UNTAC's resources were thrown into polling in the dangerous areas bordering Khmer Rouge territory, with the psychological advantage that by this time no amount of Khmer Rouge disruption could question the results or their legitimacy.[174] This was an astounding success: 89.56 per cent of the eligible voting population voted at the 1400 polling stations in every district of Cambodia, save two, deep in Khmer Rouge territory. They resulted in a Funcinpec victory, with 45.47 per cent of the vote, and were validated by the UNTAC election monitors and endorsed by the UN.[175]

Its determination to implement the Paris Agreement to the letter made UNTAC an impediment to the Khmer Rouge's manipulation of the peace process. Co-operating with UNTAC would have been disastrous for a movement with no political existence independent of its military wing: 'The Khmer Rouge is the NADK: if you demobilise the entire army, there is no Khmer Rouge. So [demobilization] would have been an act of self-destruction, suicidal'.[176] Force Commander General Sanderson commented in retrospect: 'It would only have been suicidal if [the Khmer Rouge] hadn't been able to put the guys through the cantonment, get them away somewhere and reform the army in secret in the bush. I think [UNTAC] came in much greater strength and with much greater determination than they anticipated, and they couldn't do that'.[177] Its first response was to alter its tactics to refuse UNTAC access to Khmer Rouge territory and deny it inventories of its forces and weapons.[178] It justified this by alleging that UNTAC had not complied with the Paris Agreements, failing to rigorously verify the complete repatriation of Vietnamese forces and implement quadripartite control of the five key administrative fields through the SNC.[179] It further alleged that the elections would be biased and serve only to legitimate the SoC–Vietnamese occupation of Cambodia.[180]

While it was not co-operating, the Khmer Rouge was wary of alienating the international community. At all stages, it protested 'its unswerving commitment to the Paris Agreement'.[181] It made several attempts to reassert its ability to manipulate the weaknesses in the peace process. These were in the form of demands for various measures before it would rejoin the peace process.[182] Khmer Rouge negotiators avoided all attempts at negotiating a compromise over their demands, and refused to seriously consider any other proposals.[183] The Khmer Rouge subsequently withdrew from the SNC and its Phnom Penh headquarters, making it even more difficult for UNTAC to seek its co-operation.[184] Finally, the Khmer Rouge resorted to direct attacks against UNTAC. As the peace process continued around it, the Khmer Rouge radio became increasingly hostile towards the UN presence.[185] It began to fire on UNTAC helicopters and personnel,[186] and it sought to expand the territory under its control.[187] In these ways, the Khmer Rouge chose tactics of non-cooperation and obstructionism to take advantage of UNTAC's weakness, its reliance on co-operative behaviour by the Cambodian parties. Yet the Khmer Rouge was unable to further frustrate the mission due to the strengths in UNTAC's mission design. The Khmer Rouge, aware of the strong and cohesive international support for the mission, was not prepared to attack the peacekeepers and election monitors other than in isolated incidents. For these reasons, the ability of the mission design to compensate for weaknesses within its mandate allowed UNTAC to salvage much of the Cambodian peace process.

Links and External Support

While international pressure on the Khmer Rouge was not able to force it back into the peace process, it was enough to discourage the group from attacking UNTAC while it implemented as much of the Paris Agreements as it could. The UNTAC operation was able to do this because it enjoyed perhaps the highest level of international support of any post-Cold War peacekeeping operation. The Paris Agreements were universally acclaimed, and at the time of UNTAC's deployment, the US,[188] China,[189] the ASEAN States,[190] and India[191] all expressed support for its mission. As UNTAC confronted Khmer Rouge non-cooperation, the Chinese sought to use their leverage over the movement to induce it back into the peace process, making contacts as high as Pol Pot within the Khmer Rouge leadership.[192] Chinese Foreign Minister Qian Qichen publicly warned the Khmer Rouge that it would be 'completely isolated' if it sabotaged the peace process.[193] However, '[p]rivately, Chinese officials claim[ed] that they [could] exert little real influence over the Khmer Rouge leadership',[194] and their appeals had little influence on modifying the Khmer Rouge tactics of boycotting the election process. Its withdrawal from Phase II prompted the Secretary-General to appeal to the states at the Rio de Janeiro UN Conference on Environment and Development to support UNTAC's efforts to implement the election process.[195] Meanwhile, Thailand and Japan held a series of meetings with the Khmer Rouge to attempt to mediate its concerns on the role of the SNC and secure its re-entry into the peace process.[196] The

Co-Chairmen of the Paris Conference, France and Indonesia, convened a ten-state conference with the Khmer Rouge in Beijing, to urge its co-operation with the demobilization and election processes.[197] These links to the Khmer Rouge which the international community was willing to use on behalf of UNTAC, did not provide enough leverage to compel its co-operation, but supplied enough restraint on behalf of the Khmer Rouge to allow UNTAC to salvage much of the mission despite its weaknesses.

The Khmer Rouge's ability to resist this international pressure on it to co-operate derived from its considerable self-reliance. By the beginning of the 1990s, the international dynamic driving the Cambodian civil war had collapsed, as former sponsors of the factions became more interested in rapprochement and establishing links than thwarting each other in Cambodia. As the superpowers ended their involvement in the conflict, China, the Khmer Rouge's major supporter, found itself isolated in supporting a genocidal group, and deprived of its anti-Vietnamese justification for this support.[198] Chinese involvement in the Permanent Five resolution efforts, and its gradual withdrawal of support from the Khmer Rouge, had begun to isolate its major client. This factor was significant in compelling the Khmer Rouge's signature of the Paris Agreement, but was insufficient to secure its co-operation with the provisions of the Agreement on the ground. The Khmer Rouge's military potential to disrupt the peace process, stockpiled and secure from attack in the north-west border regions, was not immediately affected by the end of Chinese assistance, particularly to masters of guerrilla warfare like the Khmer Rouge.[199] Elements of the Thai military continued to provide the Khmer Rouge with military supplies in exchange for timber and gemstones[200] despite the Thai government's efforts to comply with the Paris Agreements and the logging and gemstone moratorium.[201] For an insurgent movement as fiercely independent and well-equipped as the Khmer Rouge, isolation from a major sponsor had little effect on its determination to pursue a patient campaign of guerrilla disruption of the peace process.

Mission Durability and Belligerent Morale and Cohesion

UNTAC's ability to salvage much of the peace process derived also from the durability of the mission despite its weaknesses. UNTAC was able to rely on strong cohesion within the UN generally, and the Security Council specifically, behind its efforts to implement the Paris Agreements. The operation was careful to maintain strict neutrality and transparency in its relationship with the parties and to the Security Council. It was meticulous in faithfully carrying out the wishes of the Security Council, order to maintain this cohesion behind its actions.[202] General Sanderson saw that maintaining force cohesion was a key goal, because 'maintaining the unity of the force is the key to maintaining the base of your negotiating position and contention that you are representing the entire international community'.[203] At all stages of its deployment, UNTAC was able to rely on instantaneous contact in Phnom Penh with the ambassadors of the Permanent Five of the Security Council, as well as the Australian, Japanese, Thai, Vietnamese, and Indonesian ambassadors, and could rely on their advice and endorsements for certain actions.[204] UNTAC assigned one of its personnel to act as a liaison presence at UN headquarters in New York, thereby minimizing misunderstandings and maintaining cohesion behind the field operation. The unanimous support for Security Council Resolution 766 (1992)[205] was intended 'to communicate to the parties that UNTAC should implement its mandate vigorously and to the full'.[206] UNTAC's maintenance of the strong support of the UN coalition for its efforts gave it the confidence and inventiveness to reconfigure its mission to cope with Khmer Rouge non-cooperation.

The Khmer Rouge's confidence to defy the UNTAC mission and resist the international pressure to co-operate derived partly from its strict control over its cadre. The insurgents were able to continue their non-cooperation with the peace process by maintaining rigid control over Khmer Rouge soldiers and the population in the territory they held. Although it is loosely organized on regional commands,[207] the Khmer Rouge combines terror, ideological indoctrination, and the use of political commissars to preserve discipline with the commands of its leadership.[208] Following the unsatisfactory outcome of the Paris Peace Conference, it is reasonable to speculate that the moderate faction within the Khmer Rouge, led by Son Sen and Khieu Samphan, had begun to lose credibility; and that it adopted the policy of the hawks, led by Pol Pot and Ieng Sary, of non-cooperation and planning for the military seizure of power. Once this hard-line policy was adopted, it was strictly enforced among the Khmer Rouge militias, with general political directives passed on to regional commanders by mobile political commissars and the Khmer Rouge radio station, 'The Voice of the Greater Union Front of Cambodia'.[209] The regional commanders, in turn, used a variety of methods of command and terror to maintain discipline to the new line among the ranks.[210] In these ways, the Khmer Rouge was able to maintain its predominance in the military balance, and a cohesive and disciplined resistance to the peace process that UNTAC was trying to implement.

The May 1993 Cambodian elections yielded a popular government legitimated in the eyes of the international community, and endorsed by almost all Cambodian factions. Yet UNTAC's success was partial: it withdrew in September 1993, leaving Cambodians to fight on against a Khmer Rouge of undiminished strength and unmoderated ferocity. The major weakness in the mission that allowed the group to escape the peace process was its inappropriate response, based on a peace agreement that was the result of a deficient negotiating procedure. The mediators, and then UNTAC's sponsoring coalition, had failed to recognize that an agreement can only be *forced* if it can be *enforced*. UNTAC's weakness was that it was sent to implement a forced agreement, and configured to rely on the parties' co-operation rather than compulsion. The Khmer Rouge was secure and confident in its military position and the inevitability of its military reconquest of power. Doctrinally and philosophically unprepared for and opposed to disarmament and elections, it was inevitable that it would choose to take advantage of UNTAC's weaknesses. The importance of UNTAC's achievement, however, was that it was able to rely on a strong mission design, and the constant endorsement of its sponsoring coalition, to work around Khmer Rouge non-cooperation and salvage as much of the Paris Agreements as it could. What it achieved despite its weaknesses was an internationally endorsed government able to undertake a concerted, legitimate campaign against the guerrillas. That the war still continues is due not only to the Khmer Rouge's military abilities, but also to the parsimony and short attention span of the international community.

CONCLUSION

The incomplete success of both UNAVEM II and UNTAC in securing the goals they had been set shows the difficulty of successfully conducting elections to resolve civil wars. Yet between UNAVEM II and UNTAC there is a considerable difference in the extent to which they were able to achieve part of their mandates. Comparing how the missions coped with their weaknesses in the face of concerted resistance and manipulation from within the conflict dynamics yields some interesting conclusions about the location of weaknesses and their ultimate effects on the outcomes of the missions. The importance of UNAVEM II's vulnerabilities in its mission design in rendering it impotent to do anything about the weaknesses within its own mandate is thrown into relief by comparing it with UNTAC's robust mission design, which was able to be used to compensate for deeper weaknesses within its objectives and presence.

Both missions were based on deficient peace agreements which ultimately made their mandates dependent on the full co-operation of all disputants. The weaknesses in both missions arose from the same source: the great powers' misreading of both civil wars by assuming that their conflict dynamics would collapse towards resolution as soon as the great powers had ended their competitive interventions. They therefore assumed in dispatching UNAVEM II and UNTAC that the full co-operation of the parties with the peace process would be assured by their own restraint. This became a significant weakness for both missions when they confronted conflict dynamics which were powerful, and independently driven. The Angolan and Cambodian parties, especially Unita and the Khmer Rouge, had no previous psychological disposition towards submitting to the democratic choice of the people, and were thus almost certain to reject peace processes whose viability depended on their consent. Inevitably, these weaknesses were transferred to the presence of the missions once they deployed. UNAVEM II's restricted role and weak presence did not threaten Unita, but neither did it have any effect on its defaulting on the peace process. As soon as it became clear that UNTAC took seriously its role in implementing the Paris Agreements faithfully, and that it could not be manipulated, the Khmer Rouge saw it as a threat that had to be avoided. Both belligerents' resistance and manipulation of the peace processes were encouraged and enabled by their strong military positions within their conflict dynamics.

The difference between UNAVEM II and UNTAC, in terms of their abilities to salvage failing peace processes, was in their mission designs. UNTAC's mission design provided it with the confidence, resourcing, support, and ability to reconfigure the mission to compensate for the weaknesses in its mandate. Its reconfiguration in effect allowed it to implement the Paris Agreements around Khmer Rouge obstructionism. In doing this, it salvaged much of its mandate as well as the rationale for the mission, by marginalizing and delegitimizing the Khmer Rouge, and opening the possibilities of a military solution to the insurgency by an internationally endorsed and supported government. By contrast UNAVEM II's restricted role, resources, and support resulted in it becoming marginalized and impotent as the peace process broke down around it. Like UNTAC, it decided to go ahead with the election despite serious problems with preparing a neutral election environment. The difference was that UNTAC adjusted to counteract these problems; UNAVEM II made no adjustments to the elections to account for Unita's consistent flouting of the pre-election processes. Thus its mission design was unable to have the slightest effect on alleviating Unita's actions to take advantage of the weaknesses in the peace process and its mission. The durability of both missions played a supporting role in the adequacy of their mission designs. The lack of international interest in, and restricted size of UNAVEM II only compounded its impotence, whereas UNTAC's support and resourcing provided it with the ability and confidence to reconfigure to deal with difficult circumstances. In both missions, external links were unable to play a significant role in modifying the defaulting parties' behaviour. Rather, Unita's and the Khmer Rouge's non-cooperation was bolstered either by a confidence in their ability to survive without external support, or with continuing small amounts of outside assistance. This military factor, along with their internal cohesion and discipline, made both groups ideally suited to resist and manipulate the mission weaknesses.

5 Conclusion

The six case studies analysed in this book are not intended to be complete accounts of what went wrong and what went right in those UN missions. Rather, each forms a part of a search for commonalities in the causes of failure of UN missions. They are also a part of a search for similarities among the civil wars they were sent to resolve which can contribute to explaining the common causes of their failures. The inclusion of the successful missions as case studies is to provide a type of experimental control, to test the relevance of these common weaknesses to mission failure, by searching for their presence, or more accurately their absence, in successful UN missions. The case studies found that there are indeed common causes of failure present within a wide range of recent UN missions to civil wars. It also found that these weaknesses, when present, tend to be accentuated by similar aspects within the vastly different conflicts they are exposed to, and that the aggravation of these weaknesses cause varying levels of mission failure. Further, a search for these weaknesses, and their aggravation by these civil war aspects in successful missions, found them to be largely absent.

The rationale of this study is that the identification of the presence of these common weaknesses, and the assessment of their vulnerability to certain aspects of the civil wars they are intended to resolve, is important to increasing the effectiveness of UN missions as international policy responses. Implicit in this whole exercise is the value-judgement that UN mediation, peacekeeping, and peacebuilding missions are an invaluable contribution to global peace and the local alleviation of suffering. This study has demonstrated that the failure of these international policy instruments is directly attributable to misuse, and that it is not, as is commonly believed, caused by flaws in the policy instrument itself. Consequently, if the weaknesses are eliminated by stopping the misuse of UN missions by the international community, UN missions will be able to continue to play an active and valuable role against the wars that plague the planet. This conclusion does two things. It draws out of the case studies the common weaknesses and the most common problematic conflict aspects that accentuate them, and assesses their rate of occurrence and their culpability for mission failures. It also suggests practical measures to address these weaknesses that have been raised by the analyses in this book.

The most regular and prominent weakness in missions that ran into difficulties when introduced into civil wars was the inappropriateness of their response to the civil war. The way these missions were conceived and configured was not relevant to the constraints to and possibilities of resolving the conflicts that they were sent to end. This basic weakness dogged the ICFY mediators in Bosnia, UNOSOM II in Somalia, UNAVEM II in Angola, and to some extent, UNTAC in Cambodia. The possibilities for resolution at that time present in the Bosnian conflict were explicitly rejected by the UN. In Somalia, Angola, and Cambodia, no genuine opportunities existed to secure a peace of the kind advocated by the international community, using UN missions. Yet in all of these cases, missions were dispatched that assumed opportunities existed for resolution in those aspects of the conflicts where only constraints to resolution existed. This became a mission weakness in two ways. It deprived the missions of a purpose that was achievable given their capabilities, and thereby denied them the ability to succeed or progress. It also translated the mission's intervention in the conflict into something other than a facilitator of peace: either an impediment, an irrelevance, or an exploitable commodity. The inappropriateness of the response, then, is a crucial weakness, because it determined how the conflict dynamic reacted to other aspects or vulnerabilities in the mission.

The inappropriateness of the mission response was most often the direct result of a misdiagnosis of the conflict by the mission's sponsoring coalition. This was the case in Bosnia, Angola, Somalia, and Cambodia. These misdiagnoses were attributable to one, or both, of two sources. One cause was spurious assumptions among the international community about civil wars, that led them to misunderstand the basis of the conflict in disputed commodities or ideas; to make precipitate judgements on the indivisibility and desirable form of states; or to assume that peaceful adjudication and compromise is immediately and automatically substitutable for war. The other source of misdiagnoses was that judgements were often informed heavily by extraneous influences, such as state-centrism or the overestimation of the responsibility of international sponsorship on the civil war. In Bosnia, the sponsoring coalition's diagnosis was skewed by geopolitical and alliance rivalries; in Cambodia and Angola, by too great an emphasis on the proxy aspects of the war and their linkage to surrounding peace dynamics. This led to an often disastrous underestimation of the domestic drives and bases of the civil wars and the resilience of their conflict dynamics to resolution. An added caution was suggested by examining the UNTAC and UNAVEM II missions. This was the need to guard against confidence in solutions embodied in peace agreements. In both Cambodia and Angola, the belligerents' initial putative consent to the agreements did not necessarily connote genuine agreement or commitment to peace, or the correctness of the diagnosis of the conflict and its resolution opportunities embodied in that agreement.

The common mission weaknesses identified in the case studies proved most vulnerable to one particularly prominent aspect of the civil wars: the basic resistance of the conflict dynamic to resolution or peace. This was attributable to two causes. The first was when one or more of the belligerents in the civil war was committed to the further use of violence to pursue its interests. At first the FMLN used violence to advance its negotiations, but abandoned this as the peace process advanced. The USC-SNA, however, remained committed to violence as its primary policy instrument, used to pursue a variety of interests, including the expulsion of UNOSOM II, and was unwilling to substitute war for adjudication or peaceful methods of securing its interests. The second cause was when one or more of the belligerents continued to operate under what can be termed a 'conquest mindset'. This mindset predisposed the belligerent to expect and to strive for the seizure of undisputed and sole power over the state, using its own devices, be they violence or other means. The conquest mindset was largely incompatible with concepts of representation of populations, the sharing of power, and political compromise. It was held by the Bosnian Serbs, Unita, and the Khmer Rouge, and contributed to their determined resistance to the resolution of the conflict by UN missions advocating peace, demobilization, and democracy. The resistance of the conflict dynamic was the aspect that most accentuated the mission weaknesses of misdiagnosis and the inappropriateness of response. The importance of resistance to resolution is demonstrated by its absence from the Mozambican conflict. There the weaknesses that appeared in the ONUMOZ mission design did not cause the failure of the mission because of the extreme pliability of the conflict dynamic, and the unwillingness of the belligerents to exploit the weaknesses to the full. The government's and Renamo's willingness to surrender violence as a policy instrument, and to forgo the conquest of uncontested power allowed ONUMOZ to function effectively despite its weaknesses.

Such luxuries were not available to the ICFY mediators, UNOSOM II, or UNAVEM II. All of these missions were assigned with mandates that were not configured to address the significant internal disputes over commodities or ideas at the base of these civil wars. The missions became stranded and irrelevant. They were fundamentally unequipped to resolve the conflicts to which they were sent, which were inter-ethnic, or inter-clan wars. This suggests that at the time they were dispatched, the international community was unprepared for, and deeply misunderstood the nature and basis of ethnic conflict. Few states in the international system have experienced war over identity and for survival,[1] or are able to understand the passions with which they are fought or the issues of importance to the disputants.[2] The international community was clearly more at home with responding to conflicts left over from the Cold War and in dealing with ideologically motivated belligerents, as it was these types of conflicts over which states had fought and competed for the past half-century. Clearly UN member-states understood better the conflicts in El Salvador and Mozambique, as well as what was necessary to resolve them. In this way, missions that were weakened by being inappropriately equipped to deal with ethnic conflicts, were also casualties of excessive state-centrism in diagnosis and response within the UN.

The other side of the difficulties experienced with resistant conflict dynamics was how forgiving pliable conflict dynamics were of mission weaknesses. Among the Salvadoran and Mozambican belligerents there was a perception of the futility of war for securing their vital interests. This was attended by a previous heavy dependence on external sponsors and the loss, or fear of losing, this support. These attributes imparted an extreme pliability onto the conflict dynamic. The difference between the effect of pliable and resistant conflict dynamics on UN mission weaknesses is startling when the progress of UNOSOM II and ONUMOZ are juxtaposed.

A weakness that rarely appeared, but which was catastrophic when it did, was divisions among the missions' sponsoring coalitions. Nowhere did such divisions contribute so strongly to a mission's failure as in Bosnia. In that case, a divided, competing, and acrimonious coalition resulted directly in an inappropriately restrained response; prevented a concerted international effort to create the conditions for the success of the mediation mission; deprived the mediators of the confidence to be creative or forceful in advancing their mediation frameworks; and encouraged the obduracy of the Bosnian Serbs. It also operated at a later stage of the UNOSOM II operation in Somalia, acting to shatter all mission cohesion and morale as it came under attack. However, the absence of this weakness does not necessarily translate into a mission strength. Indeed, strong and cohesive coalition support was invaluable to the missions sent to El Salvador and Cambodia in providing them with the leverage, durability, and the confidence to formulate creative mission designs to deal with at times problematic conflict dynamics. But the ONUMOZ and UNAVEM II operations learned only too clearly that converging interests within the sponsoring coalition are of little value when attended by parsimony or lack of interest. So unity within the sponsoring coalition is a requirement, rather than a condition, of success.

Similarly, parsimony or lack of interest within the sponsoring coalition was not, on its own, a significant liability for missions it attended. In the ONUMOZ operation, parsimony proved to be a weakness that was transitory and surmountable. However, in the UNAVEM II operation, sponsoring states' lack of interest and willingness to become involved combined with other, deeper weaknesses in the diagnosis and response to contribute to the mission's marginalization and failure. This comparison also demonstrated that ONUMOZ was lucky that its weaknesses were exposed to a pliable conflict dynamic, whereas UNAVEM II's impotence and irrelevance was seized on and exploited by an extremely resistant dynamic. The investigation of the effects of parsimony also reveals that a mission's appropriate configuration to a conflict's resolution possibilities is more important to the mission's success than its size or level of resourcing, or weaponry. The best illustration of this is the comparison of the highly successful 7500-strong ONUMOZ force in Mozambique, with the spectacular failure of the 30 800-strong, heavily armed and resourced UNOSOM II force in Somalia. The importance of appropriate configuration is a condition of the diplomatic status of UN missions and their reliance on consent. This condition requires that their success is necessarily based on their ability to work with, rather than against, the interests of the belligerents.

In seeming paradox to this observation was another common weakness in less successful UN missions: the overestimation of the capabilities and leverage of missions by the UN coalitions that dispatched them. The Bosnia mediators, UNOSOM II, UNTAC, and UNAVEM II, were all assigned mandates that they did not have the means to achieve in the civil wars in which they intervened. These missions lacked either centrality to, or control or oversight of, viable peace processes, or simply did not possess the ability to apply sufficient leverage to secure immensely ambitious mandates over the resistance of extremely robust conflict dynamics. Such recurring recipes for failure had to be linked to misdiagnosis of the civil war, and an underestimation of the difficulties inherent in resolving some of these conflicts. The saga of UNOSOM II illustrates clearly the relationship between persistent misunderstanding of the conflict and improperly resourcing and inappropriately mandating a peacekeeping mission. When it was first dispatched, UNOSOM II, even with its 30 800 personnel and heavy armament, was not doctrinally equipped to secure its mandate, the building of a viable polity from a fractured and violent clan war. When the Security Council altered its mandate to respond forcefully to resistance from within the conflict dynamic, UNOSOM II's sponsoring coalition showed its continuing misreading of the Somali civil war and misunderstanding of the nature of the peacekeeping mechanism. In changing UNOSOM II's mandate to counter-insurgency, it in effect widened the gap between the mission's mandate and capabilities, rather than, as the Security Council thought it had done, giving the mission the instruments it needed to secure its mandate. UNTAC's story throws this malaise into sharper relief. When that mission was faced by resistance from within the conflict dynamic it showed greater understanding of the conflict by reconfiguring in such a way as to minimize the impact on the mission of those weaknesses open to Khmer Rouge manipulation. So an overestimation of mission capabilities can be a serious weakness, and often seems to arise from familiar attributes within the sponsoring coalitions: apathy, eagerness to spread expenses, or just plain misunderstanding of the consensual diplomatic bases of UN conflict resolution missions.

A weakness that repeatedly exposed the missions examined to direct attack or resistance, rather than just benign marginalization, was when they were charged with implementing a normative solution that threatened the interests of a powerful belligerent. This was the fate of the missions sent to Bosnia, Somalia, and Cambodia. These normative instructions imparted on their missions the vulnerability of being seen as an impediment or a danger to the interests of the most powerful belligerents, and motivated the belligerents to either exploit or attack the mission's weaknesses. Such 'solutions by diktat' to civil wars were the product of state-centrism, and an emphasis on what sort of resolution was acceptable to the international community, rather than what solution was most viable given the particular conditions of each conflict. They were a combination of other weaknesses: state-centrism, mistaken assumptions about civil wars, and the overestimation of the capabilities of UN missions to lead resistant belligerents towards a preferred solution.

All of these common weaknesses that haunt UN missions to civil wars logically share common sources. They also suggest some important, and necessary measures to correct these weaknesses by addressing their causes. All of the weaknesses identified by this study have their basis in the structure of how UN missions are designed and dispatched. Specifically, most of these weaknesses can ultimately be traced to the too-intimate involvement of distracted and competing member-states in the formulation of mission mandates and the launching of missions. There are several direct connections between this structural configuration and the weaknesses in the missions. The first is through misdiagnosis. Nearly all 'fatal' or 'near-fatal' mission weaknesses were attended by the misunderstanding of the nature and resolution possibilities of civil wars by sponsoring coalitions. Most of these misdiagnoses were caused by extraneous concerns among the member-states. This suggests the urgent need for establishing a specialist conflict analysis capability that can provide independent advice to sponsoring coalitions on the conflicts in which the UN is considering intervening. Such advice would need to include analysis and understanding of the conflicts and the possibilities and likelihood of their resolution by UN mission.

The Conflict Analysis Unit within the UN Secretariat would need direct input into decision-making on the design and dispatch of UN missions. Although an embryonic Planning and Co-ordination cell and a Situation Monitoring Centre have been established within the Department of Peacekeeping Operations, these have clearly not impacted on decisions. Data collection, sophisticated research, and systematic result collation and analysis needs to constantly co-ordinate information from conflicts and inform the UN's decisions on when and how to intervene. There is also the need to develop an intelligence capability within the UN Secretariat. There exists within the UN's culture a shyness of intelligence gathering, stemming from fears that this will impair the impartiality of missions in the eyes of the disputants. However, the complexity of the civil wars with which it has to deal makes the collection, analysis, and secure distribution of sophisticated intelligence essential to the informed design and dispatch of missions. The UN can benefit greatly from developing its own, as well as making use of member-states' human and signals intelligence capabilities. There remain practical difficulties with intelligence-sharing in multilateral operations, such as the need for operational security or the fear of compromising sources. Yet these problems are not insurmountable, and even if they are, UN conflict analysis from information collected from open sources and missions on the ground could make an enormous difference to the effective use of UN missions.

There is already a fledgeling capability for this sort of conflict analysis within the Secretariat. Reports were made by Under-Secretary for Political Affairs Marrack Goulding and others before the Bosnia and Somalia interventions[3] that recommended against the introduction of UN missions at those times. However, these were overridden by a Security Council determined to act because of compelling member-state interests. This suggests that the UN Secretariat's analysis role should be formalized as a check on the ability of the UN's member-states to dispatch UN missions at will. This system of checks, informed by independent expertise and understanding of the conflict, is needed to ensure that UN responses are determined by the missions' capabilities and appropriateness to the resolution possibilities of the conflict, rather than by knee-jerk responses to perceived UN 'responsibilities' by apathetic and parsimonious member-states. This should also help counteract the misuse of UN missions in inappropriate contexts sent to carry out unachievable tasks.

Independent conflict appraisal should also alert the UN's member-states to a paradox of UN multilateralism: that UN endorsement is needed to legitimate the application of normative solutions to conflicts, but that UN missions are incapable of applying these solutions over local resistance. Rather than succumbing to apathy over this seeming contradiction, the UN's member-states need to make greater use of the Gulf War model, where an intervention is legitimated by a UN vote, but is implemented by more muscular multilateral means. Excellent previous examples of this have been provided by UNITAF in Somalia and IFOR in Bosnia.

The use of UN missions has again subsided after a period of their heaviest utilization in UN history. This is partly attributable to the high rate of failures among those missions that have been dispatched to civil wars, which has attracted considerable criticism of the UN and opposition to its use of these missions. This is a misguided overreaction that threatens to throw the baby out with the bathwater. UN peace missions have played an invaluable role in stabilizing points of international tension and alleviating human suffering during the first fifty years of the organization's existence. As brutal conflicts show no sign of dying out or receding into human history, the international community is still in dire need of mechanisms that can resolve them. In UN missions, it has a developed and experienced policy response. There is a continued need for UN missions, in conjunction with other methods and mechanisms. There is, however, also a prior need to iron out their problems and increase their success rate. It is only through such changes that the UN will be saved from becoming another casualty of the new world order, and be able to move into its second fifty years continuing to play a vital role in saving succeeding generations from the scourge of war.

Notes

1 Introduction

1. See Kenneth N. Waltz, *Theory of International Politics* (Massachusetts: Addison-Wesley Publishing Company, 1979).
2. Hans J. Morgenthau, *Politics Among Nations: The Struggle for Power and Peace* (5th edn) (New York: Alfred A. Knopf, 1978), p. 481.
3. Within the complex debate on sovereignty and international organizations, there exists a body of opinion that a member-state does surrender a measure of sovereignty by joining the UN and ratifying its Charter. For example, a member-state renounces its independence to go to war for territorial aggrandizement by ratifying Article 2(4) on the renunciation of the use or threat of force. However, it is highly questionable whether some member-states, notably *apartheid*-era South Africa (Angola, Mozambique), the Soviet Union (Czechoslovakia, Afghanistan), the United States (Vietnam, Panama), or Iraq (Iran, Kuwait) take these theoretical restrictions on their sovereignty as practical impediments to their freedom of action.
4. Alan James, 'The United Nations', in David Armstrong and Eric Goldstein (eds), *The End of the Cold War* (London: Frank Cass, 1990), p. 186.
5. Certainly each of the permanent five have first-hand experience of the effectiveness of insurgency or the pain of counter-insurgency: consider the PRC's own birth in insurgency, the US's and France's traumatic embroilment in Indochina, the Soviet Union's slow bleeding in Afghanistan, the Russian Federation's embroilment in Chechenya, and the United Kingdom's less successful imperial disentanglements, from Palestine to Northern Ireland.
6. See for example, Mikhail Gorbachev, 'Foreign Relations – USSR: The Democratization of World Politics', 1 May 1988, George Bush, 'Aggression in the Gulf: A Partnership of Nations', 1 October 1990, and François Mitterand, 'The Rule of Law', 15 October 1990.
7. John J. Mearsheimer sees the possibility of such trends as suggested by Iraq's invasion of Kuwait in his essay, 'Disorder Restored', in Graham Allison and Gregory F. Treverton (eds), *Rethinking America's Security: Beyond Cold War to New World Order* (New York: W.W. Norton and Company, 1992), p. 234.
8. This is most persuasively argued by Barry Buzan, *People, States and Fear: An Agenda for Security Studies in the Post-Cold War Era* (2nd ed) (New York: Harvester Wheatsheaf, 1991), p. 155.
9. Apart from the strains they place on resources and infrastructure, refugee flows can also include significant criminal or insurgent elements. Examples of the seriousness with which states regard refugee flows can be seen from Zaire's reaction to Rwandan refugee camps, and even from the alarmed reactions of European states, some among the world's richest, over flows of refugees from the former Yugoslavia. See also Caroline Thomas, *New States, Sovereignty and Intervention* (Aldershot: Gower, 1985).
10. Witness the emotive public reactions to the massacre of Muslims in Bosnia

in Islamic countries, and the responses of some of the most autocratic regimes in the world: Iran, Saudi Arabia, Libya.

11. Pierre Hassner, 'Beyond Nationalism and Internationalism: Ethnicity and World Order', *Survival*, Vol. 35, No. 2, Summer 1993, p. 60.
12. Anthony Lake, 'From Containment to Enlargement', *Vital Speeches of the Day*, Vol. 60, No. 1, 15 October 1993, p. 17.
13. See Lawrence Freedman and Efraim Karsh, *The Gulf Conflict 1990–1991: Diplomacy and War in the New World Order* (London: Faber and Faber, 1993).
14. Inis L. Claude Jr, 'Collective Legitimation as a Political Function of the United Nations', *International Organization*, Vol. 20, No. 3, 1966, p. 367.
15. Ramesh Thakur, *International Peacekeeping in Lebanon: United Nations Authority and Multinational Force* (Boulder: Westview Press, 1987), p. 147.
16. Edward N. Luttwak, 'Where Are the Great Powers?', *Foreign Affairs*, Vol. 73, No. 4, July/August 1994, pp. 23–8.
17. As testified by the wave of reconfigurations sweeping military establishments, particularly of the Western powers, after the Cold War, towards downsizing and strengthening rapid response and peacekeeping components.
18. This view was emphasized by former United Kingdom Permanent Representative to the UN, Sir David Hannay in an interview, New York City, 29 March 1994.
19. Arthur A. Stein, *Why Nations Co-operate: Circumstance and Choice in International Relations* (Ithaca: Cornell University Press, 1990), pp. 28–34.
20. This consideration was obviously manifest in the formation of a non-UN coalition such as the Western Contact group on Bosnia, which included those states most interested in the conflict, but which nevertheless had diametrically opposed interests in the conflict.
21. For a full discussion on coalition-building, side-payments, and the divisibility of outcomes, see Mancur Olson, *The Logic of Collective Action: Public Goods and the Theory of Groups* (Cambridge: Harvard University Press, 1965).
22. See Ole R. Holsti, P. Terrence Hopmann, and John D. Sullivan, *Unity and Disintegration in International Alliances: Comparative Studies* (New York: John Wiley and Sons, 1973), pp. 74–5.
23. Joseph M. Grieco, 'Anarchy and the Limits of Cooperation: A Realist Critique of the Newest Liberal Institutionalism', *International Organization*, Vol. 42, No. 3, Summer 1988, p. 486.
24. Witness the caucus group that formed in the Security Council to try to lift the weapons embargo on the Bosnian government, including the United States, Iran, and Libya. See 'UN Council Blocks Arms for Bosnians', *New York Times*, 30 June 1993.
25. Sydney D. Bailey, 'The United Nations and the Termination of Armed Conflict, 1946–64', *International Affairs*, Vol. 58, No. 3, Summer 1982, pp. 20–1.
26. Even the more authoritarian states of the UN system claim some method of endorsement from their societies, be they based on socio-economic or religious solidarity: witness the preoccupation of authoritarian states, such as North Korea, with placing the word 'Democratic' prominently within the official names of their states. While states continue to support insurgencies

in enemy states, it appears that the days of supporting subversion for ideological reasons have passed.

27. A cursory glance at the Charter demonstrates the founding of the UN on ideals of Western democracy: the preamble begins with 'We the people of the United Nations . . .'; its endorsement of human rights; its bestowal of sovereign equality on its members; and its techniques of parliamentary diplomacy and decision by majority vote.
28. Sydney D. Bailey, *How Wars End: The United Nations and the Termination of Armed Conflict 1946–1964 Volume I* (Oxford: Clarendon Press, 1982), p. 2.
29. The difference between actually resolving the issues at the base of a conflict, and just suppressing their manifestation – the actual fighting – is made by John Burton, *Conflict: Resolution and Provention* (Basingstoke: Macmillan, 1990).
30. As will be seen in the case study of UNAVEM II in Chapter 4, this ill-conceived mission failed and saw the ushering in of a phase of the Angolan civil war of unprecedented brutality, in which as many as 1000 Angolans lost their lives per day.
31. Hedley Bull, *The Anarchical Society: A Study of Order in World Politics* (Basingstoke: Macmillan, 1977), p. 17.
32. Boutros Boutros-Ghali, 'UN Multilateralism: A Cure for Ugly New Nationalisms', *International Herald Tribune*, 21 August 1993, p. 6.
33. As will be seen in the case study, the obvious exception to this rule was the case of the former Yugoslavia, where the EC and the UN attempted to use the recognition of the break-up of a sovereign state as a low-cost and low-commitment substitute to actual conflict resolution on the ground. Subsequent to the failure of this gambit, UN member-states reverted to type, advocating solutions in Bosnia to preserve the territorial entirety of that now-unviable state.
34. Inis L. Claude Jr, *Swords Into Ploughshares: The Problems and Progress of International Organization* (London: University of London Press Ltd., 1965), p. 200.
35. John W. Burton, 'The History of International Conflict Resolution', in John W. Burton and Edward Azar (eds), *International Conflict Resolution: Theory and Practice* (Sussex: Wheatsheaf Books, 1986), p. 45.
36. See Boutros Boutros-Ghali, *An Agenda for Peace* (New York: United Nations, 1992); *Report on the Work of the Organization 1992*; 'Beyond Peacekeeping', Conference at New York University, 20 January 1993; 'UN Peacekeeping in a New Era: A New Chance for Peace', *World Today*, Vol. 49, No. 4, April 1993; 'An Agenda for Peace: One Year Later', *Orbis*, Vol. 37, No. 3, Summer 1993; see also Andrei Kozyrev and Gennadi Gatilov, 'The UN Peacemaking System: Problems and Prospects', *International Affairs (USSR)*, No. 12, December 1990; Eric Stein, 'The United Nations and the Enforcement of Peace', *Michigan Journal of International Law*, Vol. 10, No. 1, Winter 1989; Charles Dobbie, 'A Concept for Post-Cold War Peacekeeping', *Survival*, Vol. 36, No. 3, Autumn 1994.
37. Claude, *Swords Into Ploughshares*, p. 375.
38. Alan James, *The Politics of Peacekeeping* (London: Chatto and Windus, 1969), pp. 195–6.
39. Claude, *Swords Into Ploughshares*, p. 218.

40. Many of the doctrines of guerrilla warfare preach self-sufficiency for the movement, and the reliance on the countryside and its populace for food and shelter. The low intensity of many insurgencies, and the insurgents' reliance on captured weapons from the incumbent forces, often free them from dependence on outside assistance. The more sophisticated insurgencies have developed their own weapons manufacturing capabilities: the PLO maintained its own SAM-7 factory for some time.
41. Sir David Hannay, UK Permanent Representative to the UN, Interview, New York City, 29 March 1994.
42. Boutros Boutros-Ghali, 'Agenda for Peace: One Year Later', *Orbis*, Vol. 37, No. 3, Summer 1993, p. 328.
43. Johan Jorgen Holst, 'Enhancing Peacekeeping Operations', *Survival*, Vol. 32, No. 3, May/June 1990, pp. 268–70.
44. Mats Berdal, 'Wither UN Peacekeeping?', *Adelphi Paper 281* (London: Brasseys, 1993), p. 32.
45. Claude, *Swords Into Ploughshares*, p. 375.
46. Another variation among civil wars is their objectives: some are for control of the entire state such as in Nicaragua, others are waged by secessionist or irredentist groups for the right to break away from the state, such as in Eritrea.
47. States such as Somalia could be said to be truly anarchic, with no group possessing the attributes of central and administrative control necessary to call them the government.
48. L.J. MacFarlane, *Violence and the State* (London: Nelson, 1974), p. 76.
49. Paul Wilkinson, *Terrorism and the Liberal State* (Basingstoke: Macmillan, 1986), pp. 81–92.
50. Che Guevara, *Guerrilla Warfare* (Harmondsworth: Penguin, 1961), p. 13.
51. Kenneth N. Waltz, 'The Structure of Anarchy', in Robert O. Keohane (ed.), *Neorealism and Its Critics* (New York: Columbia University Press, 1986), p. 127.
52. Robert Taber, *The War of the Flea: A Study of Guerrilla Warfare Theory and Practice* (St Albans: Paladin, 1970), p. 45.
53. Julian Lider, *On the Nature of War* (Farnborough: Saxon House, 1977), p. 92.
54. Robert Gilpin, *War and Change in World Politics* (Cambridge: Cambridge University Press, 1981), p. 19.
55. For example, when SWAPO in Namibia was offered the opportunity of achieving Namibian independence from South Africa by complying with a UN peace process based on SCR 435, it committed itself to the abandonment of war and cooperation with the peace process which culminated in Namibian independence and a SWAPO election victory in 1989.
56. Carl von Clausewitz, *On War* (trans. Anatol Rapoport) (Harmondsworth: Penguin, 1982), p. 402.
57. Michael Howard, *The Causes of Wars and Other Essays* (London: Temple Smith, 1983), p. 8.
58. Clausewitz, *On War*, p. 410.
59. *ibid.*, p. 400.
60. Raymond Aron, *Peace and War: A Theory of International Relations* (trans. Richard Howard and Annette Baker Fox), (London: Wiedenfeld and Nicolson, 1966), p. 25.

61. Clausewitz, *On War*, p. 125.
62. Thomas C. Schelling, *Arms and Influence* (New Haven: Yale University Press, 1966), pp. 142–3.
63. Alvaro de Soto, Political Adviser to the Special Representative for the United Nations Secretary-General, quoted on BBC News and Current Affairs, 'Revolution on the 37th Floor', BBC Radio 4, 22 April 1993, 8 p.m.
64. Alan James, 'Peacekeeping and Ethnic Conflict', unpublished paper, October 1993.
65. Hedley Bull, *The Anarchical Society: A Study of Order in World Politics* (Basingstoke: Macmillan, 1977), p. 207.
66. Bailey, *How Wars End*, p. 2.
67. I. William Zartman, *Ripe for Resolution: Conflict and Intervention in Africa* (New York: Oxford University Press, 1989), p. 10.
68. Alan James, 'The Problems of Internal Peacekeeping', *Diplomacy and Statecraft*, Vol. 5, No. 1, March 1994, pp. 27–8.

2 Mediation

1. United Nations Legal Affairs Codification Division, *Handbook on the Peaceful Settlement of Disputes Between States* (New York: United Nations, 1992), p. 40.
2. Jacob Bercovitch, 'International Mediation: A Study of the Incidence, Strategies and Conditions of Successful Outcomes', *Cooperation and Conflict*, Vol. 21, No. 3, 1986, p. 156.
3. Vivienne Jabri, 'The Western Contact Group as Intermediary in the Conflict Over Namibia', in C.R. Mitchell and K. Webb (eds), *New Approaches to International Mediation* (New York: Greenwood Press, 1988), pp. 103–4.
4. Vratislav Pechota, *The Quiet Approach: A Study of the Good Offices Exercised by the United Nations Secretary-General in the Cause of Peace* (New York: United Nations Institute for Training and Research, 1972), p. 48.
5. A former UN mediator sent to the Cyprus conflict stated: '[Any settlement] must be consistent with the provisions of the UN Charter, of which the following in particular seems relevant: the purposes, principles and obligations relating to the maintenance of international peace and security, the peaceful settlement of disputes, respect for human rights and fundamental freedoms, recognition of the sovereign equality of member-states, abstention from the threat or use of force against the territorial integrity or political independence of any member-state, and respect for treaty obligations not in conflict with those of member-states under the Charter.' See Rosalyn Higgins, *The Development of International Law Through the Political Organs of the United Nations* (London: Oxford University Press, 1963), pp. 6–12.
6. Saadia Touval and I. William Zartman, 'Introduction: Mediation in Theory', in Saadia Touval and I. William Zartman, *International Mediation in Theory and Practice* (Boulder: Westview Press, 1985), p. 12.
7. John Burton, *Conflict: Resolution and Provention* (Basingstoke: Macmillan, 1990), pp. 6–7.
8. I. William Zartman and Maureen Berman, *The Practical Negotiator* (New Haven: Yale University Press, 1982), p. 13.
9. Pechota, *The Quiet Approach*, pp. 53–4.

10. I. William Zartman and Saadia Touval, 'Conclusion', in Touval and Zartman, *International Mediation*, p. 245.
11. Jacob Bercovitch, 'The Structure and Diversity of Mediation in International Relations', in Jacob Bercovitch and Jeffery Z. Rubin (eds), *Mediation in International Relations: Multiple Approaches to Conflict Management* (Basingstoke: Macmillan, 1992), p. 8.
12. *ibid.*, p. 4.
13. Zartman and Berman, *The Practical Negotiator*, pp. 57–8.
14. Fred Charles Ikle, *How Nations Negotiate* (New York: Harper and Row, 1976), pp. 16–18.
15. Hereafter shortened to 'Bosnia'.
16. The referendum, held from 29 February to 1 March 1992, was boycotted by the 31% of the population that were ethnic Serbs, but returned a 90% result in favour of independence from Yugoslavia.
17. The US and the EU recognized Bosnia on 17 April 1992, and it was accepted as a member of the UN on 22 May 1992.
18. This plan had originated in the Serb-Croat civil war that accompanied the Second World War. See Branka Magas, *The Destruction of Yugoslavia: Tracking the Break-Up 1980–92* (London: Verso, 1993), p. 324.
19. Noll Scott and Derek Jones (eds), *Bloody Bosnia: A European Tragedy* (London: The Guardian and Channel Four Television, 1994); see also Alex N. Dragnich, *Serbs and Croats: The Struggle in Yugoslavia* (San Diego: Harcourt, Brace and Co., 1993).
20. Roy Gutman, *A Witness to Genocide: The First Inside Account of Ethnic Cleansing in Bosnia* (Shaftsbury: Element, 1993); see also Salahi Ramadan Sonyel, *The Muslims of Bosnia: The Genocide of a People* (Markfielf: The Islamic Foundation, 1994).
21. SCR 713 (1991), 25 September 1991.
22. Cyrus Vance had earlier been appointed by Perez de Cuellar as Special Envoy to the former Yugoslavia on 8 October 1991.
23. Statement by the President of the Security Council, 10 April 1992.
24. Report of the Secretary-General, S/24795, 11 November 1992, pp. 3–4.
25. I am indebted to Joanne Wright for this observation.
26. Germany advocated recognizing the seceding republics of the former Yugoslavia as a cheap way of stopping the hostilities. This adds an additional level of parsimony to the Bosnia coalition.
27. After the failure of the EU peace plan, the UK, France, Belgium, and Austria requested UN involvement in resolving the Yugoslav wars on 18 October 1991.
28. In late 1995, it was revealed that the UK and France had acceded to German proposals to recognize the breakaway Yugoslav republics in return for German lenience on the questions of opting out on the currency integration and the Social Charter proposed in the Maastricht Treaty.
29. The end of the Cold War had placed great internal strains on the alliance, and a great deal of debate had attended speculation on the future shape, configuration, and purpose of the alliance.
30. American policy was originally defined by James Baker's June 1991 speech in Belgrade, which advocated the continued existence of the state of Yugoslavia. However, once convinced to recognize the seceding republics, US

policy on Bosnia was informed by legalistic considerations of sovereignty, and was sensitive to domestic demands to respond meaningfully to the conflict.

31. As a compromise and a way to deflect divisions within NATO, the US Secretary of State Warren Christopher proposed the use of US troops in a preventative deployment in Macedonia in a NATO meeting in Athens on 10 June 1993. US forces duly took up their preventative role in Macedonia.
32. This acrimony has been particularly bitter between Britain, France, and the US, and is exemplified by French Foreign Minister Alain Juppe's pointed remarks on 27 May 1993: 'I haven't agreed with the so-called division of labour between those who are in the sky and those who are on the ground. I wish that all of the great powers who are involved in the painful drama would assume their responsibility.'
33. British and French frustration with Germany paralleled their frustration with the US. They were aware that they acceded to German pressure to recognize the Yugoslav republics initially, and that Germany was able to respond freely to the internal pressures of right-wing groups and expatriate Croatians while escaping the responsibility of assuming these positions by knowing well that because of Nazi atrocities in the Balkans, German forces will never be invited to intervene in Bosnia, and thus will never be endangered by the positions advocated by the German government.
34. President Yeltsin, quoted in The *Independent*, 15 February 1994.
35. A good example of the operation of this consideration came on 12 April 1993, when the UN Security Council postponed a vote on strengthening sanctions against Serbia until after the 25 April referendum on the popularity of the Yeltsin government.
36. There were numerous calls for enforcement action and a lifting of the arms embargo, such as that issued by the Islamic Conference Organization of 13 July 1993, A/47/977 and S/26112.
37. This coincidence has led to such anomalies as the 29 June 1993 Security Council vote on lifting the arms embargo against Bosnia, where the US was supported by Iran and Libya in voting for the draft resolution, which failed to be adopted through lack of votes. See 'UN Council Blocks Arms for Bosnians', *New York Times*, 30 June 1993.
38. David Rieff, *Slaughterhouse: Bosnia and the Failure of the West* (New York: Simon and Schuster, 1995), pp. 9–15.
39. As evidenced by the regular meetings between the US, the UK, Russia, France, and Spain, to negotiate joint strategies on Bosnia.
40. On 27–28 June 1992, President Bush had a series of telephone conversations with Russia's Yeltsin, Britain's Major, and Canada's Mulroney on the possibility of a Gulf War-type multilateral enforcement action in Bosnia.
41. SCR 775 (1992), 20 May 1992.
42. SCR 787 (1992), 16 November 1992.
43. SCRs 836 (1993), 4 June 1993; 838 (1993), 10 June 1993; and 859 (1993), 24 August 1993.
44. Report of the Secretary-General, S/25248, 8 February 1993, pp. 1–2.
45. Report of the Secretary-General, S/24795, 11 November 1992, p. 13.
46. SCR 836 (1993), 4 June 1993.
47. Sabrina Petra Ramet, 'War in the Balkans', *Foreign Affairs*, Vol. 71, No. 4, Fall 1992, pp. 79–98.

48. Joint Action Program, S/25829, 24 May 1993, p. 2.
49. SCR 787 (1992), 16 November 1992.
50. *ibid.*
51. SCR 836 (1993), 4 June 1993.
52. SCR 859 (1993), 24 August 1993.
53. Laura Silber and Allan Little, *The Death of Yugoslavia* (London: Penguin Books, 1995), pp. 226–40.
54. 'Eye of the Balkan Storm', *The Sunday Times*, 20 February 1994.
55. Lawrence Freedman, 'Lifting Embargo Risks Hurting Bosnians Most', *The Times,* 15 September 1994.
56. Ed Vulliamy, *Seasons in Hell: Understanding Bosnia's War* (New York: St. Martin's Press, 1994), pp. 58–61.
57. Report of the Secretary-General, S/25479, 26 March 1993, p. 4.
58. John Zamentica, 'The Yugoslav Conflict', *Adelphi Paper 270* (London: IISS, 1992), p. 22.
59. Noel Malcolm, *Bosnia: A Short History* (London: Macmillan, 1991), p. 248.
60. Quoted in The *International Herald Tribune,* 2 December 1993.
61. Patrick Moore, 'Bosnian Impasse Poses Problems for Diplomacy', *Radio Free Europe*, Vol. 2, No. 14, 2 April 1993, p. 28.
62. ICFY Co-Chairmens' Report, S/26066, 8 July 1993, p. 4.
63. ICFY Co-Chairmens' Report, S/26233, 3 August 1993, p. 2.
64. 'Plan to Split Bosnia Challenges Serbs', *International Herald Tribune*, 9–10 July 1994.
65. See especially the ICFY Co-Chairmens' response to the Serb-Croat peace plan 'on behalf of the Muslim people', S/26066, 8 July 1993.
66. Zamentica, 'The Yugoslav Conflict', 1992, p. 27.
67. See A/48/92 and S/25341, 26 February 1993.
68. While the Serbs were not the only combatants practising ethnic cleansing – evidence abounds of these activities by government and Croat forces – the Serbs have received most of the international opprobrium and condemnation.
69. See SCRs 769 (1992), 7 August 1992; 771 (1992), 13 August 1992; 798 (1992), 18 December 1992; and 808 (1993) 22 February 1993.
70. Edith S. Klein, 'Obstacles to Conflict Resolution in the Territories of the Former Yugoslavia', in David A. Charters (ed.), *Peacekeeping and the Challenge of Civil Conflict Resolution* (New Brunswick: University of New Brunswick, 1994), p. 161.
71. Ruger Thurow and Tony Horwitz, 'Paranoid and Vengeful, Serbs Claim Their War is to Right Old Wrongs', *Wall Street Journal*, 18 September 1992.
72. Former UNPROFOR II Commander Phillipe Morillon, 'UN Operations in Bosnia: Lessons and Realities', *RUSI Journal*, Vol. 138, No. 6, December 1993, p. 34.
73. Klein, 'Obstacles to Conflict Resolution', p. 160.
74. Report of the Secretary-General, S/25221, 2 February 1993, p. 2.
75. Report of the Secretary-General, S/25248, 8 February 1993, p. 2.
76. Report of the Secretary-General, S/25221, 2 February 1993, p. 27.
77. The mediators reported that by March 1993 'the position of the Bosnian Serbs had hardened appreciably since the Geneva round of negotiations in January on many of the political aspects of an overall settlement'. See Report of the Secretary-General, S/25479, 26 March 1993, p. 5.

78. Michael Wesley, 'Blue Berets or Blindfolds? Peacekeeping and the Hostage Effect', *International Peacekeeping*, Vol. 2, No. 4, Winter 1995, pp. 473–6.
79. David Gompert, 'How to Defeat Serbia', *Foreign Affairs*, Vol. 73, No. 4, July/August 1994, p. 40.
80. SCR 758 (1992), 8 June 1992.
81. ICFY Co-Chairmens' Report, S/26066, 8 July 1993, p. 5.
82. UNDPI, 'The UN and the Situation in the Former Yugoslavia', DPI/1312/Rev.2, March 1994, p. 27.
83. SCRs 757 (1992), 30 May 1992 and 787 (1992), 16 November 1992, applied mandatory sanctions against Serbia and Montenegro, and explicitly linked the lifting of these sanctions to Bosnian Serb co-operation with peace plans.
84. 'Bosnia Faces Ultimatum to Accept Peace Plan', *International Herald Tribune*, 6 July 1994.
85. Opening statement of Cyrus Vance to the January 1993 peace talks in Geneva, quoted in Report of the Secretary-General, S/25050, 6 January 1993, p. 7.
86. Report of the Secretary-General, S/25221, 2 February 1993, p. 13.
87. 'Draft Agreement Relating to Bosnia and Herzegovina', S/25050, 6 January 1993, p. 16.
88. While the Vance–Owen plan ruled out ethnically pure cantons, it did recognize that each canton would be dominated by one of the ethnic groups through its predominance in numbers. It was thought that this compromise would secure agreement to a plan that rejected ethnic cleansing.
89. Silber and Little, *The Death of Yugoslavia*, pp. 306–7.
90. 'Next in Bosnia', *The Economist*, 23 January 1993, p. 19.
91. Malcolm, *Bosnia*, pp. 247–8.
92. ICFY Co-Chairmens' Report, S/26066, 8 July 1993, p. 4.
93. *ibid.*
94. ICFY Co-Chairmens' Report, S/26260, 6 August 1993, p. 3.
95. *International Herald Tribune*, 6 July 1994.
96. Silber and Little, *The Death of Yugoslavia*, pp. 374–80.
97. James Gow, 'Towards a Settlement in Bosnia: The Military Dimension', *The World Today*, Vol. 50, No. 5, May 1994, p. 97.
98. Malcolm, *Bosnia*, p. 249.
99. David B. Ottaway, 'Bosnian Serbs Seem Poised to Spurn Partition Plan', *International Herald Tribune*, 19 July 1994.
100. Quoted in *Facts on File*, Vol. 52, No. 2712, 12 November 1992, p. 849.
101. 'After Owen–Vance', *New Statesman and Society*, 7 May 1993, p. 5.
102. ICFY Co-Chairmens' Report, S/26260, 6 August 1993, p. 2.
103. Bosnian Government Official, quoted in William Pfaff, 'Really, the Only Bosnia Plan on the Table', *International Herald Tribune*, 9–10 July 1994.
104. 'Serbs in Bosnia Ready to Reject Peace at Polls', *International Herald Tribune*, 29 August 1994.
105. A full account of the mechanics and fluctuations between the Bosnia coalition partners would fill volumes. But many public moments of tension dot the history of the UN's involvement in Bosnia: the visit of Senator Bob Dole to Europe in December 1994, President Yeltsin's belligerent warnings in September 1994, the numerous votes in the US Congress to force the lifting of the embargo, the tensions over the hostages crises in December 1994 and

May 1995, and the controversy over the American refusal to share intelligence on the Balkans with its European coalition partners in late 1994.

106. Beginning with the visit to Belgrade by Russian Deputy Foreign Minister Vitaly Churkin in March 1993.
107. Russian warnings against aiding the Muslims have often been belligerent: in June 1994 Foreign Minister Andrei Kozyrev warned that secret arms shipments to the Muslims could ignite a 'new world war'; see 'Bosnia Arms Could Spark World War', *International Herald Tribune*, 15 June 1994. The European powers, particularly Britain, France, and Germany, were also adamant on this issue, with French Foreign Minister Alain Juppe calling American proposals to lift the embargo 'an absurdity'; see 'America and Europe Clash Over Arms Ban', *Daily Telegraph*, 12 September 1994.
108. Diplomats and media sources collected a growing corpus of circumstantial evidence that Serbia was breaking its own embargo against the Bosnian Serbs. Observers saw elite Serbian paramilitary units such as the Tigers entering the Bihac pocket in November 1994, while advanced anti-aircraft weapons systems appeared in the Krajina following NATO airstrikes at the same time. See John Pomfret, 'Belgrade Suspected of Breaking Its Embargo', *International Herald Tribune*, 10–11 December 1994.
109. See, for example, 'Bosnian Serbs Seek Map Change and Further Talks', *International Herald Tribune*, 22 July 1994.
110. Heightened tensions within the Contact Group were noticeable on many occasions during changes in the tempo of the war, such as during the Muslim offensive and Serb counter-offensive around the Bihac pocket in late 1994; see Michael Sheridan, 'UN Takes Stock of Muslim Offensive', The *Independent*, 8 November 1994.
111. Gompert, 'How To Defeat Serbia', p. 37.
112. First introduced to the Security Council in April 1993.
113. OCI Communiqué, A/47/977 and S/26112, 19 July 1993.
114. See Dan Williams, 'Biding Time, Big Powers Seek New Sanctions on Serbs', *International Herald Tribune*, 1 August 1994.
115. Gompert, 'How to Defeat Serbia', p. 38.
116. This point was bitterly noted by Vance and Owen in their report to the Security Council after the final rejection of the Vance–Owen plan. See ICFY Co-Chairmen's Report, S/26066, 8 July 1993, p. 3.
117. For example, Stoltenberg and Owen made the angry observation in May 1993 that during American, Russian, British, French, and Spanish meetings with the Bosnian parties that month, 'Unfortunately the conception was conveyed . . . that the roll-back of the Bosnian Serbs was no longer a priority position on the international agenda', an impression diametrically opposed to that the mediators had been assuring the parties was the case. See ICFY Co-Chairmen's Report, S/26066, 8 July 1993.
118. Malcolm, *Bosnia*, p. 249.
119. Klein, 'Obstacles to Conflict Resolution', p. 153.
120. Yigal Chazan, 'Paranoia and Apathy Grip Pale', *Guardian*, 8 November 1994.
121. Malcolm, *Bosnia*, p. 250.
122. Klein, 'Obstacles to Conflict Resolution', p. 154.
123. The five core groups forming the FMLN were the Communist Party of

El Salvador (PCES), the Farabundo Marti Popular Forces of Liberation (FPL), the People's Revolutionary Army (ERP), the Armed Forces of Popular Resistance (FARN), and the Revolutionary Party of Central American Workers (PRTC). Close links were formed with other, non-military front and political organizations, such as the Democratic Revolutionary Front (FDR).

124. From a Radio Venceremos broadcast, 7 December 1988, quoted in Christina Meyer, *Underground Voices: Insurgent Propaganda in El Salvador, Nicaragua, and Peru* (Santa Monica, RAND, 1991), p. 5.
125. James Dunkerley, *The Long War: Dictatorship and Revolution in El Salvador* (London: Junction Books, 1982), p. 168.
126. These initiatives began with the Contadora process in 1983 and continued through the Esquipulas agreements and various regional contact groups. These efforts were acknowledged and encouraged by the Security Council in Resolution 530 (1983) and General Assembly 38/10 (1983).
127. In the Declaration of San Isidrio Coronado in December 1989, the five Central American Presidents (Mexico, Guatemala, El Salvador, Honduras, Nicaragua, and Costa Rica) appealed to the Secretary-General to facilitate talks between the Salvadoran government and the FMLN.
128. Security Council Resolution 637 (1989).
129. See, for example, the Guatemala Peace Plan signed by Costa Rica, Guatemala, El Salvador, Honduras, and Nicaragua of 7 August 1987, and the statements of officials at the Summit, *Facts on File*, 14 August 1987, pp. 581–4.
130. The Contadora Group, of Colombia, Mexico, Panama, and Venezuela, joined by Argentina, Brazil, Peru, and Uruguay formed in January 1983 into a pressure group for peace in Central America. Its efforts within the UN resulted in Security Council Resolution 530 (1983) and General Assembly Resolution 38/10 (1983) supporting the peace efforts in Central America and asking the Secretary-General to keep the Organization informed of their progress.
131. The Esquipulas Group, comprised of Costa Rica, Guatemala, El Salvador, Nicaragua, and Honduras, formed in August 1987 to co-operatively remove structural impediments to the resolution of the region's civil wars.
132. See Bob Woodward, *Veil: The Secret Wars of the CIA 1981–1987* (London: Headline, 1987).
133. This request was one of the subjects of a joint communiqué issued by the two on 1 August 1991.
134. United Nations Briefing Paper, 'United Nations Observer Mission in El Salvador', DPI/1306/Rev.2, 31 October 1993, p. 27.
135. David Holiday and William Stanley, 'Building the Peace: Preliminary Lessons From El Salvador', *Journal of International Affairs*, Vol. 46, No. 2, Winter 1993, p. 418.
136. In 1988 and 1989, ARENA had beaten competitors from the left in national elections, among them former members of the FDR, the FMLN's political wing.
137. George R. Vickers, 'The Political Reality After Eleven Years of War', in Joseph S. Tulchin with Gary Bland (eds), *Is There A Transition to Democracy in El Salvador?* (Boulder: Lynne Rienner Publishers, 1992), pp. 27–9.
138. Stephen Baranyi and Liisa North, *Stretching the Limits of the Possible: United Nations Peacekeeping in Central America: Aurora Papers 15* (Ontario: Canadian Centre for Global Security, 1992), pp. 26–7.

139. Jose Z. Garcia, 'Democratic Consolidation in El Salvador', *Current History*, Vol. 87, No. 533, December 1988, p. 422.
140. Quoted in Yvonne Grenier, 'Understanding the FMLN: A Glossary of Five Words', *Conflict Quarterly*, Spring 1991, p. 59.
141. Francisco A. Alvarez, 'Transition Before the Transition: The Case of El Salvador', *Latin American Perspectives*, Issue 56, Vol. 15, No. 1, Winter 1988, p. 83.
142. Grenier, 'Understanding the FMLN', p. 58.
143. Michael Radu and Vladimir Tismaneanu, *Latin American Revolutionaries: Groups, Goals, Methods* (Washington: Pergammon Brassey's, 1990), pp. 187–234.
144. Linda Robinson, 'Why Central America is Still Not Democratic', *SAIS Review*, Vol. 12, No. 2, Summer–Fall 1992, p. 89.
145. Democratic Revolutionary Front Communiqué, quoted in *Facts on File*, 30 October 1987, p. 799.
146. Thomas Anderson, 'El Salvador's Dim Prospects', *Current History*, Vol. 85, No. 507, January 1986, p. 36.
147. Report of the Secretary-General, S/22031, 21 December 1990, pp. 1–2.
148. The right, through its death squads, as well as the left in El Salvador, had demonstrated particular skills at terrorism and guerrilla methods.
149. See, for example, Security Council Resolution 637 (1989) and General Assembly Resolution 38/10.
150. United Nations Department of Public Information, 'The Peace Process in El Salvador and the United Nations: Fact Sheet 1', DPI/1149A–40697, 1 July 1991, p. 1.
151. Klepak, 'Peacekeeping in Central America', in Charters, *Peacekeeping*, p. 84.
152. Baranyi and North, *Stretching the Limits of the Possible*, p. 24.
153. Heavy use of United Nations verification mechanisms for monitoring compliance with the agreements as they were reached was also recognized by Perez de Cuellar as a vital component of progress in the negotiations. See UNDPI, 'Peace Process in El Salvador', p. 3.
154. SCR 693 (1991).
155. Report of the Secretary-General, S/22494, 16 April 1991, pp. 2–5.
156. Grenier, 'Understanding the FMLN', p. 54.
157. Joseph G. Sullivan, 'How Peace Came to El Salvador', *Orbis*, Vol. 38, No. 1, Winter 1994, p. 83.
158. Jose Z. Garcia, 'Democratic Consolidation in El Salvador', *Current History*, Vol. 87, No. 533, December 1988, p. 423.
159. Grenier, 'Understanding the FMLN', p. 57.
160. FMLN/FDR, 'Proposal of the FMLN/FDR', *Latin American Perspectives*, Issue 55, Vol. 14, No. 4, Fall 1987, pp. 481–6.
161. See Security Council Resolution 637 (1989) and General Assembly Resolution 44/10 (1989).
162. United Nations, *El Salvador Agreements: The Path to Peace* (New York: United Nations, 1992), pp. iv–v.
163. Enrique Baloyra-Herp, 'The Persistent Conflict in El Salvador', *Current History*, Vol. 90, No. 554, March 1991, p. 122.
164. United Nations, *El Salvador Agreements*, pp. 1–6.

165. Report of the Secretary General, A/46/713; S/23256, 2 December 1991, pp. 1–2.
166. Sullivan, 'How Peace Came to El Salvador', p. 84.
167. *ibid.*, p. 89.
168. UNDPI, Press Release, SG/SM/4426 of 4 April 1990.
169. Sullivan, 'How Peace Came to El Salvador', p. 96.
170. *ibid.*, p. 85.
171. Holiday and Stanley, 'Building the Peace', p. 418.
172. Grenier, 'Understanding the FMLN', pp. 62–3.
173. *ibid.*, p. 63.
174. Sullivan, 'How Peace Came to El Salvador', p. 81.
175. Pamela Constable, 'How Peace Came to El Salvador', *Current History*, Vol. 92, No. 572, March 1993, p. 107.
176. *Facts on File*, 16 February 1990, p. 111.
177. Sullivan, 'How Peace Came to El Salvador', p. 85.
178. See S/22693, and A/46/713 and S/23256, 2 December 1991, p. 3.
179. Report of the Secretary-General, A/46/713 and S/23256, 2 December 1991, p. 3.
180. At the US–Soviet Malta summit on 2–3 December 1989, and later in an hour-long telephone conversation on 7 December 1989, James Baker and Eduard Schevardnadze explored ways to completely isolate the FMLN from its suppliers, following Baker's demand that there would be a 'political price to pay' if greater Soviet co-operation was not forthcoming. See *Facts on File*, 15 December 1989, p. 926.
181. See for example their Presidents' 'Declaration on the Situation in El Salvador', A/45/906 and S/22032, pp. 17–19.
182. Sullivan, 'How Peace Came to El Salvador', pp. 93–4.
183. See, for example, Report of the Secretary-General, S/22031, 21 December 1990, and SCR 714 (1991).
184. Department of Social Sciences Universidad de El Salvador, 'An Analysis of the Correlation of Forces in El Salvador', *Latin American Perspectives*, Issue 55, Vol. 14, No. 4, Fall 1987, p. 431.
185. Anderson, 'El Salvador's Dim Prospects', p. 36.
186. Report of the Secretary-General, S/23999, 26 May 1992.
187. Michael Radu, 'The Structure of the Salvadoran Left', *Orbis*, Vol. 28, No. 4, Winter 1985, p. 677.
188. *ibid.*, p. 681.
189. Sullivan, 'How Peace Came to El Salvador', p. 90.

3 Peacekeeping

1. International Peace Academy, *Peacekeeper's Handbook* (New York: Pergamon Press, 1984), p. 22.
2. William J. Durch, 'Introduction', in William J. Durch (ed.), *The Evolution of United Nations Peacekeeping: Case Studies and Comparative Analysis* (London: Macmillan, 1994), p. 4.
3. John Gerard Ruggie, 'Wandering in the Void', *Foreign Affairs*, Vol. 72, No. 5, November/December 1993, p. 29.
4. Ramesh Thakur, 'From Great Power Collective Security to Middle Power

Peacekeeping', in Hugh Smith (ed.), *Australia and Peacekeeping* (Canberra, ADSC, 1990), p. 8.

5. Alan James, 'Peacekeeping and Ethnic Conflict: Theory and Evidence', unpublished paper, October 1993.
6. See Boutros Boutros-Ghali, *Agenda for Peace* (New York: United Nations, 1992), p. 6.
7. Somalis all belong to the same ethnic group, have a common religion, and speak the same language. Somali society is therefore organized around various territorially based clans or sub-clans, between which there has been a history of incessant feuding and warfare. Featuring all of the closeness and often chauvinism of ethnic groups, inter-clan warfare in Somalia showed itself to be every bit as desperate and bloody as inter-ethnic conflict elsewhere. See Abdi Ismael Samatar, 'Destruction of State and Society in Somalia: Beyond the Tribal Convention', *Journal of Modern African Studies*, Vol. 30, No. 4, 1992, pp. 625–41.
8. The main political clan groups that attended the January 1992 peace conference in Addis Ababa were: the Somali Africans Muki Organization (SAMO), the Somali Democratic Alliance (SDA), the Somali Democratic Movement (SDM), the Somali National Democratic Union (SNDU), the Somali National Front (SNF), the Somali National Movement (SNM), the Somali National Union (SNU), the Somali Patriotic Movement (SPM), the Somali Salvation Democratic Front (SSDF), the Southern Somali National Movement (SSNM), the United Somali Front (USF), the United Somali Party (USP), and the United Somali Congress (USC).
9. Kenneth Freed, 'Chewing the Fat, With a Side of Qat', *Los Angeles Times*, 26 December 1992.
10. Mark Yost, 'A Short History of Somalia', *Wall Street Journal*, 19 October 1993.
11. See Bush's address to the American people, 'Conditions in Somalia', 4 December 1992.
12. New US Secretary of State Warren Christopher met with UN Secretary-General Boutros-Ghali on 1 February 1993 to press of a UN operation to relieve UNITAF.
13. For an example of a typical coalition member's misreading of the conflict, see Bill Clinton's address to the American people, 'Somalia: Why Our Troops Will Leave by March 31 1994', 7 October 1993.
14. SCR 897 (1994) 4 February 1994.
15. Report of the Secretary-General, S/25354, 3 March 1993, p. 9.
16. Report of the Secretary-General, S/23693, 11 March 1992, p. 4.
17. Report of the Secretary-General, S/1994/12, 6 January 1994, p. 12.
18. Addis Ababa Agreement, Permanent Mission of Ethiopia to the UN, 28 December 1993, pp. 2–5.
19. Report of the Secretary-General, S/23829, 21 April 1992, pp. 7, 11, 13.
20. SCR 814 (1993), 26 March 1993.
21. Report of the Secretary-General, S/26317, 17 August 1993, p. 17.
22. *New York Times*, 23 January 1992.
23. Rakiya Omaar, 'Somalia: At War With Itself', *Current History*, Vol. 91, No. 565, May 1992, p. 233; for the concept of the security dilemma in ethnic conflicts see Barry R. Posen, 'The Security Dilemma and Ethnic Conflict', *Survival*, Vol. 35, No. 1, Spring 1993, pp. 27–47.

24. The Djibouti Accords, brokered by Djibouti's President Hassan Gouled Aptidon in June 1991, agreed to instal Ali Mahdi for the duration of the final push against Siad Barre forces in southern Somalia. Ali Mahdi was to retain the title long after the Siad Barre forces had been defeated.
25. Report of the Secretary-General, S/26317, 17 August 1993.
26. While the USC originally voted for the installation of Ali Mahdi as interim President, and Aideed was later elected chairman of the USC, the breakaway USC-SNA fiercely contested Ali Mahdi's position.
27. Aideed had been formerly the Chief of Police in Mogadishu, the Armed Forces Chief of Staff, and fought in the Ogaden War against Ethiopia. A talented, Soviet-trained officer, he had defected to the anti-Siad Barre forces in 1989, in which he played a decisive role in toppling the dictator's regime.
28. Inquiries into USC-SNA attacks on UNOSOM II revealed sophisticated ambush techniques to establish killing zones, well thought out flank protection, extremely tight firing discipline, and advanced crossfire tactics to maximize casualties among the peacekeepers. See Report of the Secretary-General, S/1994/653 Annex, 1 June 1994.
29. Bernard Morris, 'Somali Mercy Mission Turns Into a Bloodbath', *Sunday Times*, 28 February 1993.
30. Robert M. Press, 'UN Pursues Talks With Somali Clans', *Christian Science Monitor*, 22 September 1993.
31. Report of the Secretary-General, S/1994/653, 1 June 1994, p. 41.
32. John Gerard Ruggie, 'Wandering in the Void: Chartering the UN's New Strategic Role', *Foreign Affairs*, Vol. 72, No. 5, November/December 1993, p. 29.
33. Admiral Jonathon T. Howe, Special Representative of the Secretary-General to Somalia, quoted in *UN World Chronicle*, No. 517, 23 September 1993.
34. Professor Tom Farer, Report of the Secretary-General, S/26351, 24 August 1993, p. 6.
35. *New York Times*, 3 January 1993.
36. Peter Biles, 'Anarchy Rules', *Africa Report,* Vol. 37, No. 4, July/August 1992, p. 32.
37. Report of the Secretary-General, S/23829/Add.1, 21 April 1992, p. 11.
38. Report of the Secretary-General, S/23829, 21 April 1992, p. 4.
39. Report of the Secretary-General, S/23693, 11 March 1992, p. 6; and Report of the Secretary-General, S/23829, 21 April 1992, p. 5.
40. Report of the Secretary-General, S/23829, 21 April 1992, p. 4.
41. Rakiya Omaar, 'Somalia: At War With Itself', *Current History*, Vol. 91, No. 565, May 1992, p. 234.
42. UNDPI, 'The United Nations and the Situation in Somalia', p. 2.
43. Report of the Secretary-General, S/23693, 11 March 1992, p. 10.
44. Report of the Secretary-General, S/24992, 19 December 1992, p. 7.
45. Letter from the Secretary-General to the Security Council, S/24859, 27 November 1992, p. 1.
46. During a four-hour trip to Mogadishu on 3 January 1993, Boutros-Ghali was forced to cancel a visit to the UN compound by an Aideed-inspired riot, which showered his entourage with rocks and held signs calling him 'the father of famine and death'.
47. Mark Huband, 'When Yankee Goes Home', *Africa Report*, Vol. 38, No. 2, March/April 1993, p. 23.

48. Ali Mahdi Mohammed openly encouraged UNOSOM II attacks against Aideed, repeatedly claiming that Aideed's arrest was the only realistic avenue to peace in Somalia. See Robert Block, 'Former Envoy Criticises UN Actions in Somalia', *The Independent*, 16 June 1993.
49. Brigadier M.B. Page, 'Somalia: background and prospects', *RUSI Journal*, October 1993, p. 11.
50. Captain Johnson of the US contingent of the UNITAF Force, quoted in Geoffrey York, 'Somalia's Bloody Web of Clanship', *Scotland on Sunday*, 21 February 1993.
51. See Mark Huband, 'UN Troops Kill Protesters', *The Guardian*, 14 June 1993; hostility reached such a level in Mogadishu that a group calling itself Muslim Voice was distributing leaflets urging Somalis to 'kill all foreigners', and Somalis working for the UN in Mogadishu were ritually executed. See Peter Hillmore, 'UN Succumbs to the Curse of Somalia', The *Observer*, 18 July 1993.
52. Report of the Secretary-General, S/1994/12, 6 January 1994, p. 8.
53. Jonathon Stevenson, 'Hope Restored in Somalia?', *Foreign Policy*, No. 91, Summer 1993, p. 149.
54. Interview With Lamine Sise, Somalia Desk, UN Department of Political Affairs, New York, 19 April 1994.
55. UN Official, quoted in Keith Richburg, 'Marines "Ready" For UN Handover', *The Guardian*, 5 February 1993.
56. See Leslie H. Gelb, 'US Forces Should Go To Somalia', *International Herald Tribune*, 20 November 1992.
57. The Secretary-General's Special Envoy to Somalia was quoted as saying as late as February 1993, 'It's not a secure environment. [US marines] can't leave yet.' See Keith Richburg, 'Marines "Ready" For UN Handover'.
58. Report of the Secretary-General, S/25168, 26 January 1993, Annex II, pp. 11, 14.
59. Letter from the Secretary-General to the Security Council, S/24859, 27 November 1992, p. 2.
60. Report of the Secretary-General, S/24480, 24 August 1992, p. 3.
61. Letter from the Secretary-General to the Security Council, S/24868, 30 November 1992, p. 1.
62. Under-Secretary-General for African Affairs James Jonah, quoted in *Facts on File*, 23 January 1993.
63. Report of the Secretary-General, S/23693, 11 March 1992.
64. Admiral Jonathon T. Howe, quoted in Mark Huband, 'The Politics of Violence', *Africa Report*, Vol. 38, No. 5, September/October 1993, p. 18.
65. Admiral Jonathon T. Howe, quoted in *UN World Chronicle*, No. 517, 23 September 1993.
66. Letter from the Secretary-General to the Security Council, S/24868, 30 November 1992, p. 1.
67. Report of the Secretary-General, S/24992, 19 December 1992, p. 10.
68. *ibid.*, p. 3.
69. See Statement by the President of the Security Council, S/PV.3089, 30 June 1992.
70. See, for example Mark Huband, 'Italians "Failed to Help Fellow UN Troops"', *The Guardian*, 6 September 1993.

71. For the problems of mounting an urban counter-insurgency, see Jennifer Morrison Taw and Bruce Hoffman, *The Urbanisation of Insurgency: The Potential Challenge to US Army Operations* (Santa Monica: RAND, 1994).
72. The Somali militias and bandit gangs were all heavily armed as a result of the large amount of Cold War weapons transfers to the region, and the broad distribution of arms carried out by the anti-Siad Barre insurgents. The range of weaponry ranged from the ubiquitous AK-47 to sophisticated rocket-propelled grenades and 'technicals', or all-terrain vehicles mounted with heavy-calibre machine guns, rocket launchers, or anti-tank guns.
73. Report of the Secretary-General, S/1994/653 Annex, 1 June 1994, p. 41.
74. 'UN Troops Fire on Women and Children', *The Scotsman*, 10 September 1993.
75. Caleb Baker, 'Manhunt for Aideed: Why the Rangers Came Up Empty-Handed', *Armed Forces Journal*, December 1993, p. 18.
76. See Report of the Commission of Inquiry, S/1994/653, 1 June 1994.
77. Report of the Secretary-General, S/26351, 24 August 1993, pp. 6–7.
78. See Richard Dowden, 'UN Troops Died "Trying to Take Somali Radio Station"', *The Independent*, 8 June 1993; and Richard Ellis, 'Can "Delta Farce" Now Get It Right?', *Sunday Times*, 5 September 1993.
79. Letter from the Secretary-General to the Security Council, S/24859, 27 November 1992, p. 7.
80. Report of the Secretary-General, S/26351, 24 August 1993, p. 5.
81. Report of the Secretary-General, S/26022, 1 July 1993, p. 3.
82. Report of the Secretary-General, S/26351, 24 August 1993, p. 7.
83. SCR 837 (1993), 6 June 1993.
84. Report of the Secretary-General, S/26022, 1 July 1993, p. 5.
85. In one incident after the attack on the Pakistanis, Pakistani troops fired into a rioting crowd, killing 14 civilians. See Nicholas Hinton, 'UN's Humanitarian Goal Lost in the Smoke of Battle', *The Guardian*, 14 June 1993.
86. In a dawn raid on what was thought to be a USC-SNA safe house on 30 August 1993, 400 US Rangers and the elite Delta Force seized personnel from the UNDP, and French volunteers serving with Action Against Hunger. See Martin Walker, 'UN Raid "Not a Mistake"', *The Guardian*, 31 August 1993.
87. Report of the Secretary-General, S/26738, 12 November 1993, pp. 14, 16.
88. SCR 885 (1993), 16 November 1993.
89. Mats Berdal, 'Fateful Encounter: The United States and UN Peacekeeping', *Survival*, Vol. 36, No. 1, Spring 1994, pp. 30–50.
90. UNDPI, Press Release No. 5147, 18 October 1993, p. 2.
91. Report of the Secretary-General, S/1994/12, 6 January 1994, p. 12.
92. Frances Harris and Bruce Johnston, 'Italians Join Rush to Pull Out of UN Forces', *Daily Telegraph*, 14 October 1993.
93. SCR 733 (1992), 23 January 1992.
94. Report of the Secretary-General, S/23829, 21 April 1992, p. 11.
95. Elliott, 'The Making of a Fiasco', p. 11.
96. Baker, 'Manhunt for Aideed', p. 18.
97. SCR 886 (1993), 18 November 1993.
98. Italy, France, Belgium, Sweden, Norway, and Germany all withdrew or threatened to withdraw their contingents, and following the battle of Bakhara

Market, the US pledged to withdraw its contingent by March 1994. See Peter Hillmore, 'UN Succumbs to the Curse of Somalia', *The Observer*, 18 July 1993.

99. Report of the Secretary-General, S/26317, 17 August 1993.
100. In particular, the Italian contingent under General Bruno Loi, later relieved of his command by the UN, refused to take part in offensive operations. See David Willey, 'Rome Bestows Laurels on the General Who Won't Hit Back', *The Observer*, 18 July 1993.
101. In September 1993, the Nigerian contingent accused the Italian contingent of failing to provide assistance when it was ambushed by USC-SNA forces. See Mark Huband, 'Italians "Failed to Help Fellow UN Troops"', *The Guardian*, 6 September 1993.
102. Scott Peterson, 'UN Draws Up Deadline to Quit Somalia', *Daily Telegraph*, 27 September 1994.
103. Samatar, 'Destruction of State and Society in Somalia', p. 637.
104. Report of the Secretary-General, S/23829, 21 April 1992, p. 15.
105. Letter from the Secretary-General to the Security Council, S/24868, 30 November 1992, p. 2.
106. See Paul L. Moorcraft, *African Nemisis: War and Revolution in Southern Africa* (London: Brasseys, 1984); and Abiodun Alao, *Brothers at War* (London: British Academic Press, 1994).
107. Renamo was used not only to cripple the Mozambican government, but to disrupt the vital transport corridors from the Indian Ocean to the landlocked members of the SADCC, Zambia, and Zimbabwe, thereby making them more dependent on South Africa for ports for their trade.
108. Robert Jasper, 'Mozambique: Whose Interests do the Saboteurs Serve?', *International Herald Tribune*, 20 June 1985.
109. Victoria Brittain, 'Rebels Without a Cause', *The Guardian*, 22 April 1991.
110. Emily MacFarquhar, 'The Killing Fields of Mozambique', *U.S. News and World Report*, 2 May 1988.
111. Robert Gersony, in a Report to the US State Department that was to prove crucial in denying Renamo aid from the US government, reported that Renamo classified its areas of control into three regions: (1) 'tax areas', of relative security from government attack, where supplies, recruits, porters, and concubines could be regularly extracted; (2) 'control areas', in proximity to a base, in which the inhabitants were forced into slave labour to erect defences and grow food; and (3) 'destruction areas', which were designated for violent, wholesale, and thorough devastation.
112. E.A. Wayne, 'Mozambique Rebels Deny Charges of Civilian Abuses', *Christian Science Monitor*, 25 April 1988.
113. See *General Peace Agreement for Mozambique*, 4 October 1992, S/24635 Annex, 8 October 1992.
114. SCR 797 (1992), 16 December 1992.
115. The Soviet and Chinese relationship with the Mozambican government was at best arm's length, and any assistance was at best desultory. The Frelimo government consistently denied Soviet requests to build a military base on Mozambican territory, while Mozambique's application to join Comecon was denied in 1981.
116. The Reagan administration resisted pressure from various right-wing organ-

izations, and from Republican Senators Bob Dole and Jesse Helms, to begin aiding Renamo in the same way as the US was arming Unita, the Contras, and the Mujahadin. This resistance was exemplified by the 1985 visit to the White House of Mozambican President Samora Machel.

117. Peter G. Hemsch, 'How Mozambique's Guns Were Silenced', *Christian Science Monitor*, 7 October 1992.
118. SCR 782 (1992), 13 October 1992.
119. SCRs 797 (1992), 16 December 1992; 818 (1993), 13 April 1993; and 850 (1993), 9 July 1993.
120. Report of the Secretary General, S/24892, 3 December 1992, p. 6.
121. SCR 882 (1993), 5 November 1993.
122. SCR 797 (1992), 16 December 1992.
123. Malyn Newitt, *A History of Mozambique* (Bloomington: Indiana University Press, 1995), pp. 565–7.
124. Thomas H. Henriksen, *Revolution and Counterrevolution: Mozambique's War of Independence 1964–1974* (Westport: Greenwood Press, 1983), pp. 195–7.
125. M. Hall and T. Young, 'Recent Constitutional Developments in Mozambique', *Journal of African Law*, Vol. 35, Nos. 1–2, 1991, p. 107.
126. Newitt, *A History of Mozambique*, p. 573.
127. Tom Young, 'The MNR/Renamo: External and Internal Dynamics', *African Affairs*, Vol. 89, No. 357, October 1990, p. 501.
128. Mario Azaredo, *Historical Dictionary of Mozambique* (New Jersey: The Scarecrow Press, 1991), p. 110.
129. Quoted in Chris Alden and Mark Simpson, 'Mozambique: A Delicate Peace', *The Journal of Modern African Studies*, Vol. 31, No. 1, 1993, p. 122.
130. Peter G. Hemsch, 'How Mozambique's Guns Were Silenced', *Christian Science Monitor*, 7 October 1992.
131. Alex Vines, *Renamo: Terrorism in Mozambique* (Bloomington: Indiana University Press, 1991), p. 131.
132. *ibid.*, p. 132.
133. *General Peace Agreement for Mozambique*, 4 October 1992, S/24635 Annex, 8 October 1992, p. 17.
134. See Chris McGreal, 'Renamo Puts £66 m Price on Keeping Peace', *The Guardian*, 10 June 1993; and Barnaby Phillips, 'Mozambique Leader Lifts Threat to Boycott Poll', *Daily Telegraph*, 21 September 1994.
135. *General Peace Agreement for Mozambique*, 4 October 1992, S/24635 Annex, 8 October 1992, p. 2.
136. *ibid.*, p. 42.
137. Report of the Secretary-General, S/24642, 9 October 1992, p. 3.
138. Report of the Secretary-General, S/1994/89, 28 January 1994, p. 5.
139. Report of the Secretary-General, S/24892, 3 December 1992, pp. 5, 7.
140. Report of the Secretary-General, S/26034, 30 June 1993, p. 2.
141. Andrew Meldrum, 'Peace At Last', *Africa Report*, Vol. 38, No. 2, March/April 1993, p. 49.
142. Report of the Secretary-General, S/25518, 2 April 1993, p. 2.
143. Report of the Secretary-General, S/26666, 1 November 1993, p. 11.
144. See Report of the Secretary-General, S/26385, 30 August 1993, p. 3; and Report of the Secretary-General, S/26666, 1 November 1993, pp. 7–8.

145. SCR 882 (1993), 5 November 1993.
146. Hemsch, 'How Mozambique's Guns Were Silenced'.
147. Frelimo had long looked for ways to end the war non-militarily: its diplomatic offensive and the conclusion of the Nkomati Accord in the 1980s attest to its realization that the rebels could not be silenced by its own military forces.
148. Vines, *Renamo*, p. 130.
149. Interview with Jose M. da Silva Campino, UN Department of Political Affairs, New York, 11 March 1994.
150. SCR 797 (1992), 16 December 1992.
151. *General Peace Agreement for Mozambique*, 4 October 1992, p. 2.
152. The UN in late 1992-early 1993 was sponsoring its three largest peacekeeping operations of all time – the 20 500-strong UNTAC force in Cambodia, the 39 000-strong UNPROFOR forces in the former Yugoslavia, and was preparing to launch the 30 800-strong UNOSOM II force into Somalia, and at the same time maintaining an unprecedented number of smaller operations around the world.
153. Report of the Secretary-General, S/25518, 2 April 1993, p. 3.
154. Report of the Secretary-General, S/26666, 1 November 1993, pp. 7–8.
155. Report of the Secretary-General, S/25518, 2 April 1993, p. 3.
156. Report of the Secretary-General, S/1994/89, 28 January 1994, p. 6.
157. Report of the Secretary-General, S/26666, 1 November 1993, p. 5.
158. *General Peace Agreement for Mozambique*, 4 October 1992, pp. 34–5.
159. SCR 818 (1993), 14 April 1993.
160. Report of the Secretary-General, S/24992, 3 December 1992, pp. 4, 7.
161. Report of the Secretary-General, S/26666, 1 November 1993, p. 11.
162. Report of the Secretary-General, S/26385, 2 April 1993, p. 11.
163. Report of the Secretary-General, S/24992, 3 December 1992, p. 7.
164. Report of the Secretary-General, S/25518, 2 April 1993, p. 11.
165. Report of the Secretary-General, S/26385, 30 August 1993, p. 3.
166. Report of the Secretary-General, S/26034, 30 June 1993, p. 2.
167. *General Peace Agreement for Mozambique*, 4 October 1992, pp. 34–5.
168. David Beresford, 'Mozambican Rebels Make Peace Pledge', *The Guardian*, 27 October 1994.
169. UNDPI, 'Mozambique: Out of the Ruins of War', *Africa Recovery Briefing Paper No. 8*, May 1993, p. 13.
170. Barnaby Phillips, 'Mozambique Leader Lifts Threat to Boycott Poll', *Daily Telegraph*, 21 September 1994.
171. David Beresford, 'Mozambican Rebels Make Peace Pledge', *The Guardian*, 27 October 1994.
172. Interview with Joan T. Seymour, UN Department of Political Affairs, New York, 11 March 1994.
173. Martin Walker, 'UN To Remain After Election', *The Guardian*, 15 October 1994.
174. The biggest contributors to the Trust Fund were Italy, the US, Denmark, and Norway.
175. Newitt, *A History of Mozambique*, pp. 572–3.
176. Hemsch, 'How Mozambique's Guns Were Silenced'.
177. Patrick Brogan, *World Conflicts: Why and Where They Are Happening* (London: Bloomsbury, 1992), pp. 65–6.

178. Karl Maier, 'Between Washington and Pretoria', *Africa Report*, Vol. 33, No. 6, November–December 1988, p. 44.
179. The event with the greatest impact was the news of Renamo's July 1991 massacre of up to 1000 civilians in Nampula.
180. Comprised of the 1988 Angola–Namibia Accords, Namibian independence in 1989, the dismantling of *apartheid*, and the 1991 Angolan peace treaty.
181. Hemsch, 'How Mozambique's Guns Were Silenced'.
182. SCR 818 (1993), 14 April 1993.
183. SCR 898 (1994), 23 February 1994.
184. Newitt, *A History of Mozambique*, pp. 573–4.
185. Vines, *Renamo*, p. 132.
186. *ibid.*
187. Campino interview, 11 March 1994.
188. See Report of the Secretary-General, S/24892, 3 December 1992, pp. 6–8.

4 Election Monitoring

1. David Stoelting, 'The Challenge of UN-Monitored Elections in Independent Nations', *Stanford Journal of International Law*, Vol. 28, No. 2, Spring 1992, pp. 417–18.
2. Boutros Boutros-Ghali, *An Agenda For Peace* (New York, United Nations, 1992), p. 11.
3. Report of the Secretary-General, 'Implementation of the Recommendations Contained in "An Agenda for Peace"', A/47/695 and S/25944, 15 June 1993, p. 8.
4. Robin Hay, *Civilian Aspects of Peacekeeping: A Summary of Workshop Proceedings, Ottawa 9–10 July 1991* (Working Paper 36), (Ottawa: Canadian Institute for International Peace and Security, 1991), p. 21.
5. Allan D. Cooper, 'UN-Supervised Elections in Namibia: A Critical Analysis', *Without Prejudice*, Vol. 3, No. 1, 1990, p. 67.
6. This is particularly prevalent in the 'enlargement' doctrine of the Clinton administration; see National Security Adviser Anthony Lake, 'From Containment to Enlargement', *Vital Speeches of the Day*, Vol. IX, No. 1, 15 October 1993, p. 16.
7. Beginning with the operation in Namibia, the United Nations has implemented or attempted to implement elections or plebiscites in seven of the fifteen post-Cold War interventions; and advocated elections eventually in Bosnia and Somalia.
8. I. William Zartman, *Ripe for Resolution: Conflict and Intervention in Africa* (New York: Oxford University Press, 1989), p. 279.
9. Hay, *Civilian Aspects of Peacekeeping*, p. 19.
10. Report of the Secretary-General, 'Implementation of the Recommendations Contained in "An Agenda for Peace"', pp. 8–9.
11. J. McCoy, L. Garber, and R. Pastor, 'Pollwatching and Peacemaking', *Journal of Democracy*, Vol. 2, No. 4, Fall 1991, p. 104.
12. *ibid.*, p. 110–11.
13. Stoetling, 'The Challenge of UN-Monitored Elections in Independent Nations', p. 397.
14. McCoy, Garber, and Pastor, 'Pollwatching and Peacemaking', p. 107.

15. G. O'Donnell and P.C. Schmitter, *Transitions From Authoritarian Rule: Tentative Conclusions About Uncertain Democracies* (Baltimore: Johns Hopkins University Press, 1986), p. 61.
16. Melinda N. Hodgson, 'When to Accept, When to Abstain: A Framework for UN Election Monitoring', *New York University Journal of International Law and Politics*, Vol. 25, No. 1, Fall 1992, p. 149.
17. Martin Harrop and William L. Miller, *Elections and Voters: A Comparative Introduction* (Basingstoke: Macmillan, 1987), p. 259.
18. Barry Munslow, 'Democratisation in Africa', *Parliamentary Affairs*, Vol. 46, No. 4, October 1993, p. 480.
19. McCoy, Garber, and Pastor, 'Pollwatching and Peacemaking', p. 108.
20. See Fred Halliday, *The Making of the Second Cold War* (London: Verso, 1986).
21. *Movimento Popular para a Libertacao de Angola*, founded in 1956 by Agostinho Neto to struggle against Portuguese rule.
22. The other movement, Holden Roberto's FNLA, was to be quickly destroyed in the ensuing civil war.
23. Allister Sparks, 'Toll Rises in Angola's Civil War', *Washington Post*, 15 March 1987.
24. US support for Unita has been estimated to have averaged at $15 million per year during the 1980s.
25. Of particular use to Unita were shipments of Stinger anti-aircraft and TOW anti-tank missiles.
26. David B. Ottaway and Patrick E. Tyler, 'Superpowers Raise Ante As Fighting Intensifies', *Washington Post*, 27 July 1986.
27. Patrick E. Tyler, 'Rebel Success Turns on South African Aid', *Washington Post*, 30 July 1986.
28. The Brazzaville Accord between South Africa, Angola, and Cuba, mediated by the United States, was signed on 13 December 1988 linking the withdrawal of Cuban troops from Angola to South African withdrawal and independence for Namibia.
29. 'Peace Accords for Angola', S/22609 Enclosure, 17 May 1991, pp. 2–3.
30. SCR 696 (1991), 30 May 1991.
31. SCR 747 (1992), 24 March 1992.
32. See Roger E. Kanet and Garth A. Katner, 'From New Thinking to the Fragmentation of Consensus in Soviet Foreign Policy: The USSR and the Developing World', in Roger E. Kanet, Deborah Nutter Miner, and Tamara J. Resler (eds), *Soviet Foreign Policy in Transition* (Cambridge: Cambridge University Press, 1992), p. 129; and Mikhail Gorbachev, 'International Affairs: Asia and the Pacific Region', Vladivostok, 28 July 1986, *Vital Speeches of the Day*, Vol. 52, No. 23, 15 September 1986, p. 711.
33. Much of the linking was a result of the operation of the ANC and the PAC from sanctuaries in the frontline states and South Africa's response, to destabilize those states harbouring these groups.
34. So much so that even while it was supporting the Unita insurgents, the US remained Angola's biggest trading partner for oil and related products.
35. Thomas G. Weiss and Meryl A. Kessler, 'Resurrecting Peacekeeping: The Superpowers and Conflict Management', *Third World Quarterly*, Vol. 12, No. 3, July 1991.
36. Statement by the President of the Security Council, 9 September 1992.

37. SCR 804 (1993), 29 January 1993.
38. SCR 747 (1992), 24 March 1992.
39. For example, Security Council debate at its 3168th Meeting, 29 January 1993, S/PV.3168, features almost universal agreement on the legitimacy of the electoral process as a substitute for warfare, and condemnation of Unita's rejection of the election results and its return to war.
40. SCR 785 (1992), 30 October 1992.
41. Statement by the President of the Security Council, 3115th Meeting, 18 September 1992.
42. Special Representative of the Secretary-General Margaret Anstee had planned to take the Angolan election monitoring team to oversee the Mozambican elections pending the successful conclusion of the Angolan process. As it turned out, the failure of the Angolan elections cast grave doubts over the similar process in Mozambique eighteen month afterwards.
43. 'Peace Accords for Angola', S/22609 Enclosure, 17 May 1991, p. 50.
44. SCRs 696 (1991), 30 May 1991, and 747 (1992), 24 March 1992.
45. James Hamill, 'Angola's Road From Under the Rubble', *The World Today*, Vol. 50, No. 1, January 1994, p. 7.
46. James D. Sidaway and David Simon, 'Geopolitical Transition and State Formation: the Changing Political Geographies of Angola, Mozambique and Namibia', *Journal of Southern African Studies*, Vol. 19, No. 1, March 1993, pp. 13–14.
47. Patrick Smith, 'Angola: Free and Fair Elections!', *Review of African Political Economy*, Vol. 55, November 1992, p. 104.
48. Report of the Secretary-General, S/24858, 25 November 1992, p. 16.
49. Linda M. Heywood, 'Unita and Ethnic Nationalism in Angola', *Journal of Modern African Studies*, Vol. 27, No. 1, 1989, p. 64.
50. 'Peace Accords for Angola', S/22609 Enclosure, 17 May 1991, p. 47.
51. In particular South Africa had regularly pressured Angola to admit Unita into a power-sharing government, and as recently as 30 December 1989, Angolan President Jose Eduardo dos Santos ruled out the possibility of a multiparty democracy in Angola.
52. After the breakdown of the peace process, the MPLA was adamant that in any agreement bringing Unita back into the peace process, Savimbi was to be excluded from any possibility of holding political office.
53. Gillian Gunn, 'Unfulfilled Expectations in Angola', *Current History*, Vol. 89, No. 547, May 1990, pp. 216–34.
54. See 'Unita Calls Off Offensive', *New York Times*, 10 March 1989.
55. Unita calculated that the MPLA had become very unpopular because of the continuing war, the harshness of its rule, the failure of Marxist economics, and the growing number of revelations of embezzlement, corruption, and fraud among ministers.
56. Keith Somerville, 'Angola: An End to the Misery in Sight?', *The World Today*, Vol. 47, No. 5, May 1991, p. 73.
57. Hamill, 'Angola's Road From Under the Rubble', p. 7.
58. Unita based its support and objectives on promoting the goals of the Ovimbundu, Chokwe, Ganguela, and Ovambo tribes of the central Angolan highlands in their rivalry against coastal, white, and mixed-race Angolans. See Heywood, 'Unita and Ethnic Nationalism in Angola'.

59. Unita exploited the widespread rural resentment that the MPLA government had failed to deliver even minimal assistance to rural Angolans (over three-quarters of the population) and their desires for an alternative government. See Gerald J. Bender, 'Peacemaking in Southern Africa: The Luanda-Pretoria Tug-of-War', *Third World Quarterly*, Vol. 11, No. 2, April 1989, p. 17.
60. Hamill, 'Angola's Road From Under the Rubble', p. 7.
61. For an excellent analysis of the nature of ethnic conflict and competition in a democracy, see Donald L. Horowitz, *Ethnic Groups in Conflict* (Berkeley: University of California Press, 1985).
62. 'Concepts for Resolving the Issues Still Pending Between the Government of the People's Republic of Angola and UNITA', 'Peace Accords for Angola', S/22609 Attachment III, 17 May 1991, p. 45.
63. Report of the Secretary-General, S/22627, 20 May 1991, p. 5.
64. 'Peace Accords for Angola', S/22609 Enclosure, 17 May 1991, p. 48.
65. 'United Nations Angola Verification Mission II', PS/DPI/5/Rev.2, March 1992, p. 2.
66. Report of the Secretary-General, S/24858, 25 November 1992, pp. 2–4.
67. Virginia Page Fortna, 'United Nations Angola Verification Mission II', in William J. Durch (ed.) *The Evolution of United Nations Peacekeeping: Case Studies and Comparative Analysis* (London: Macmillan, 1994), p. 389.
68. Hamill, 'Angola's Road From Under the Rubble', p. 7.
69. SCR 696 (1991), 30 May 1991.
70. SCR 811 (1993) of 12 March 1993 and other Security Council calls afterwards expressed unreserved support for the Peace Accords and their results.
71. Report of the Secretary-General, S/22627, 20 May 1991, p. 6.
72. Fortna, 'United Nations Angola Verification Mission II', p. 399.
73. 'Peace Accords for Angola', S/22609 Enclosure, 17 May 1991, pp. 4, 6, 9.
74. Appendix 4, 'Peace Accords for Angola', S/22609 Enclosure, 17 May 1991, pp. 28–30.
75. Interview with Jose M. da Silva Campino, Department of Political Affairs, United Nations Headquarters, New York City, 11 March 1994.
76. United Nations Angola Verification Mission, 'Notes for the Guidance of Military/Police Observers on Assignment', UNST.ADM/GS/FOD (02), Field Operations Division, June 1991, pp. 5–6.
77. Statement by the President of the Security Council, S/PV.3115, 18 September 1992.
78. Chris Simpson, 'The Undemocratic Game', *Africa Report*, Vol. 38, No. 4, July–August 1993, p. 51.
79. United Nations Press Release SG/1966, 19 October 1992, p. 2.
80. Report of the Secretary-General, S/24858, 25 November 1992, p. 6.
81. *ibid.*, pp. 2–3.
82. SCR 793 (1992), 30 November 1992.
83. Statement by the President of the Security Council, S/PV.3126, 27 October 1992.
84. 'Peace Accords for Angola', S/22609 Enclosure, 17 May 1991, p. 10.
85. Report of the Secretary-General, S/24858, 22 November 1992, p. 13.
86. Report of the Secretary-General, S/22627, 20 May 1991, p. 5.
87. Report of the Secretary-General, S/24858, 25 November 1992, p. 2.
88. 'Statement of the President of the Security Council', S/PV.3092, 7 July 1992.

89. Report of the Secretary-General, S/24858, 25 November 1992, p. 4.
90. Special Representative of the Secretary-General Margaret Anstee, Press Statement, SG/1966, 19 October 1992, p. 3.
91. Inge Tvedten, 'U.S. Policy Towards Angola Since 1975', *Journal of Modern African Studies*, Vol. 10, No. 1, 1992, p. 49.
92. 'Peace Accords for Angola', S/22609 Enclosure, 17 May 1991, p. 47.
93. In an interview with journalist Karl Maier on 20 September 1992, Jonas Savimbi stated 'If Unita does not win the elections, it has to be rigged', see 'Urgent Talks Seek to Avoid War in Angola', *The Independent*, 7 October 1992.
94. See *Facts on File*, 17 October 1991 and 8 October 1992.
95. Somerville, 'Angola: An End to the Misery in Sight?', p. 73.
96. Report of the Secretary-General, S/24858, 22 November 1992, p. 13.
97. Vicki R. Finkel, 'Brothers in Arms', *Africa Report*, Vol. 37, No. 2, March–April 1992, p. 62.
98. *Facts on File*, 8 October 1992.
99. Report of the Secretary-General, S/24858, 25 November 1992, p. 4.
100. Letter from the Secretary-General to the Security Council, S/24996, 21 December 1992, p. 2.
101. Hamill, 'Angola's Road From Under the Rubble', p. 9.
102. For example, on 1 June 1992, South African President F.W. DeKlerk, during a mission to the Russian Federation, signed a communiqué with Russian President Boris Yeltsin stressing the importance of free elections in Angola.
103. See *Facts on File*, 30 June 1993.
104. Karl Maier, 'Urgent Talks Seek to Avert War in Angola'.
105. Fortna, 'United Nations Angola Verification Mission II', p. 389.
106. Richard Dowden, 'Clinton Finally Pulls Plug on Angola Rebels', *The Independent*, 21 May 1993.
107. Victoria Brittain and David Pallister, 'Wounded Mercenaries Expose S. African Aid Line to Unita', *The Guardian*, 13 March 1993.
108. Smith, 'Angola: Free and Fair Elections!', p. 102.
109. *Keesing's Record of World Events*, Vol. 40, 1994, R3.
110. Heywood, 'Unita and Ethnic Conflict in Angola', p. 60.
111. Statement by the President of the Security Council, S/PV.3092, 7 July 1992.
112. SCR 696 (1991) of 30 May 1991.
113. *New York Times*, 11 May 1992.
114. Report of the Secretary-General, S/24858, 25 November 1992, p. 6.
115. *ibid.*, p. 6.
116. Statement of the President of the Security Council, S/PV.3126, 27 October 1992.
117. Tvedten, 'U.S. Policy Towards Angola Since 1975', p. 45.
118. Victoria Brittain, 'Luanda Seeks to Isolate Unita', *The Guardian*, 24 May 1993.
119. Hamill, 'Angola's Road From Under the Rubble', p. 10.
120. Report of the Secretary-General, S/25124, 25 January 1993, pp. 2, 8.
121. Mikhail Gorbachev, 'International Affairs: Asia and the Pacific Region', Vladivostok, 28 July 1986, *Vital Speeches of the Day*, Vol. 52, No. 23, 15 September 1986, p. 711.
122. Ben Kiernan (ed.), *Genocide and Democracy in Cambodia: The Khmer*

Rouge, the United Nations and the International Community (New Haven: Yale University Southeast Asia Studies, 1993), p. 195.

123. Britain was the largest contributor among the NATO powers of lethal and non-lethal military aid to the Cambodian non-Communist insurgents; while in the US in 1989, Congress pressured President Bush to stop aiding these insurgents and seek to end the conflict.
124. For an excellent account of the Paris Conference negotiations, see Michael Haas, *Genocide by Proxy: Cambodian Pawn on a Superpower Chessboard* (New York: Praeger, 1991).
125. Interview with Lieutenant-Colonel Damien Healey, ADF, 14 December 1993.
126. SCR 745 (1992), 28 February 1992. Italics in original.
127. SCR 826 (1993), 20 May 1993.
128. Permanent Five, Statement on Cambodia, Paris, 13 March 1993.
129. Report of the Secretary-General, S/23613, 19 February 1992, p. 14.
130. Report of the Secretary-General, S/22059, 11 January 1991, pp. 15–16.
131. SCR 826 (1993), 20 May 1993.
132. Judy Ledgerwood, 'Patterns of CPP Political Repression and Violence During the UNTAC Period', in Steve Heder and Judy Ledgerwood (eds), *Propaganda, Politics, and Violence in Cambodia: Democratic Transition Under United Nations Peacekeeping* (Armonk: M.E. Sharp, 1996), p. 117.
133. Khieu Kanharith, 'The Cambodian Factions in the Democratic Process', in Kiernan, *Genocide and Democracy in Cambodia*, pp. 294–7.
134. Jarat Chopra, John Mackinlay, and Larry Minear, *Report on the Cambodian Peace Process* (Oslo: Norwegian Institute of International Affairs, 1993), p. 16.
135. Lieutenant-Colonel Healey, Interview, 14 December 1993.
136. The Khmer Rouge introduced a proposal to alter the peace process after its withdrawal from Phase II. This was to expand the SNC to include equal numbers of representatives of the four resistance groups, and to give it control of five key fields of administration in Cambodia: foreign affairs, defence, finance, public security, and information. It believed that its influence over the non-Communist resistance would give it a 75% say in all decisions in the administration, and ultimately allow it to seize power in its own right through infiltration and intimidation.
137. Report of the Secretary-General, S/24286, 14 July 1992, p. 3.
138. Gary Klintworth, *Cambodia's Past, Present, and Future*, Working Paper No. 268, (Canberra: SDSC, 1993), p. 3.
139. Trisha Thomas, 'Into the Unknown: Can the United Nations Bring Peace to Cambodia?', *Journal of International Affairs*, Vol. 44, No. 1, Spring 1990, pp. 507–7.
140. Interview with Lieutenant-General John Sanderson, ADF, formerly UNTAC Force Commander, 15 December 1993.
141. David Chandler, *Brother Number One: A Political Biography of Pol Pot* (Boulder: Westview Press, 1992), pp. 88–93.
142. Quoted in Ben Kiernan, 'The Inclusion of the Khmer Rouge in the Cambodian Peace Process: Causes and Consequences', in Kiernan, *Genocide and Democracy in Cambodia*, p. 237.
143. John Pedler, 'Cambodia: Danger and Opportunity for the West', *The World Today*, Vol. 45, No. 2, February 1989, p. 19.

144. Haas, *Genocide by Proxy*, p. 215.
145. The SoC had accepted that it would never defeat the Khmer Rouge on its own after the Vietnamese withdrawal, while the non-Communist resistance, even as its partners in the CGDK, had endured the Khmer Rouge's brutality for years in the western Cambodian jungles.
146. Interview with Lieutenant-Colonel Healey, 14 December 1993.
147. Report of the Secretary-General, S/23613, 19 February 1992, p. 12.
148. Proposed Structure for Cambodia Agreements, S/22059 Annex III, 11 January 1991, p. 37.
149. Permanent Five Statement on Cambodia, S/21689, 31 August 1990, p. 10.
150. Report of the Secretary-General, S/24286, 14 July 1992, p. 4.
151. At the apex of the disarmament process on 10 September 1992, UNTAC had disarmed and cantoned 42 368 CPAF troops, 3445 ANKI troops, and 6479 KPNLAF troops, but no Khmer Rouge.
152. Report of the Secretary-General, S/24286, 14 July 1992, p. 3.
153. Report of the Secretary-General, S/25124, 25 January 1993, p. 23.
154. Report of the Secretary-General, S/24800, 15 November 1992, p. 6.
155. Report of the Secretary-General, S/25719, 3 May 1993, p. 27.
156. SCR 783 (1992), 13 October 1992.
157. Report of the Secretary-General, S/24286, 14 July 1992, p. 2.
158. Reported in Report of the Secretary-General, S/24800 Annex I, 15 November 1992, p. 10.
159. On 3 June 1993, the Secretary-General addressed a personal appeal to Khieu Samphan which was rejected in a reply on 5 June. See Report of the Secretary-General, S/24090, 12 June 1992, p. 3.
160. SCRs 766 (1992) of 21 July 1992 and 783 (1992) of 13 October 1992.
161. Report of the Secretary-General, S/24286, 14 July 1992, p. 5.
162. Interview with Lieutenant-Colonel Healey, 14 December 1993.
163. Report of the Secretary-General, S/24578, 21 September 1992, p. 1.
164. SCR 783 (1992), 13 October 1992.
165. SCR 792 (1992), 30 November 1992.
166. Report of the Secretary-General, S/25719, 3 May 1993, p. 28.
167. Report of the Secretary-General, S/5124, 25 January 1993, p. 10.
168. Interview with Lieutenant-General Sanderson, 15 December 1993.
169. Interview with Lieutenant-Colonel Healey, 14 December 1993.
170. Interview with Lieutenant-General Sanderson, 15 December 1993.
171. Report of the Secretary-General, S/24800, 15 November 1992, p. 6.
172. SCR 810 (1993), 8 March 1993.
173. For example, Terry McCarthy, 'Khmer Rouge Plays on Old Fears in Cambodia', *The Independent*, 14 October 1992.
174. Michael Wesley, 'The Cambodian Waltz: The Khmer Rouge and United Nations Intervention', *Terrorism and Political Violence*, Vol. 7, No. 4, Winter 1995, p. 75.
175. SCR 880 (1993), 4 November 1993.
176. Interview with Lieutenant-General Sanderson, 15 December 1993.
177. *ibid.*
178. Report of the Secretary-General, S/24090, 12 June 1992, p. 4.
179. Report of the Secretary-General, S/24578, 21 September 1992, p. 1.
180. Khmer Rouge spokesman Mak Ben, quoted in Klintworth, *op. cit.*, 1993, p. 12.

181. Report of the Secretary-General, S/24800 Appendix II, 15 November 1992.
182. These included increased UNTAC patrolling of the border with Vietnam, the cessation of funds to the SoC government, the replacement of the SNC with a five-member body consisting of UNTAC and the four factions, the dismantling of the SoC administrative structure, and the disenfranchisement of non-ethnic Cambodians. See Klintworth, *Cambodia's Past, Present, and Future*, p. 6.
183. See for example the report of the Thai and Japanese diplomats on their attempts to negotiate with the Khmer Rouge, Report of the Secretary-General, S/24800, 15 November 1992, pp. 11–12.
184. Report of the Secretary-General, S/25719, 3 May 1993, p. 4.
185. Report of the Secretary-General, S/24578, 21 September 1992, p. 14.
186. Note by the President of the Security Council, S/25822, 22 May 1993, p. 1.
187. Report of the Secretary-General, S/25719, 3 May 1993, p. 2.
188. Raoul M. Jennar, 'UNTAC: 'International Triumph' in Cambodia?', *Security Dialogue*, Vol. 25, No. 2, 1994, p. 145.
189. David Roberts, 'Cambodia: Problems of a UN-Brokered Peace', *The World Today*, Vol. 48, No. 7, July 1992, p. 30.
190. Gerhard Will, 'The Elections in Cambodia: Taking Stock of a UN Mission', *Aussenpolitik*, Vol. 44, No. 4, 1993, p. 394.
191. John Pedler, 'Cambodia: Danger and Opportunity for the West', *The World Today*, Vol. 45, No. 2, February 1989, p. 21.
192. Kiernan, 'Inclusion of the Khmer Rouge', in Kiernan, *Genocide and Democracy in Cambodia*, p. 202.
193. Klintworth, *Cambodia's Past, Present, and Future*, p. 18.
194. Nayan Chanda, 'Civil War in Cambodia?', *Foreign Policy*, Vol. 76, Fall 1989, p. 38.
195. Report of the Secretary-General, S/24090, 12 June 1992, p. 3.
196. Report of the Secretary-General, S/24800, 15 November 1992, pp. 1, 9–11.
197. Will, 'Elections in Cambodia', p. 393.
198. William S. Turley, 'The Khmer War: Cambodia After Paris', *Survival*, Vol. 32, No. 5, September/October 1990, pp. 488–9.
199. Chopra, Mackinlay, and Minear, *Report on the Cambodian Peace Process*, p. 9.
200. Jennar, 'UNTAC: International Triumph', p. 150.
201. Letter from the Royal Thai Government, S/24873 Annex, 30 November 1992, p. 2.
202. Interview with Lieutenant-Colonel Healey, 14 December 1993.
203. Interview with Lieutenant-General Sanderson, 15 December 1993.
204. *ibid.*
205. SCR 766 (1992) demanded Khmer Rouge (although unnamed in the resolution) co-operation with Phase II, and reaffirmed its full support for UNTAC's efforts in carrying out its mandate fully.
206. Report of the Secretary-General, S/24578, 21 September 1992, p. 16.
207. Craig Etcheson, 'Civil War and the Coalition Government of Democratic Kampuchea', *Third World Quarterly*, Vol. 9, No. 1, January 1987, p. 200.
208. Interview with Lieutenant-Colonel Healey, 14 December 1993.
209. *ibid.*
210. Interview with Lieutenant-General Sanderson, 15 December 1993.

5 Conclusion

1. Those that have that come to mind include Israel, South Africa, and perhaps Bangladesh.
2. This was demonstrated by the ineffectiveness of the economic sanctions applied to various sides in the Yugoslav wars in restraining their violent promotion of their ethnic identity and survival.
3. In Bosnia, both Boutros-Ghali and Goulding opposed the introduction of peacekeepers, see Report of the Secretary-General, S/23900, 1992, while in Bosnia, Special Representative Mahommed Sahnoun cautioned against withdrawing US marines and substituting peacekeepers see Keith Richburg, 'Marines "Ready" for UN Handover', *The Guardian*, 5 February 1993.

Bibliography

Primary Sources: Interviews and Speeches

Albright, Madeleine K., Testimony before the House Appropriations Subcommittee on Foreign Operations, 5 May 1994, United States Information Service, London, 9 May 1994.

Baker, James III, 'International Efforts for a Peaceful Cambodia', Washington D.C.: Bureau of Public Affairs, US Department of State, 30 July 1989.

Boutros-Ghali, Boutros, 'Beyond Peacekeeping', Conference at New York University School of Law on the Future of Collective Security, 20 January 1993.

'Challenges and Opportunities for the United Nations Towards the Twenty-First Century', United Nations University Symposium, Tokyo, 18 February 1993.

Bush, George, 'Aggression in the Gulf: A Partnership of Nations', Delivered at the United Nations General Assembly, New York, 1 October 1990, *Vital Speeches of the Day*, Vol. 62, No. 1, 15 October 1990.

Address to the American people, 'Conditions in Somalia', 4 December 1992, *Vital Speeches of the Day*, Vol. 65, No. 6, 1 January 1993.

Campino, Jose M. da Silva, United Nations Department of Political Affairs, Interviewed at United Nations Headquarters, New York City, 11 March 1994.

Clinton, Bill, Address to the American People, 'Somalia: Why Our Troops Will Leave by March 31 1994', 7 October 1993, *Vital Speeches of the Day*, Vol. 70, No. 2, 1 November 1993.

'Reforming the United Nations: The United States Intends to Remain Engaged and Lead', Speech delivered to the 48th Session of the United Nations General Assembly, 27 September 1993, *Vital Speeches of the Day*, Vol. 60, No. 1, 15 October 1993.

Gorbachev, Mikhail, 'Foreign Relations – USSR: The Democratization of World Politics', *Vital Speeches of the Day*, Vol. 54, No. 14, 1 May 1988.

Hannay, Sir David, United Kingdom Permanent Representative to the United Nations, Interview Conducted at United Kingdom Permanent Mission to the United Nations, New York City, 29 March 1994.

Healey, Lieutenant-Colonel Damien, Australian Defence Force, Formerly Chairman, UNTAC Mixed Military Working Group, Interview Conducted in Canberra, 14 December 1993.

Kirkpatrick, Jeane J., 'Projecting and Protecting U.S. Interests in the United Nations: U.N. Strategy and Its Relations to U.S. Foreign Policy', *Vital Speeches of the Day*, Vol. 54, No. 8, 1 February 1988.

Lake, Anthony, 'From Containment to Enlargement', *Vital Speeches of the Day*, Vol. 60, No. 1, 15 October 1993.

Mitterand, François, 'The Rule of Law', speech delivered to the 45th Session of the United Nations General Assembly, 24 September 1990, *Vital Speeches of the Day*, Vol. 57, No. 1, 15 October 1990.

Pelletier, Michel, United Nations Department of Peacekeeping Operations, Interviewed at United Nations Headquarters, New York City, 30 March 1994.

Reagan, Ronald, Address to the General Assembly of the United Nations, 26 September 1983, General Assembly Official Records, A/38/PV.5.
Sanderson, Lieutenant-General John, Australian Defence Force, Formerly UNTAC Force Commander, Interview Conducted in Canberra, 15 December 1993.
Seymour, Joan T., Special Assistant to the Under-Secretary-General, Department of Political Affairs, Interview Conducted on 11 March 1994 at United Nations Headquarters, New York City.
Sise, Lamine, Somalia Desk, Department of Political Affairs, Interviewed at United Nations Headquarters, New York City, 19 April 1994.

Primary Sources: Official Documents

Addis Ababa Agreement of the First Session of the Conference on National Reconciliation in Somalia, 27 March 1993.
Agreements on a Comprehensive Political Settlement of the Cambodia Conflict, Paris, 27 September 1991.
Boutros-Ghali, Boutros, Report on the Work of the Organization From the Forty-Sixth to the Forty-Seventh Session of the General Assembly, September 1992 (New York: United Nations, 1992).
An Agenda For Peace: Preventative Diplomacy, Peacemaking and Peace-keeping: Report of the Secretary-General Pursuant to the Statement Adopted by the Summit Meeting of the Security Council on 31 January 1992 (New York: United Nations, 1992).
Department of Foreign Affairs and Trade, *Cambodia: An Australian Peace Proposal* (Canberra: Australian Government Publishing Service, 1990).
Perez de Cuellar, Javier, Report of the Secretary-General on the Work of the Organization, 1984 (New York: United Nations, 1984).
United Nations High Commission for Refugees: Office of the Special Envoy for the Former Yugoslavia, 'Information Notes on Former Yugoslavia', No. 1/94, January 1994.

General Assembly Documents

General Assembly Resolution 41/71, 3 December 1986.
General Assembly Resolution 43/160B, 9 December 1988.
Letter dated 6 July 1989 from the Secretary-General Addressed to the President of the General Assembly, 'The Situation in Central America: Threats to International Peace and Security and Peace Initiatives', A/44/375, 7 July 1989.
General Assembly Resolution 45/37, 28 November 1990.
'Comprehensive Review of the Whole Question of Peacekeeping Operations in All Their Aspects', General Assembly Official Records, A/46/254, 18 June 1991.
General Assembly Resolution 47/29, 25 November 1992.

Security Council Documents

Security Council Resolution 435 (1978), 29 September 1978.
Security Council Resolution 566 (1985), 19 June 1985.
Letter dated 27 August 1987 from the Permanent Representatives of Costa Rica, El Salvador, Guatemala, and Nicaragua to the United Nations Addressed to the Secretary-General, A/42/521 and S/19085, 31 August 1987.

Letter dated 19 January 1988 from the Permanent Representatives of Costa Rica, El Salvador, Guatemala, and Nicaragua to the United Nations Addressed to the Secretary-General, A/42/911 and S/19447, 22 January 1988.
Letter dated 27 February 1989 from the Permanent Representatives of Costa Rica, El Salvador, Guatemala, and Nicaragua to the United Nations Addressed to the Secretary-General, A/44/140 and S/20491, 27 February 1989.
Letter dated 14 April 1989 from the Secretary-General Addressed to the Ministers for Foreign Affairs of Costa Rica, El Salvador, Guatemala, Honduras and Nicaragua, A/44/288 and S/20643 Annex, 18 May 1989.
Letter dated 8 May 1989 from the Permanent Representative of Guatemala to the United Nations Addressed to the Secretary-General, A/44/289 and S/20644, 18 May 1989.
Letter dated 18 May 1989 from the Permanent Representatives of Costa Rica, El Salvador, Guatemala, and Nicaragua to the United Nations Addressed to the Secretary-General, A/44/287 and S/20642, 18 May 1989.
Security Council Resolution 637 (1989), 27 July 1989.
Letter dated 9 August 1989 from the Permanent Representatives of Costa Rica, El Salvador, Guatemala, and Nicaragua to the United Nations Addressed to the Secretary-General, A/44/451 and S/20778, 9 August 1989.
Letter dated 28 August 1989 from the Secretary-General Addressed to the President of the Security Council, S/20856, 21 September 1989.
Security Council Resolution 644 (1989), 7 November 1989.
'Declaration of San Isidrio de Coronado', A/44/872 and S/21019 Annex, 12 December 1989.
Letter dated 13 February 1990 from the Representatives of China, France, the Union of Soviet Socialist Republics, the United Kingdom of Great Britain and Northern Ireland and the United States of America to the United Nations Addressed to the Secretary-General, 'The Situation In Kampuchea: Question of Peace, Stability and Co-operation in South-East Asia', A/45/127 and S/21149, 15 February 1990.
Letter dated 16 March 1990 from the Representatives of China, France, the Union of Soviet Socialist Republics, the United Kingdom of Great Britain and Northern Ireland and the United States of America to the United Nations Addressed to the Secretary-General, 'The Situation In Kampuchea: Question of Peace, Stability and Co-operation in South-East Asia', A/45/167 and S/21196, 16 March 1990.
'Toncontin Agreement', S/21206 Annex, 26 March 1990.
Security Council Resolution 650 (1990), 27 March 1990.
'Montelimar Declaration', S/21235, 9 April 1990.
'Declaration by Mr Khieu Samphan, President of the Democratic Kampuchea Party and Vice-President of Cambodia in Charge of Foreign Affairs Condemning the Vietnamese Aggressors and Their Lackeys for Making an Attempt on the Life of His Royal Highness Prince Norodom Sihanouk, President of Cambodia', A/45/220 and S/21253 Annex, 14 April 1990.
Security Council Resolution 653 (1990), 20 April 1990.
Statement by the Secretary-General in Informal Consultations of the Security Council Held on 19 April 1990, S/21259 Annex, 20 April 1990.
Security Council Resolution 654 (1990), 4 May 1990.
Letter dated 29 May 1990 from the Representatives of China, France, the Union

of Soviet Socialist Republics, the United Kingdom of Great Britain and Northern Ireland and the United States of America to the United Nations Addressed to the Secretary-General, 'The Situation In Kampuchea: Question of Peace, Stability and Co-operation in South-East Asia', A/45/293 and S/21318, 29 May 1990.

Security Council Resolution 656 (1990), 8 June 1990.

Letter dated 23 July 1990 from the Representatives of China, France, the Union of Soviet Socialist Republics, the United Kingdom of Great Britain and Northern Ireland and the United States of America to the United Nations Addressed to the Secretary-General, 'The Situation In Kampuchea: Question of Peace, Stability and Co-operation in South-East Asia', A/45/353 and S/21404, 23 July 1990.

Letter dated 30 August 1990 from the Permanent Representatives of China, France, the Union of Soviet Socialist Republics, the United Kingdom of Great Britain and Northern Ireland and the United States of America to the United Nations Addressed to the Secretary-General, 'The Situation In Kampuchea: Question of Peace, Stability and Co-operation in South-East Asia', A/45/472 and S/21689, 31 August 1990.

Letter dated 11 September 1990 from the Permanent Representatives of France and Indonesia to the United Nations Addressed to the Secretary-General, 'The Situation in Kampuchea', A/45/490 and S/21732, 17 September 1990.

Security Council Resolution 668 (1990), 20 September 1990.

Letter dated 25 October 1990 from the Permanent Representatives of China, France, the Union of Soviet Socialist Republics, the United Kingdom of Great Britain and Northern Ireland and the United States of America to the United Nations Addressed to the Secretary-General, 'The Situation In Kampuchea: Question of Peace, Stability and Co-operation in South-East Asia', A/45/671 and S/21908, 25 October 1990.

Press Statement of the Co-Chairmen of the Paris Conference on Cambodia, S/21940 Annex, 10 November 1990.

Letter dated 8 January 1991 from the Permanent Representatives of France and Indonesia to the United Nations Addressed to the Secretary-General, 'The Situation In Cambodia', A/46/61 and S/22059, 11 January 1991.

Security Council Resolution 691 (1991), 6 May 1991.

'Letter Dated 17 May 1991 From the Charge d'Affairs A.I. of the Permanent Mission of Angola to the United Nations Addressed to the Secretary-General', S/22609, 17 May 1991.

'Peace Accords for Angola', S/22609 Annex, 17 May 1991.

'Letter Dated 17 May 1991 From the Permanent Representative of Portugal to the United Nations Addressed to the Secretary-General', S/22617, 18 May 1991.

Security Council Resolution 693 (1991), 20 May 1991.

Security Council Resolution 696 (1991), 30 May 1991.

Final Communiqué of the Meeting of the Supreme National Council of Cambodia in Pattaya (Thailand), A/46/271 and S/22740 Annex, 26 June 1991.

Communiqué of the Co-Chairmen of the Paris Conference on Cambodia and the Five Permanent Members of the United Nations Security Council, Issued at Beijing on 18 July 1991, A/46/340 and S/22889 Annex, 5 August 1991.

Communiqué Issued on 30 August 1991 by the Co-Chairmen of the Paris Conference on Cambodia and the Five Permanent Members of the United Nations Security Council, A/46/418 and S/23011 Annex, 4 September 1991.

Security Council Resolution 713 (1991), 25 September 1991.
Letter dated 24 September 1991 from the Permanent Representatives of China, France, the Union of Soviet Socialist Republics, the United Kingdom of Great Britain and Northern Ireland and the United States of America to the United Nations Addressed to the Secretary-General, 'The Situation In Cambodia', A/46/508 and S/23087, 27 September 1991.
Security Council Resolution 714 (1991), 30 September 1991.
Security Council Resolution 717 (1991), 16 October 1991.
Security Council Resolution 718 (1991), 31 October 1991.
Security Council Resolution 719 (1991), 6 November 1991.
'Concept for a United Nations Peacekeeping Operation in Yugoslavia, as Discussed with Yugoslav Leaders by the Honourable Cyrus R. Vance, Personal Envoy of the Secretary-General and Marrack Goulding, Under-Secretary-General for Special Political Affairs', S/23280 Annex III, 12 December 1991.
Security Council Resolution 728 (1992), 8 January 1992.
Security Council Resolution 729 (1992), 14 January 1992.
Letter dated 20 January 1992 from the Charge D'Affaires A.I. of the Permanent Mission of Somalia to the United Nations Addressed to the President of the Security Council, S/23445, 20 January 1992.
Security Council Resolution 733 (1992), 23 January 1992.
Security Council Resolution 745 (1992), 28 February 1992.
Security Council Resolution 746 (1992), 17 March 1992.
Security Council Resolution 747 (1992), 24 March 1992.
Security Council Resolution 749 (1992), 7 April 1992.
Statement by the President of the Security Council, S/23802, 10 April 1992.
Statement by the President of the Security Council, S/25646, 24 April 1992.
Security Council Resolution 751 (1992), 24 April 1992.
Security Council Resolution 752 (1992), 15 May 1992.
Security Council Resolution 755 (1992) 20 May 1992.
Security Council Resolution 757 (1992), 30 May 1992.
Security Council Resolution 758 (1992), 8 June 1992.
Note by the President of the Security Council, S/24091, 12 June 1992.
Letter dated 23 June 1992 from the Secretary-General Addressed to the President of the Security Council, S/24179, 25 June 1992.
Letter dated 23 June 1992 from the Secretary-General to the President of the Security Council, S/24180, 29 June 1992.
'Bahir Dar Declaration of the All-Party Meeting on Somalia', S/24184, 25 June 1992.
Security Council Resolution 761 (1992), 29 June 1992.
Statement by the President of the Security Council, S/24249, 7 July 1992.
Security Council Resolution 764 (1992), 13 July 1992.
Security Council Resolution 766 (1992), 21 July 1992.
Security Council Resolution 767 (1992), 27 July 1992.
Security Council Resolution 770 (1992), 13 August 1992.
Security Council Resolution 775 (1992), 28 August 1992.
Statement by the President of the Security Council, S/24573, 18 September 1992.
Statement by the President of the Security Council, S/24623, 8 October 1992.
'General Peace Agreement for Mozambique', S/24635 Annex, 8 October 1992.
'Report of the Chairman of the Working Group on Confidence and Security-

Building and Verification Measures to the Co-Chairmen of the Steering Committee of the International Conference on the Former Yugoslavia', S/24364 Annex, 8 October 1992.
Security Council Resolution 781 (1992), 9 October 1992.
Security Council Resolution 782 (1992), 13 October 1992.
Statement by the President of the Security Council, S/24683, 19 October 1992.
Statement by the President of the Security Council, S/24720, 27 October 1992.
Letter dated 11 November 1992 from the Secretary-General Addressed to the President of the Security Council, S/24805, 13 November 1992.
Security Council Resolution 787 (1992), 16 November 1992.
Letter dated 24 November 1992 from the Secretary-General Addressed to the President of the Security Council, S/24859, 27 November 1992.
'Position of the Royal Thai Government With Regard to Security Council Resolution 792 (1992) on Cambodia', S/24873 Annex, 30 November 1992.
Security Council Resolution 793 (1992), 30 November 1992.
Letter dated 29 November 1992 from the Secretary-General Addressed to the President of the Security Council, S/24868, 30 November 1992.
Statement by the President of the Security Council, S/24884, 2 December 1992.
Security Council Resolution 794 (1992), 3 December 1992.
Security Council Resolution 795 (1992), 11 December 1992.
Security Council Resolution 797 (1992), 16 December 1992.
'Letter Dated 18 December 1992 from the Secretary-General Addressed to the President of the Security Council', S/24996, 21 December 1992.
Security Council Debate, 'The Situation in Cambodia', S/PV.3153, 22 December 1992.
Statement by the President of the Security Council, S/25002, 22 December 1992.
Letter dated 7 January 1993 from the Secretary-General Addressed to the President of the Security Council, S/25078, 9 January 1993.
Statement by the President of the Security Council, S/25162, 25 January 1993.
Security Council Resolution 804 (1993), 29 January 1993.
Letter dated 29 January 1993 from the Secretary-General Addressed to the President of the Security Council, S/25200, 29 January 1993.
Letter dated 26 January 1993 from the Secretary-General Addressed to the President of the Security Council, S/25241, 4 February 1993.
Security Council Resolution 808 (1993), 22 February 1993.
Statement by the President of the Security Council, S/25334, 25 February 1993.
Letter dated 3 March 1993 from the Permanent Representative of Bosnia and Herzegovina to the United Nations Addressed to the Secretary-General, A/47/901 and S/25362, 3 March 1993.
Security Council Resolution 810 (1993), 8 March 1993.
Security Council Resolution 811 (1993), 12 March 1993.
Security Council Resolution 814 (1993), 26 March 1993.
Security Council Resolution 816 (1993), 31 March 1993.
Statement by the President of the Security Council, S/25520, 3 April 1993.
Note by the President of the Security Council, S/25530, 5 April 1993.
Statement by the President of the Security Council, S/25557, 8 April 1993.
Security Council Resolution 818 (1993), 14 April 1993.
Security Council Resolution 819 (1993), 16 April 1993.
Security Council Resolution 820 (1993), 17 April 1993.

Letter dated 26 April 1993 from the Secretary-General Addressed to the President of the Security Council, S/25669, 27 April 1993.
Statement by the President of the Security Council, SC/5601, 27 April 1993.
Security Council Resolution 823 (1993), 30 April 1993.
Report of the Security Council Mission Established Pursuant to Resolution 819 (1993), S/25700, 30 April 1993.
Security Council Resolution 824 (1993), 6 May 1993.
Statement by the President of the Security Council, S/25746, 10 May 1993.
Statement by the President of the Security Council, SC/5617, 14 May 1993.
Security Council Resolution 826 (1993), 20 May 1993.
'Agreement on the Cessation of Hostilities in Bosnia and Herzegovina Concluded Between Gen. Milivoj Petkovic and Gen. Sefer Halilovic on 12 May 1993 in the Presence of Lt-Gen. Philippe Morillon and ECMM/EEC Jean-Pierre Thebault', S/25824 Annex, 22 May 1993.
Letter dated 24 May 1993 from the Permanent Representatives of France, the Russian Federation, Spain, the United Kingdom of Great Britain and Northern Ireland and the United States of America Addressed to the President of the Security Council, S/25829, 24 May 1993.
Security Council Resolution 832 (1993), 27 May 1993.
'Note by the President of the Security Council', S/25859, 28 May 1993.
Statement by the Special Representative of the Secretary-General for Cambodia at the Supreme National Council of Cambodia, S/25879 Annex, 29 May 1993.
Letter dated 28 May 1993 from the Secretary-General Addressed to the President of the Security Council, S/25871, 1 June 1993.
Security Council Resolution 834 (1993), 1 June 1993.
Security Council Resolution 835 (1993), 2 June 1993.
Security Council Resolution 836 (1993), 4 June 1993.
Security Council Resolution 837 (1993), 6 June 1993.
Statement by the President of the Security Council, S/25899, 8 June 1993.
Letter dated 8 June 1993 from the Secretary-General Addressed to the President of the Security Council, S/25901, 8 June 1993.
Note by the President of the Security Council, S/25896, 8 June 1993.
Security Council Resolution 840 (1993), 15 June 1993.
Statement by the President of the Security Council, SC/5662, 30 June 1993.
Letter dated 22 June 1993 from the Secretary-General Addressed to the President of the Security Council, S/25988, 22 June 1993.
Draft Resolution, S/25997, 29 June 1993 (Not Adopted).
Letter dated 8 July 1993 from the Secretary-General Addressed to the President of the Security Council, S/26052, 8 July 1993.
'Report of the Co-Chairmen of the Steering Committee of the International Conference on the Former Yugoslavia', S/26066 Annex, 8 July 1993.
Security Council Resolution 850 (1993), 9 July 1993.
Security Council Resolution 851 (1993), 15 July 1993.
'Communiqué of the OIC Special Ministerial Meeting of the Bureau of the Islamic Conference of Foreign Ministers Enlarged to Members of the Contact Group and States Contributing Troops to the UNPROFOR, Islamabad, 13 July 1993', A/47/977 and S/26112 Annex I, 19 July 1993.
Statement by the President of the Security Council, S/26134, 22 July 1993.
'Report of the Co-Chairmen of the Steering Committee of the International Conference on the Former Yugoslavia', S/26233 Annex, 3 August 1993.

'Report of the Co-Chairmen of the Steering Committee of the International Conference on the Former Yugoslavia', S/26260 Annex, 6 August 1993.
'Report of the Co-Chairmen of the Steering Committee of the International Conference on the Former Yugoslavia', S/26337 Annex, 20 August 1993.
Security Council Resolution 859 (1993), 24 August 1993.
Security Council Resolution 860 (1993), 27 August 1993.
Security Council Resolution 863 (1993), 13 September 1993.
Security Council Debate, 'The Situation in Angola', S/PV.3277, 15 September 1993.
Security Council Resolution 864 (1993), 15 September 1993.
Security Council Resolution 865 (1993), 22 September 1993.
Statement by the President of the Security Council, SC/5706/Rev.1, 24 September 1993.
Security Council Resolution 868 (1993), 29 September 1993.
Security Council Resolution 783 (1992), 13 October 1993.
Security Council Resolution 878 (1993), 29 October 1993.
Security Council Resolution 879 (1993), 29 October 1993.
Security Council Resolution 785 (1992), 30 October 1993.
Statement by the President of the Security Council, S/26677, 1 November 1993.
Letter dated 3 November 1993 from the Secretary-General Addressed to the President of the Security Council, S/26689, 3 November 1993.
Security Council Resolution 880 (1993), 4 November 1993.
Security Council Resolution 882 (1993), 5 November 1993.
Security Council Resolution 885 (1993), 16 November 1993.
Security Council Resolution 886 (1993), 18 November 1993.
Security Council Resolution 888 (1993), 30 November 1993.
Letter dated 7 December 1993 from the Secretary-General Addressed to the President of the Security Council, S/26865, 11 December 1993.
Security Council Resolution 890 (1993), 15 December 1993.
Statement by the President of the Security Council, S/PRST/1994/1, 7 January 1994.
Security Council Resolution 897 (1994), 4 February 1994.
Statement by the President of the Security Council, S/PRST/1994/7, 10 February 1994.
Security Council Resolution 898 (1994), 23 February 1994.
Security Council Resolution 900 (1994), 4 March 1994.
Statement by the President of the Security Council, S/PRST/1994/10, 14 March 1994.
Security Council Resolution 903 (1994), 16 March 1994.
Letter dated 28 March 1994 from the Secretary-General Addressed to the President of the Security Council, S/1994/361, 30 March 1994.
Letter dated 21 April 1994 from the Secretary-General Addressed to the President of the Security Council, S/1994/486, 21 April 1994.
Security Council Resolution 913 (1994), 22 April 1994.
Security Council Resolution 920 (1994), 26 May 1994.
Security Council Resolution 922 (1994), 31 May 1994.
Security Council Resolution 923 (1994), 31 May 1994.
Security Council Resolution 932 (1994), 30 June 1994.
Security Council Resolution 941 (1994), 23 September 1994.
Security Council Resolution 942 (1994), 23 September 1994.
Security Council Resolution 946 (1994), 30 September 1994.

'Report of the Security Council Mission to Somalia on 26 and 27 October 1994', S/1994/1245, 3 November 1994.
Security Council Resolution 960 (1994), 21 November 1994.
Security Council Resolution 976 (1995), 8 February 1995.

Economic and Social Council Documents
Economic and Social Council Resolution 2100 (LXIII), 3 August 1977.
Economic and Social Council Resolution 1979/54, 2 August 1979.

Secretary-General's Reports

Angola
'Report of the Secretary-General on the United Nations Angola Verification Mission', S/22627, 20 May 1991.
'Further Report of the Secretary-General on the United Nations Angola Verification Mission II (UNAVEM II)', S/24858, 25 November 1992.
'Further Report of the Secretary-General on the United Nations Angola Verification Mission II (UNAVEM II)', S/25840, 25 May 1993.
'Further Report of the Secretary-General on the United Nations Angola Verification Mission II (UNAVEM II)', S/26060, 12 July 1993.
'Report of the Secretary-General on the United Nations Angola Verification Mission (UNAVEM II)', S/26872, 14 December 1993.
'Report of the Secretary-General on the United Nations Angola Verification Mission (UNAVEM II)', S/1995/97, 1 February 1995.
'First Progress Report of the Secretary-General on the United Nations Angola Verification Mission (UNAVEM III)', S/1995/177, 5 March 1995.

Bosnia-Herzegovina
'Report of the Secretary-General Pursuant to Security Council Resolution 721 (1991)', S/23280, 11 December 1991.
'Report of the Secretary-General Pursuant to Security Council Resolution 749 (1992)', S/23836, 24 April 1992.
'Report of the Secretary-General Pursuant to Security Council Resolution 757 (1992)', S/24075, 6 June 1992.
'Further Report of the Secretary-General Pursuant to Security Council Resolutions 757 (1992), 758 (1992) and 761 (1992)', S/24263, 10 July 1992.
'Report of the Secretary-General on the Situation in Bosnia and Herzegovina', S/24540, 10 September 1992.
'Report of the Secretary-General Pursuant to Security Council Resolution 781 (1992)', S/24767, 5 November 1992.
'Report of the Secretary-General on the International Conference on the Former Yugoslavia', S/24795, 11 November 1992.
'Report of the Secretary-General on the Activities of the International Conference on the Former Yugoslavia', S/25050, 6 January 1993.
'Report of the Secretary-General on the Activities of the International Conference on the Former Yugoslavia', S/25050, 2 February 1993.
'Report of the Secretary-General on the New York Round of the Peace Talks on Bosnia and Herzegovina (3–8 February 1993)', S/25248, 8 February 1993.
Note by the Secretary-General, 'The Situation of Human Rights in the Territory of the Former Yugoslavia', A/48/92 and S/25341, 26 February 1993.

'Report of the Secretary-General on the Activities of the International Conference on the Former Yugoslavia: Peace Talks on Bosnia and Herzegovina', S/25479, 26 March 1993.
'Report of the Secretary-General Pursuant to Security Council Resolutions 802, 807 and 815 (1993)', S/25555, 8 April 1993.
'Report of the Secretary-General Pursuant to Security Council Resolution 836 (1993)', S/25939, 14 June 1993.

Cambodia
'Report of the Secretary-General on Cambodia', S/23097, 30 September 1991.
'Report of the Secretary-General on Cambodia', S/23613, 19 February 1992.
'First Progress Report of the Secretary-General on the United Nations Transitional Authority in Cambodia', S/23870, 1 May 1992.
'Special Report of the Secretary-General on the United Nations Transitional Authority in Cambodia', S/24090, 12 June 1992.
'Second Special Report of the Secretary-General on the United Nations Transitional Authority in Cambodia', S/24286, 14 July 1992.
'Second Progress Report of the Secretary-General on the United Nations Transitional Authority in Cambodia', S/24578, 21 September 1992.
'Report of the Secretary-General on the Implementation of Security Council Resolution 783 (1992)', S/24800, 15 November 1992.
'Third Progress Report of the Secretary-General on the United Nations Transitional Authority in Cambodia', S/25124, 25 January 1993.
'Report of the Secretary-General on the Implementation of Security Council Resolution 792 (1992)', S/25289, 13 February 1993.
'Fourth Progress Report of the Secretary-General on the United Nations Transitional Authority in Cambodia', S/25719, 3 May 1993.
'Report of the Secretary-General in Pursuance of Paragraph 6 of Security Council Resolution 810 (1993)', S/25784, 15 May 1993.
'Report of the Secretary-General on the Conduct and Results of the Elections in Cambodia', S/25913, 10 June 1993.

El Salvador
Report of the Secretary-General, 'Central America: Efforts Towards Peace', S/22031, 21 December 1990.
Report of the Secretary-General, 'Central America: Efforts Towards Peace', S/22494, 16 April 1991.
'First Report of the United Nations Observer Mission in El Salvador', A/45/1055 and S/23037 Annex, 16 September 1991.
'Second Report of the United Nations Observer Mission in El Salvador', A/46/658 and S/23222 Annex, 15 November 1991.
Report of the Secretary-General, 'The Situation in Central America: Threats to International Peace and International Security and Peace Initiatives', A/46/713 and S/23256, 2 December 1991.
Report of the Secretary-General, 'Central America: Efforts Towards Peace', S/23402, 10 January 1992.
Report of the Secretary-General, 'United Nations Observer Mission in El Salvador', S/23642, 25 February 1992.

'Report of the Secretary-General on the United Nations Observer Mission in El Salvador', S/23999, 26 May 1992.
'Report of the Secretary-General on the United Nations Observer Mission in El Salvador', S/24833, 23 November 1992.
Report of the Secretary-General, 'The Situation in Central America: Procedures for the Establishment of a Firm and Lasting Peace and Progress in Fashioning a Region of Peace, Freedom, Democracy and Development', A/47/739 and S/24871, 30 November 1992.
'Report of the Secretary-General on the United Nations Observer Mission in El Salvador (ONUSAL)', S/25006, 23 December 1992.
'Report of the Secretary-General on the United Nations Observer Mission in El Salvador', S/25812, 21 May 1993.
'Report of the Secretary-General on the United Nations Observer Mission in El Salvador', S/25812/Add.1, 24 May 1993.
'Further Report of the Secretary-General on the United Nations Observer Mission in El Salvador (ONUSAL)', S/26005, 29 June 1993.
'Further Report of the Secretary-General on the United Nations Observer Mission in El Salvador (ONUSAL)', S/26371, 30 August 1993.
'Further Report of the Secretary-General on the United Nations Observer Mission in El Salvador', S/26581, 14 October 1993.
'Report of the Secretary-General on the United Nations Observer Mission in El Salvador', S/26606, 20 October 1993.
'Further Report of the Secretary-General on the United Nations Observer Mission in El Salvador', S/26790, 23 November 1993.
'Report of the Secretary-General on the United Nations Observer Mission in El Salvador', S/1994/179, 16 February 1994.
'Report of the Secretary-General on the United Nations Observer Mission in El Salvador', S/1994/304, 16 March 1994.
'Report of the Secretary-General on the United Nations Observer Mission in El Salvador', S/1994/375, 31 March 1994.
'Report of the Secretary-General on the United Nations Observer Mission in El Salvador', S/1994/536, 4 May 1994.

Mozambique

'United Nations Operation in Mozambique: Report of the Secretary-General', S/24642, 9 October 1992.
'Report of the Secretary-General on the United Nations Operation in Mozambique', S/24892, 3 December 1992.
'Report of the Secretary-General on the United Nations Operation in Mozambique', S/25518, 2 April 1993.
'Report of the Secretary-General on the United Nations Operation in Mozambique', S/26304, 30 June 1993.
'Report of the Secretary-General on the United Nations Operation in Mozambique', S/26385, 30 August 1993.
'Report of the Secretary-General on the United Nations Operation in Mozambique', S/26666, 1 November 1993.
'Report of the Secretary-General on the United Nations Operation in Mozambique', S/1994/89, 28 January 1994.
'Progress Report on the United Nations Operation in Mozambique', S/1994/1196, 21 October 1994.

'Final Report of the Secretary-General on the United Nations Operation in Mozambique', S/1994/1449, 23 December 1994.

Somalia

Report of the Secretary-General, 'The Situation in Somalia', S/23693, 11 March 1992.

Report of the Secretary-General, 'The Situation in Somalia', S/23829, 21 April 1992.

Report of the Secretary-General, 'The Situation in Somalia', S/24480, 24 August 1992.

Report of the Secretary-General Submitted in Pursuance of Paragraphs 18 and 19 of Security Council Resolution 794 (1992), 'The Situation in Somalia', S/24992, 19 December 1992.

Progress Report of the Secretary-General, 'The Situation in Somalia', S/25168, 26 January 1993.

'Further Report of the Secretary-General Submitted in Pursuance of Paragraphs 18 and 19 of Resolution 794 (1992)', S/25354, 3 March 1993.

'Report of the Secretary-General on the Implementation of Security Council Resolution 837 (1993)', S/26022, 1 July 1993.

'Further Report of the Secretary-General Submitted in Pursuance of Paragraph 18 of Resolution 814 (1993)', S/26317, 17 August 1993.

'Report Pursuant to Paragraph 5 of Security Council Resolution 837 (1993) on the Investigation into the 5 June 1993 Attack on United Nations Forces in Somalia Conducted on Behalf of the Secretary-General', S/26351, 24 August 1993.

'Further Report of the Secretary-General Submitted in Pursuance of Paragraph 19 of Resolution 814 (1993) and Paragraph A 5 of Resolution 865 (1993)', S/26738, 12 November 1993.

'Further Report of the Secretary-General Submitted in Pursuance of Paragraph 4 of Resolution 886 (1993)', S/1994/12, 6 January 1994.

'Report of the Commission of Inquiry Established Pursuant to Security Council Resolution 885 (1993) to Investigate Armed Attacks on UNOSOM II Personnel Which Led to Casualties Among Them', S/1994/653 Annex, 1 June 1994.

'Report by the Secretary-General Concerning the Situation in Somalia', S/1994/1068, 17 September 1994.

Primary Sources: Television and Radio

BBC News and Current Affairs, The Thin Blue Line: A 3-Part Series, BBC Radio 4, 8 pm, 15 April–6 May 1993, 8 p.m.

UNDPI, 'El Salvador: An Interview with Alvaro de Soto, Senior Political Advisor to the United Nations Secretary-General', United Nations World Chronicle, No. 513, 29 April 1993.

UNDPI, 'Somalia: An Interview with Admiral Jonathon T. Howe', United Nations World Chronicle, No. 517, 23 September 1993.

Secondary Sources: Books

Acharya, Amitar, Pierre Lizee, and Sorpong Peou (eds), *Cambodia – The 1989 Paris Peace Conference: Background Analysis and Documents* (New York: Kraus International Publications, 1991).

Acheson, Dean, *Present at the Creation: My Years at the State Department* (New York: Norton, 1969).
Alao, Abiodun, *Brothers at War* (London: British Academic Press, 1994).
Allison, Graham T., *Essence of Decision: Explaining the Cuban Missile Crisis* (Boston: Little, Brown and Company, 1971).
Allison, Graham T., and Gregory F. Treverton (eds), *Rethinking America's Security: Beyond Cold War to New World Order* (New York: Norton and Company, 1992).
Almond, Mark, *Europe's Backyard War: The War in the Balkans* (London: Mandarin, 1994).
Andemichael, Berhanykun, *Peaceful Settlement Among African States: Roles of the United Nations and the Organization of African Unity* (New York: UNITAR, 1972).
Armstrong, David, and Eric Goldstein (eds), *The End of the Cold War* (London: Frank Cass, 1990).
Aron, Raymond, *Peace and War: A Theory of International Relations* trans. Richard Howard and Annette Baker-Fox (London: Weidenfeld and Nicolson, 1980).
Azeredo, Mario, *Historical Dictionary of Mozambique* (New Jersey: The Scarecrow Press, 1991).
Baehr, Peter R., and Leon Gordenker, *The United Nations in the 1990s* (Basingstoke: Macmillan, 1992).
Bailey, Sydney D., *The General Assembly of the United Nations* (New York: Frederick A. Praeger, 1960).
The Procedure of the UN Security Council (Oxford: Clarendon Press, 1975).
How Wars End: The United Nations and the Termination of Armed Conflict 1946–1964 Volume I (Oxford: Clarendon Press, 1982).
Baranyi, Stephen, and Liisa North, *Stretching the Limits of the Possible: United Nations Peacekeeping in Central America: Aurora Papers 15* (Ontario: Canadian Centre for Global Security, 1992).
Barratta, Joseph Preston, *International Peacekeeping: History and Strengthening* (Washington: Centre for UN Reform Education, 1989).
Bell, Coral, *The Reagan Paradox: American Foreign Policy in the 1980s* (Aldershot: Edward Elgar, 1989).
Bennett, A. LeRoy, *International Organizations: Principles and Issues* (New Jersey: Prentice-Hall Inc., 1991).
Bercovitch, Jacob, and Jeffrey Z. Rubin (eds), *Mediation in International Relations: Multiple Approaches to Conflict Management* (Basingstoke: Macmillan, 1992).
Berridge, G.R., *Return to the UN: UN Diplomacy in Regional Conflicts* (Hampshire: Macmillan, 1991).
Berridge, G.R., and A. Jennings (eds), *Diplomacy at the United Nations* (London: Macmillan, 1985).
Bertelsen, Judy S. (ed.), *Nonstate Nations in International Politics: Comparative System Analysis* (New York: Praeger Publishers, 1977).
Blainey, Geoffrey, *The Causes of War* (London: Macmillan, 1973).
Bogdanor, Vernon, and David Butler (eds), *Democracy and Elections: Electoral Systems and their Political Consequences* (Cambridge: Cambridge University Press, 1983).
Bowett, D.W., *United Nations Forces: A Legal Study of United Nations Practice* (London: Stevens and Sons, 1964).

Brogan, Patrick, *World Conflicts: Why and Where They Are Happening* (London: Bloomsbury, 1992).

Bull, Hedley, *The Anarchical Society: A Study of Order in World Politics* (Basingstoke: Macmillan, 1977).

(ed.), *Intervention in World Politics* (Oxford: Clarendon Press, 1984).

Burton, John, *Conflict: Resolution and Prevention* (Basingstoke: Macmillan, 1990).

Burton, John W., and Edward Azar (eds), *International Conflict Resolution: Theory and Practice* (Sussex: Wheatsheaf Books, 1986).

Bustelo, Mara R., and Philip Alston, *Whose New World Order: What Role for the United Nations?* (Sydney: The Federation Press, 1991).

Buzan, Barry, *People, States and Fear: An Agenda for International Security Studies in the Post-Cold War Era* (2nd ed.) (New York: Harvester Wheatsheaf, 1991).

Brzezinski, Zbigniew, *The Grand Failure: The Birth and Death of Communism in the Twentieth Century* (New York: MacDonald, 1990).

Carr, Edward Hallett, *The Twenty Years' Crisis 1919–1939: An Introduction to the Study of International Relations* (London: Macmillan, 1970).

Chaliand, Gerard, *Minority Peoples in the Age of Nation States* (London: Pluto Press, 1988).

Chandler, David P., *The Tragedy of Cambodian History: Politics, War and Revolution Since 1945* (New Haven: Yale University Press, 1991).

Brother Number One: A Political Biography of Pol Pot (Boulder: Westview Press, 1992).

Charters, David A. (ed.), *Peacekeeping and the Challenge of Civil Conflict Resolution* (New Brunswick: University of New Brunswick, 1994).

Chopra, Jarat, John MacKinlay, and Larry Minear, *Report on the Cambodian Peace Process* (Oslo: Norwegian Institute of International Affairs, 1993).

Claude, Inis L. Jr., *Swords Into Ploughshares: The Problems and Progress of International Organization* (London: University of London Press Ltd., 1965).

Clausewitz, Carl von, *On War*, trans. Anatol Rapoport (Harmondsworth: Penguin, 1982).

Cox, David, *Exploring An Agenda For Peace: Issues Arising From the Report of the Secretary-General* (Ottawa: Canadian Centre for Global Security, 1993).

Cox, Robert W., and Harold K. Jacobson (eds), *The Anatomy of Influence: Decision Making in International Organization* (New Haven: Yale University Press, 1974).

Crnobrnja, Mihailo, *The Yugoslav Drama* (Toronto: McGill Press, 1994).

Cross, James Elliot, *Conflict in the Shadows: The Nature and Politics of Guerrilla War* (Westport: Greenwood Press Publishers, 1973).

Damrosch, Lori Fisler, and David A. Scheffer (eds), *Law and Force in the New International Order* (Boulder, Colorado: Westview Press, 1991).

da Silva, K.M., and R.J. May (eds), *Internationalization of Ethnic Conflict* (London: Pinter Publishers, 1991).

Debray, Regis, *Revolution in the Revolution? Armed Struggle and Political Struggle in Latin America* (Harmondsworth: Penguin Books, 1967).

Diehl, Paul F. (ed.), *The Politics of International Organizations: Patterns and Insights* (Chicago: Dorsey Press, 1989).

Downs, Anthony, *An Economic Theory of Democracy* (New York: Harper and Row Publishers, 1957).

Dragnich, Alex N., *Serbs and Croats: The Struggle in Yugoslavia* (San Diego: Harcourt, Brace and Co., 1993).

Durch, William J. (ed.), *The Evolution of United Nations Peacekeeping: Case Studies and Comparative Analysis* (London: Macmillan, 1994).
Dunkerley, James, *The Long War: Dictatorship and Revolution in El Salvador* (London: Junction Books, 1982).
Eckstein, Harry (ed.), *Internal War: Problems and Approaches* (New York: Free Press, 1964).
Fairbairn, Geoffrey, *Revolutionary Guerrilla Warfare: The Countryside Version* (Harmondsworth: Penguin, 1974).
Falk, Richard A. (ed.), *The International Law of Civil War* (Baltimore: Johns Hopkins University Press, 1971).
Falk, Richard A., Samuel S. Kim, and Saul H. Mendlovitz (eds), *The United Nations and a Just World Order* (Boulder, Colorado: Westview Press, 1991).
Fanon, Frantz, *The Wretched of the Earth* (London: Penguin Books, 1967).
Fawcett, James, *Law and Power in International Relations* (London: Faber and Faber, 1982).
Findlay, Trevor, *Cambodia: The Legacy and Lessons of UNTAC, SIPRI Peacekeeping Series No. 1* (Oxford: Oxford University Press, 1995).
Finkelstein, Lawrence S. (ed.), *Politics in the United Nations System* (Durham: Duke University Press, 1988).
Fleron, Frederic J. Jr., Erik P. Hoffmann, and Robbin F. Laird (eds), *Contemporary Issues in Soviet Foreign Policy From Brezhnev to Gorbachev* (New York: Aldine de Gruyter, 1991).
Freedman, Lawrence, and Efraim Karsh, *The Gulf Conflict 1990–1991: Diplomacy and War in the New World Order* (London: Faber and Faber, 1993).
Fromm, Erich, *The Anatomy of Human Destructiveness* (London: Penguin Books, 1973).
Furley, Oliver (ed.), *Conflict in Africa* (London: British Academic Press, 1994).
Gaddis, John Lewis, *Strategies of Containment: A Critical Appraisal of Postwar American National Security Policy* (Oxford: Oxford University Press, 1982).
The Long Peace: Inquiries Into the History of the Cold War (New York: Oxford University Press, 1987).
The United States and the End of the Cold War: Implications, Reconsiderations, Provocations (New York: Oxford University Press, 1992).
George, Alexander L., *Bridging the Gap: Theory and Practice in Foreign Policy* (Washington, D.C.: United States Institute of Peace Press, 1993).
Gibson, Richard, *African Liberation Movements: Contemporary Struggles Against White Minority Rule* (London: Oxford University Press, 1972).
Gilpin, Robert, *War and Change in World Politics* (Cambridge: Cambridge University Press, 1981).
Golan, Galia, *The Soviet Union and National Liberation Movements in the Third World* (Boston: Unwin Hyman, 1988).
Goodrich, Leland M., *The United Nations* (London: Stevens and Sons Ltd., 1960).
Goodrich, Leland M., and Edvard Hambro, *Charter of the United Nations: Commentary and Documents* (2nd ed) (London: Stevens and Sons Ltd., 1949).
Guevara, Che, *Guerrilla Warfare* (Harmonsdworth: Penguin, 1961).
Gutman, Roy, *A Witness to Genocide: The First Inside Account of the Horrors of Ethnic Cleansing in Bosnia* (Shaftsbury: Element, 1993).
Haas, Michael, *Genocide by Proxy: Cambodian Pawn on a Superpower Chessboard* (New York: Praeger, 1991).

Halliday, Fred, *The Making of the Second Cold War* (London: Verso, 1986).
Cold War, Third World: An Essay in Soviet–U.S. Relations (London: Hutchinson Radius, 1989).
Harbottle, Michael, *The Impartial Soldier* (London: Oxford University Press, 1970).
Harrop, Martin, and William L. Miller, *Elections and Voters: A Comparative Introduction* (Basingstoke: Macmillan, 1987).
Hay, Robin, *Civilian Aspects of Peacekeeping: A Summary of Workshop Proceedings, Ottawa 9–10 July 1991* (Working Paper 36) (Ottawa: Canadian Institute for International Peace and Security, 1991).
Heder, Steve, and Judy Ledgerwood (eds), *Propaganda, Politics, and Violence in Cambodia: Democratic Transition Under United Nations Peacekeeping* (Armonk: ME Sharp, 1996).
Henriksen, Thomas H., *Revolution and Counterrevolution: Mozambique's War of Independence 1964–1974* (Westport: Greenwood Press, 1983).
Heraclides, Alexis, *The Self-Determination of Minorities in International Politics* (London: Frank Cass, 1991).
Higgins, Rosalyn, *The Development of International Law Through the Political Organs of the United Nations* (London: Oxford University Press, 1963).
United Nations Peacekeeping 1946–1967 Documents and Commentary, Volume I The Middle East (London: Oxford University Press, 1969).
United Nations Peacekeeping 1946–1967 Documents and Commentary, Volume III Africa (Oxford: Oxford University Press, 1980).
United Nations Peacekeeping 1946–1979 Documents and Commentary, Volume IV Europe (Oxford: Oxford University Press, 1981).
Hiscocks, Richard, *The Security Council: A Study in Adolescence* (London: Longman, 1973).
Holsti, Ole R., P. Terrence Hopmann, and John D. Sullivan, *Unity and Disintegration in International Alliances: Comparative Studies* (New York: John Wiley and Sons, 1973).
Hopkinson, Nicholas, *The United Nations and the New World Disorder: Wilton Park Paper 75* (London: HMSO, 1993).
Horowitz, Donald L., *Ethnic Groups in Conflict* (Berkeley: University of California Press, 1985).
Howard, Michael, *The Causes of Wars and Other Essays* (London: Temple Smith, 1983).
Ikle, Fred Charles, *How Nations Negotiate* (New York: Harper and Row Publishers, 1976).
International Peace Academy, *Peacekeeper's Handbook* (New York: Pergammon Press, 1984).
Jabri, Vivienne, *Mediating Conflict: Decision-Making and Western Intervention in Namibia* (Manchester: Manchester University Press, 1990).
Jackson, Richard L., *The Non-Aligned, the UN and the Superpowers* (New York: Praeger, 1983).
James, Alan, *The Politics of Peacekeeping* (London: Chatto and Windus, 1969).
Peacekeeping in International Politics (London: Macmillan, 1990).
Jervis, Robert, and Seweryn Bailer (eds), *Soviet–American Relations After the Cold War* (Durham: Duke University Press, 1991).
Jonsson, Christer, *Superpower: Comparing American and Soviet Foreign Policy* (London: Frances Pinter, 1984).

Kanet, Roger E., Deborah Nutter Miner, and Tamara J. Resler (eds), *Soviet Foreign Policy in Transition* (Cambridge: Cambridge University Press, 1992).
Kegley, Charles W. (ed.), *The Long Postwar Peace: Contending Explanations and Projections* (New York: Harper Collins, 1989).
Keohane, Robert O., and Joseph S. Nye, *Power and Interdependence: World Politics in Transition* (Boston: Little, Brown and Company, 1977).
Keohane, Robert O. (ed.), *Neorealism and Its Critics* (New York: Colombia University Press, 1986).
Kiernan, Ben (ed.), *Genocide and Democracy in Cambodia: The Khmer Rouge, the United Nations and the International Community* (New Haven: Yale University Southeast Asia Studies, 1993).
Kirisci, Kemal, *The PLO and World Politics: A Study of the Mobilization of Support for the Palestinian Cause* (London: Frances Pinter, 1986).
Kissinger, Henry A., *A World Restored* (London: Victor Gollancz Ltd., 1957).
American Foreign Policy (3rd ed) (New York: W.W. Norton and Company Inc., 1977).
The White House Years (Sydney: Hodder and Stoughton, 1979).
Years of Upheaval (Boston: Little, Brown and Company, 1982).
Diplomacy (New York: Simon and Schuster, 1994).
Klintworth, Gary, *Cambodia's Past, Present, and Future, Working Paper No. 268* (Canberra: Defence Studies Centre, 1993).
Kriesberg, Louis, and Stuart J. Thorson (eds), *Timing and De-Escalation of International Conflicts* (Syracuse: Syracuse University Press, 1991).
Kubalkova, V., and A.A. Cruickshank, *Marxism and International Relations* (Oxford: Clarendon Press, 1985).
Larkin, Bruce D., *China and Africa, 1949–1970* (Berkeley: University of California Press, 1971).
Larrabee, F. Stephen (ed.), *The Volatile Powder Keg: Balkan Security After the Cold War* (Washington: American University Press, 1994).
Lider, Julian, *On the Nature of War* (Farnborough: Saxon House, 1977).
Little, Richard, *Intervention: External Involvement in Civil Wars* (London: Martin Robertson, 1970).
Liu, F.T., *United Nations Peacekeeping and the Non-Use of Force* (Boulder: Lynne Rienner Publishers, 1992).
Luard, Evan (ed.), *The International Regulation of Civil Wars* (London: Thames and Hudson, 1972).
The United Nations: How It Works and What It Does (London: Macmillan, 1982).
A History of the United Nations Volume 1: The Years of Western Domination 1945–1955 (London: Macmillan, 1982).
MacFarlane, L.J., *Violence and the State* (London: Nelson, 1974).
Mack, Andrew, David Plant, and Ursula Doyle (eds), *Imperialism, Intervention and Development* (London: Croom Helm, 1979).
MacKenzie, W.J.M., and Kenneth Robinson (eds), *Five Elections in Africa: A Group of Electoral Studies* (Oxford: Clarendon Press, 1960).
MacKinlay, John, *The Peacekeepers: An Assessment of Peacekeeping Operations at the Arab–Israeli Interface* (London: Unwin Hyman, 1989).
Magas, Branka, *The Destruction of Yugoslavia: Tracking the Break-Up 1980–92* (London: Verso, 1993).

Malcolm, Noel, *Bosnia: A Short History* (London: Macmillan, 1991).
Meyer, Christina, *Underground Voices: Insurgent Propaganda in El Salvador, Nicaragua and Peru* (Santa Monica: RAND, 1991).
Miall, Hugh, *The Peacemakers: Peaceful Settlement of Disputes Since 1945* (Basingstoke: Macmillan, 1992).
Miller, Linda B., *World Order and Local Disorder: The United Nations and Internal Conflicts* (Princeton: Princeton University Press, 1967).
Mitchell, C.R., and K. Webb (eds), *New Approaches to International Mediation* (New York: Greenwood Press, 1988).
Moorcraft, Paul L., *African Nemesis: War and Revolution in Southern Africa* (London: Brassey's, 1994).
Morgenthau, Hans J., *Politics Among Nations: The Struggle for Power and Peace* (5th ed) (New York: Alfred A. Knopf, 1978).
Morrison, Alex (ed.), *The Changing Face of Peacekeeping* (Toronto: Canadian Institute of Strategic Studies, 1993).
Moynihan, Daniel Patrick, *A Dangerous Place* (London: Secker and Warburg, 1979).
Newitt, Maylin, *A History of Mozambique* (Bloomington: Indiana University Press, 1995).
Nicholas, H.G., *The United Nations As a Political Institution* (5th ed.) (Oxford: Oxford University Press, 1975).
Nogee, Joseph L., and Robert H. Donaldson, *Soviet Foreign Policy Since World War II* (4th ed.) (New York: Macmillan Publishing Company, 1992).
O'Donnell, Guillermo, and Philippe C. Schmitter, *Transitions From Authoritarian Rule: Tentative Conclusions About Uncertain Democracies* (Baltimore: Johns Hopkins University Press, 1986).
Olson, Mancur, *The Logic of Collective Action: Public Goods and the Theory of Groups* (Cambridge: Harvard University Press, 1965).
Pechota, Vratislav, *The Quiet Approach: A Study of the Good Offices Exercised by the United Nations Secretary-General in the Cause of Peace* (New York: United Nations Institute for Training and Research, 1972).
Peschoux, Christophe, *Enquete sur les 'nouveaux' khmers rouges: essai de debrouissaillage* (Paris, 1992).
Poulton, Hugh, *The Balkans: Minorities and States in Conflict* (London: Minority Rights Publications, 1993).
Poole, J.B., and R. Guthrie (eds), *Verification 1993: Peacekeeping, Arms Control and the Environment* (London: Brassey's, 1993).
Popper, Karl R., *Conjectures and Refutations: The Growth of Scientific Knowledge* (London: Routledge and Kegan Paul, 1963).
Quaye, Christopher O., *Liberation Struggles in International Law* (Philadelphia: Temple University Press, 1991).
Radu, Michael and Vladimir Tismaneanu, *Latin American Revolutionaries: Groups, Goals, Methods* (Washington: Pergammon-Brassey's, 1990).
Raman, K. Venkata, *The Ways of the Peacemaker: A Study of the United Nations Intermediary Assistance in the Peaceful Settlement of Disputes* (New York: UNITAR, 1975).
Renner, Michael, *Critical Juncture: The Future of Peacekeeping, Worldwatch Paper 14* (Washington, D.C.: Worldwatch Institute, 1993).
Reynolds, Charles, *The Politics of War: A Study of the Rationality of Violence in Inter-State Relations* (New York: St. Martin's Press, 1989).

Rieff, David, *Slaughterhouse: Bosnia and the Failure of the West* (New York: Simon and Schuster, 1995).

Riker, William H., *The Theory of Political Coalitions* (New Haven: Yale University Press, 1962).

Rikhye, Indar Jit, and Kjell Skjelsbaek (eds), *The United Nations and Peacekeeping: Results, Limitations and Prospects: The Lessons of 40 Years of Experience* (London: Macmillan, 1990).

Rivlin, Benjamin, and Leon Gordenker (eds), *The Challenging Role of the U.N. Secretary-General: Making 'The Most Impossible Job in the World' Possible* (Westport, Connecticut: Praeger, 1993).

Roper, John, Masashi Nishihara, Olara A. Otunnu, and Enid C.B. Schoettle, *Keeping the Peace in the Post-Cold War Era: Strengthening Multilateral Peacekeeping* (New York: The Trilateral Commission, 1993).

Rosenau, James N. (ed.), *International Aspects of Civil Strife* (Princeton: Princeton University Press, 1964).

The United Nations in a Turbulent World (Boulder: Lynne Rienner Publishers, 1992).

Rothschild, Joseph, *Ethnopolitics: A Conceptual Framework* (New York: Columbia University Press, 1981).

Rubinstein, Alvin Z., *Soviet Foreign Policy Since World War II: Imperial and Global* (3rd ed.) (Glenview, Illinios: Scott, Foresman and Company, 1989).

Saksena, K.P., *The United Nations and Collective Security: A Historical Analysis* (Delhi: D.K. Publishing House, 1974).

Sandole, Dennis, J.D., and Ingride Sandole-Staroste (eds), *Conflict Management and Problem-Solving: Interpersonal and International Applications* (London: Frances Pinter, 1987).

Sartori, Giovanni (ed.), *Social Science Concepts: A Systematic Analysis* (Beverley Hills: Sage Publications, 1984).

Schelling, Thomas C., *The Strategy of Conflict* (New York: Oxford University Press, 1960).

Arms and Influence (New Haven: Yale University Press, 1966).

Scott, Andrew M., *Insurgency* (Chapel Hill: University of North Carolina Press, 1970).

Scott, Noll, and Derek Jones (eds), *Bloody Bosnia: A European Tragedy* (London: *The Guardian* and Channel Four Television, 1994).

Silber, Laura, and Allan Little, *The Death of Yugoslavia* (London: Penguin Books, 1995).

Skogmo, Bjorn, *UNIFIL: International Peacekeeping in Lebanon, 1978–1988* (Boulder: Lynne Rienner Publishers, 1989).

Smith, Hugh (ed.), *Australia and Peacekeeping* (Canberra: Australian Defence Studies Centre, 1990).

Snyder, Glenn H., and Paul Diesing, *Conflict Among Nations: Bargaining, Decision Making and System Structure in International Crises* (Princeton: Princeton University Press, 1977).

Sonyel, Salahi Ramadan, *The Muslims of Bosnia: The Genocide of a People* (Markfield: The Islamic Foundation, 1994).

Stein, Arthur A., *Why Nations Cooperate: Circumstance and Choice in International Relations* (Ithaca: Cornell University Press, 1990).

Sureda, A. Rigo, *The Evolution of the Right to Self-Determination: A Study of United Nations Practice* (Leiden: A.W. Sijthoff, 1973).

Taber, Robert, *War of the Flea: A Study of Guerrilla Warfare Theory and Practice* (St. Albans: Paladin, 1970).
Taw, Jennifer Morrison, and Bruce Hoffman, *The Urbanization of Insurgency: The Potential Challenge to U.S. Army Operations* (Santa Monica: RAND, 1994).
Thakur, Ramesh, *International Peacekeeping in Lebanon: United Nations Authority and Multinational Force* (Boulder: Westview Press, 1987).
Thomas, Caroline, *New States, Sovereignty and Intervention* (Aldershot: Gower, 1985).
Touval, Saadia, *The Peace Brokers: Mediators in the Arab–Israeli Conflict, 1948–1979* (Princeton: Princeton University, 1982).
Touval, Saadia, and I. William Zartman, *International Mediation in Theory and Practice* (Boulder: Westview Press, 1985).
Tulchin, Joseph S., with Gary Bland (eds), *Is There a Transition to Democracy in El Salvador?* (Boulder: Lynne Rienner Publishers, 1992).
United Nations, *The Blue Helmets: A Review of United Nations Peacekeeping* (New York: United Nations, 1990).
El Salvador Agreements: The Path to Peace (New York: United Nations, 1992).
United Nations Office of Legal Affairs Codification Division, *Handbook on the Peaceful Settlement of Disputes Between States* (New York: United Nations, 1992).
United Nations Department of Public Information, *Yearbook of the United Nations* (New York: United Nations, 1969–1994).
Urquhart, Brian, *Hammarskjold* (New York: Alfred A. Knopf, 1973).
A Life In Peace and War (New York: W.W. Norton and Company, 1987).
Van Ness, Peter, *Revolution and Chinese Foreign Policy: Peking's Support for Wars of National Liberation* (Berkeley: University of California Press, 1971).
Vickery, Michael, *Kampuchea: Politics, Economics and Society* (London: Frances Pinter, 1986).
Vincent, R.J., *Nonintervention and International Order* (Princeton: Princeton University Press, 1974).
Vines, Alex, *Renamo: Terrorism in Mozambique* (Bloomington: Indiana University Press, 1991).
Vulliamy, Ed, *Seasons in Hell: Understanding Bosnia's War* (London: Simon and Schuster, 1994).
Waltz, Kenneth N., *Man, the State, and War: A Theoretical Analysis* (New York: Columbia University Press, 1954).
Theory of International Politics (Massachusetts: Addison-Wesley Publishing Company, 1979).
White, N.D., *The United Nations and the Maintenance of International Peace and Security* (Manchester: Manchester University Press, 1990).
Wilkinson, Paul, *Terrorism and the Liberal State* (Basingstoke: Macmillan, 1986).
Woodward, Bob, *Veil: The Secret Wars of the CIA 1981–1987* (London: Headline, 1987).
The Commanders (New York: Simon and Schuster, 1991).
Woodward, Peter, and Murray Forsyth (eds), *Conflict and Peace in the Horn of Africa: Federalism and Its Alternatives* (Aldershot: Dartmouth, 1994).
Yoder, Amos, *The Evolution of the United Nations System* (New York: United Nations, 1989).
Zartman, I. William, *Ripe for Resolution: Conflict and Intervention in Africa* (New York: Oxford University Press, 1989).

Zartman, I. William, and Maureen Berman, *The Practical Negotiator* (New Haven: Yale University Press, 1982).

Secondary Sources: Articles

Abram, Morris B., 'The United Nations and Human Rights', *Foreign Affairs*, Vol. 47, No. 2, January 1969, pp. 363–74.

Alden, Chris, and Mark Simpson, 'Mozambique: A Delicate Peace', *Journal of Modern African Studies*, Vol. 31, No. 1, 1993, pp. 109–30.

Alvarez, Fransisco A., 'Transition Before the Transition: The Case of El Salvador', *Latin American Perspectives*, Issue 56, Vol. 15, No. 1, Winter 1988, pp. 78–92.

Anderson, Thomas P., 'El Salvador's Dim Prospects', *Current History*, Vol. 85, No. 507, January 1986, pp. 9–37.

Ayisi, Ruth Ansah, 'And Now Peace', *Africa Report*, Vol. 37, No. 6, pp. 31–3.

Bailey, Sydney D., 'New Light on Abstentions in the UN Security Council', *International Affairs*, Vol. 50, No. 4, October 1974, pp. 554–73.

'Some Procedural Problems in the UN General Assembly', *The World Today*, Vol. 31, No. 1, January 1975, pp. 24–8.

'The UN Security Council: Evolving Practice', *The World Today*, Vol. 34, No. 3, March 1978, pp. 100–6.

'The United Nations and the Termination of Armed Conflict, 1946–64', *International Affairs*, Vol. 58, No. 3, Summer 1982, pp. 465–75.

Baker, Caleb, 'Manhunt for Aideed: Why the Rangers Came Up Empty-Handed', *Armed Forces Journal*, December 1993, p. 18.

Baloyra, Enrique A., 'The Seven Plagues of El Salvador', *Current History*, Vol. 86, No. 524, December 1987, pp. 413–34.

'The Persistent Conflict In El Salvador', *Current History*, Vol. 90, No. 554, March 1991, pp. 413–34.

Bender, Gerald J., 'Peacemaking in Southern Africa: The Luanda–Pretoria Tug-of-War', *Third World Quarterly*, Vol. 11, No. 2, April 1989, pp. 15–30.

Bell-Fialkoff, Andrew, 'A Brief History of Ethnic Cleansing', *Foreign Affairs*, Vol. 72, No. 3, Summer 1993, pp. 110–21.

Berdal, Mats, 'Whither UN Peacekeeping?', *Adelphi Paper 281* (London: Brassey's and IISS, October 1993).

'Fateful Encounter: The United States and UN Peacekeeping', *Survival*, Vol. 36, No. 1, Spring 1994, pp. 30–50.

Bercovitch, Jacob, 'International Mediation: A Study of the Incidence, Strategies and Conditions of Successful Outcomes', *Cooperation and Conflict*, Vol. 21, No. 3, 1986, pp. 155–68.

'International Mediation and Dispute Settlement: Evaluating Conditions for Successful Mediation', *Negotiation Journal*, Vol. 7, No. 1, January 1991, pp. 17–30.

Bercovitch, Jacob, and Richard Wells, 'Evaluating Mediation Strategies: A Theoretical and Empirical Analysis', *Peace and Change*, Vol. 18, No. 1, January 1993, pp. 3–25.

Berkowitz, Bruce D., 'Documentation: Rules of Engagement for U.N. Peacekeeping Forces in Bosnia', *Orbis*, Vol. 38, No. 4, Fall 1994, pp. 635–46.

Biles, Peter, 'Anarchy Rules', *Africa Report*, Vol. 37, No. 4, July/August 1992, pp. 30–3.

Boerma, Maureen, 'The United Nations Interim Force in the Lebanon: Peacekeeping in a Domestic Conflict', *Millenium*, Vol. 8, No. 1, Spring 1979, pp. 51–63.
Boutros-Ghali, Boutros, 'UN Peacekeeping in a New Era: A New Chance for Peace', *The World Today*, Vol. 49, No. 4, April 1993, pp. 66–9.
'An Agenda For Peace: One Year Later', *Orbis*, Vol. 37, No. 3, Summer 1993, pp. 323–32.
Campbell, Donald T., '"Degrees of Freedom" and the Case Study', *Comparative Political Studies*, Vol. 8, No. 2, July 1975, pp. 178–93.
Carment, David, 'The International Dimensions of Ethnic Conflict: Concepts, Indicators and Theory', *Journal of Peace Research*, Vol. 30, No. 2, May 1993, pp. 137–50.
Chanda, Nayan, 'Civil War in Cambodia?' *Foreign Policy*, No. 76, Fall 1989, pp. 26–43.
Chipman, John, 'Managing the Politics of Parochialism', *Survival*, Vol. 35, No. 1, Spring 1993, pp. 143–70.
Chumakova, M., 'The Struggle Against Interventionism and Reaction in El Salvador', *International Affairs* (USSR), No. 11, November 1985, pp. 46–82.
Claude, Inis L. Jr., 'Collective Legitimation as a Political Function of the United Nations', *International Organization*, Vol. 20, No. 3, 1966, pp. 367–79.
Constable, Pamela, 'At War's End in El Salvador', *Current History*, Vol. 92, No. 572, March 1993, pp. 106–11.
Cooper, Allan D., 'UN-Supervised Elections in Namibia: A Critical Analysis', *Without Prejudice*, Vol. 3, No. 1, 1990, pp. 45–69.
Cooper, Robert, and Mats Berdal, 'Outside Intervention in Ethnic Conflicts', *Survival*, Vol. 35, No. 1, Spring 1993, pp. 118–42.
Crocker, Chester A., 'The Lessons of Somalia: Not Everything Went Wrong', *Foreign Affairs*, Vol. 74, No. 3, May/June 1995, pp. 2–8.
Daley, Tad, 'Can the UN Stretch to Fit Its Future?', *The Bulletin of Atomic Scientists*, Vol. 48, No. 3, April 1992, pp. 38–42.
Department of Social Sciences, Universidad de El Salvador, 'An Analysis of the Correlation of Forces in El Salvador', *Latin American Perspectives*, Issue 55, Vol. 14, No. 4, Fall 1987, pp. 426–52.
Dobbie, Charles, 'A Concept for Post-Cold War Peacekeeping', *Survival*, Vol. 36, No. 3, Autumn 1994, pp. 121–48.
Donnelly, Jack, 'Recent Trends in UN Human Rights Activity: Description and Polemic', *International Organization*, Vol. 35, No. 4, Autumn 1981, pp. 633–55.
'International Human Rights: A Regime Analysis', *International Organization*, Vol. 40, No. 3, Summer 1986, pp. 599–642.
Duncan, Alistair, 'Operating in Bosnia', *RUSI Journal*, June 1994, pp. 11–18.
Etcheson, Craig, 'Civil War and the Coalition Government of Democratic Kampuchea', *Third World Quarterly*, Vol. 9, No. 1, January 1987, pp. 187–202.
'The "Peace" in Cambodia', *Current History*, Vol. 91, No. 569, December 1992, pp. 413–17.
Finkel, Vicki R., 'Brothers in Arms', *Africa Report*, Vol. 37, No. 2, March–April 1992, pp. 60–4.
FMLN/FDR, 'Proposal of the FMLN/FDR', *Latin American Perspectives*, Issue 55, Vol. 14, No. 4, Fall 1987, pp. 481–6.
Fromuth, Peter J., 'The Making of a Security Community: The United Nations

After the Cold War', *Journal of International Affairs*, Vol. 46, No. 2, Winter 1993, pp. 359–60.
Fuesser, Ulrich, and Gerhard Will, 'Cambodia: No Peace in Sight', *Aussenpolitik*, Vol. 42, No. 2, 1991, pp. 200–8.
Fukuyama, Francis, 'Gorbachev and the Third World', *Foreign Affairs*, Vol. 64, No. 4, Spring 1986, pp. 715–31.
Garcia, Jose Z., 'El Salvador: Legitimizing the Government', *Current History*, Vol. 84, No. 500, March 1985, pp. 101–36.
'Democratic Consolidation in El Salvador', *Current History*, Vol. 87, No. 533, December 1988, pp. 421–38.
Gompert, David, 'How to Defeat Serbia', *Foreign Affairs*, Vol. 73, No. 4, July/August 1994, pp. 31–47.
Goulding, Marrack, 'The Evolution of United Nations Peacekeeping', *International Affairs*, Vol. 69, No. 3, 1993, pp. 451–64.
Gow, James, 'Towards a Settlement in Bosnia: The Military Dimension', *The World Today*, Vol. 50, No. 5, May 1994, pp. 96–9.
Grenier, Yvon, 'Understanding the FMLN: A Glossary of Five Words', *Conflict Quarterly*, Spring 1991, pp. 51–75.
Grieco, Joseph M., 'Anarchy and the Limits of Cooperation: A Realist Critique of the Newest Liberal Institutionalism', *International Organization*, Vol. 42, No. 3, Summer 1988, pp. 485–507.
Gunn, Gillian, 'Unfulfilled Expectations in Angola', *Current History*, Vol. 89, No. 547, May 1990, pp. 213–34.
Haaglund, Gustav, 'Peacekeeping in a Modern War Zone', *Survival*, Vol. 32, No. 3, May/June 1990, pp. 233–40.
Haas, Ernst B., 'Regime Decay: Conflict Management and International Organizations, 1945–1981', *International Organization*, Vol. 37, No. 2, Spring 1983, pp. 189–235.
Hall, M., and T. Young, 'Recent Constitutional Developments in Mozambique', *Journal of African Law*, Vol. 35, Nos. 1–2, 1991, pp. 102–115.
Halliday, Fred, '"The Sixth Great Power": On the Study of Revolution and International Relations', *Review of International Studies*, Vol. 16, No. 3, Summer 1990, pp. 207–21.
Hamill, James, 'Angola's Road From Under the Rubble', *The World Today*, Vol. 50, No. 1, January 1994, pp. 6–11.
Harbottle, Michael, 'The Strategy of Third Party Interventions in Conflict Resolution', *International Journal*, Vol. 35, No. 1, Winter 1979–80, pp. 118–31.
Hassner, Pierre, 'Beyond Nationalism and Internationalism: Ethnicity and World Order', *Survival*, Vol. 35, No. 2, Summer 1993, pp. 49–65.
Heraclides, Alexis, 'Secessionist Minorities and External Involvement', *International Organization*, Vol. 44, No. 3, Summer 1990, pp. 341–78.
'The International Dimension of Minority Separatism: An Attempt at Unravelling a Pandora Box', *Paradigms*, Vol. 6, No. 1, Spring 1992, pp. 117–39.
Hervouet, Gerard, 'The Cambodian Conflict: the Difficulties of Intervention and Compromise', *International Journal*, Vol. 45, No. 2, Spring 1990, pp. 258–91.
Heywood, Linda M., 'Unita and Ethnic Nationalism in Angola', *Journal of Modern African Studies*, Vol. 27, No. 1, 1989, pp. 47–66.
Higgins, Rosalyn, 'The New United Nations and the Former Yugoslavia', *International Affairs*, Vol. 69, No. 3, 1993, pp. 465–83.

Hodgson, Melida N., 'When to Accept, When to Abstain: A Framework for U.N. Election Monitoring', *New York University Journal of International Law and Politics*, Vol. 25, No. 1, Fall 1992, pp. 137–73.
Hoffman, Stanley, 'International Organization and the International System', *International Organization*, Vol. 24, No. 3, 1970, pp. 389–413.
Holiday, David, and William Stanley, 'Building the Peace: Preliminary Lessons From El Salvador', *Journal of International Affairs*, Vol. 46, No. 2, Winter 1993, pp. 415–38.
Holst, Johan Jorgen, 'Enhancing Peacekeeping Operations', *Survival*, Vol. 32, No. 3, May/June 1990, pp. 264–75.
Huband, Mark, 'When Yankee Goes Home', *Africa Report*, Vol. 38, No. 2, March/April 1993, pp. 20–3.
'The Politics of Violence', *Africa Report*, Vol. 38, No. 5, September/October 1993, pp. 13–19.
Huntington, Samuel P., 'How Countries Democratize', *Political Science Quarterly*, Vol. 106, No. 4, 1991–1992, pp. 579–616.
James, Alan, 'The Realism of Realism: The State and the Study of International Relations', *Review of International Studies*, Vol. 15, 1989, pp. 215–29.
'Internal Peacekeeping: A Dead End for the UN?', *Security Dialogue*, Vol. 24, No. 4, December 1993, pp. 359–68.
'The Problems of Internal Peacekeeping', *Diplomacy and Statecraft*, Vol. 5, No. 1, March 1994, pp. 21–46.
Jennar, Raoul M., 'UNTAC: "International Triumph" in Cambodia?', *Security Dialogue*, Vol. 25, No. 2, 1994, pp. 145–56.
Jonah, James O.C., 'The Military Talks at Kilometre 101: The U.N.'s Effectiveness as a Third Party', *Negotiation Journal*, Vol. 6, No. 1, January 1990, pp. 53–70.
Katz, Mark N., 'Mechanisms of Russian-American Conflict Resolution', *International Journal of Group Tensions*, Vol. 23, No. 1, 1993, pp. 25–42.
Klintworth, Gary, 'China's Indochina Policy', *Journal of Northeast Asian Studies*, Fall 1989, pp. 25–43.
Kozyrev, Andrei, and Gennadi Gatilov, 'The UN Peacemaking System: Problems and Prospects', *International Affairs* (USSR), No. 12, December 1990, pp. 79–88.
Lefever, Ernest W., 'The Limits of UN Intervention in the Third World', *Review of Politics*, Vol. 30, No. 3, January 1968, pp. 3–18.
Leifer, Michael, 'Power-Sharing and Peacemaking in Cambodia', *SAIS Review*, Vol. 12, No. 1, Winter–Spring 1992, pp. 132–48.
Luttwak, Edward N., 'Where Are the Great Powers?', *Foreign Affairs*, Vol. 73, No. 4, July/August 1994, pp. 23–8.
MacKinlay, John, 'Powerful Peacekeepers', *Survival*, Vol. 32, No. 3, May/June 1990, pp. 241–50.
Maier, Karl, 'Between Washington and Pretoria', *Africa Report*, Vol. 33, No. 6, November–December 1988, pp. 42–4.
Mason, Paul E., and Thomas F. Marsteller Jr., 'U.N. Mediation: More Effective Options', *SAIS Review*, Vol. 5, No. 2, Summer/Fall 1985, pp. 271–84.
McCoy, Jennifer, Larry Garber, and Robert Pastor, 'Pollwatching and Peacemaking', *Journal of Democracy*, Vol. 2, No. 4, Fall 1991, pp. 102–114.
McGregor, Charles, 'China, Vietnam, and the Cambodian Conflict: Beijing's End Game Strategy', *Asian Survey*, Vol. 30, No. 3, March 1990, pp. 266–83.

Meldrum, Andrew, 'Lessons From Angola', *Africa Report*, Vol. 38, No. 1, January–February 1993, pp. 22–4.
'Peace At Last', *Africa Report*, Vol. 38, No. 2, March/April 1993, pp. 47–50.
Moore, Patrick, 'Bosnian Impasse Poses Dilemmas for Diplomacy', *Radio Free Europe*, Vol. 2, No. 14, 2 April 1993, pp. 28–30.
Morgan, Glenda, 'Violence in Mozambique: Towards an Understanding of Renamo', *Journal of Modern African Studies*, Vol. 28, No. 4, 1990, pp. 603–19.
Morillon, Phillipe, 'U.N. Operations in Bosnia: Lessons and Realities', *RUSI Journal*, Vol. 138, No. 6, December 1993, pp. 31–5.
Moss, Ambler H. Jr., 'Peace in Central America?', *Survival*, Vol. 32, No. 5, September/October 1990, pp. 421–36.
Munslow, Barry, 'Democratization in Africa', *Parliamentary Affairs*, Vol. 46, No. 4, October 1993, pp. 478–90.
Omaar, Rakiya, 'Somalia: At War With Itself', *Current History*, Vol. 91, No. 565, May 1992, pp. 230–4.
Page, Brigadier M.B., 'Somalia: Background and Prospects', *RUSI Journal*, October 1993, pp. 6–14.
Parsons, Sir Anthony, 'The United Nations in the Post-Cold War Era', *International Relations*, Vol. 11, No. 3, December 1992, pp. 189–200.
Paschall, Rod, 'Tactical Exercises: The Impartial Buffer', *MHQ*, Vol. 5, No. 1, Autumn 1992, pp. 52–3.
Pazzanita, Anthony G., 'The Conflict Resolution Process in Angola', *Journal of Modern African Studies*, Vol. 29, No. 1, 1991, pp. 83–114.
Pedler, John, 'Cambodia: Danger and Opportunity for the West', *The World Today*, Vol. 45, No. 2, February 1989, pp. 19–21.
Pike, Douglas, 'The Cambodian Peace Process: Summer of 1989', *Asian Survey*, Vol. 29, No. 9, September 1989, pp. 842–52.
Posen, Barry R., 'The Security Dilemma and Ethnic Conflict', *Survival*, Vol. 35, No. 1, Spring 1993, pp. 27–47.
Radu, Michael, 'The Structure of the Salvadoran Left', *Orbis*, Vol. 28, No. 4, Winter 1985, pp. 673–84.
Ramet, Sabrina Petra, 'War in the Balkans', *Foreign Affairs*, Vol. 71, No. 4, Fall 1992, pp. 79–98.
Rifkind, Malcolm, 'Peacekeeping or Peacemaking? Implications and Prospects', *RUSI Journal*, Vol. 138, No. 2, April 1993, pp. 1–6.
Roberts, Adam, 'Humanitarian War: Military Intervention and Human Rights', *International Affairs*, Vol. 69, No. 3, 1993, pp. 429–49.
'The United Nations and International Security', *Survival*, Vol. 35, No. 2, Summer 1993, pp. 3–30.
Roberts, David, 'Cambodia: Problems of a UN-Brokered Peace', *The World Today*, Vol. 48, No. 7, July 1992, pp. 29–31.
Robinson, Linda, 'Why Central America is Still Not Democratic', *SAIS Review*, Vol. 12, No. 2, Summer–Fall 1992, pp. 81–96.
Ruggie, John Gerard, 'Wandering the Void: Charting the UN's New Strategic Role', *Foreign Affairs*, Vol. 72, No. 5, November/December 1993, pp. 26–31.
Samatar, Abdi Ismail, 'Destruction of the State and Society in Somalia: Beyond the Tribal Convention', *Journal of Modern African Studies*, Vol. 30, No. 4, 1992, pp. 111–28.
Schroeder, Paul, 'Historical Reality vs. Neorealist Theory', *International Security*, Vol. 19, No. 1, Summer 1994, pp. 108–48.

Sharp, Jane M.O., 'Intervention in Bosnia – The Case For', *The World Today*, Vol. 49, No. 2, February 1993, pp. 29–32.

Sidaway, James D., and David Simon, 'Geopolitical Transition and State Formation: the Changing Political Geographies of Angola, Mozambique and Namibia', *Journal of Southern African Studies*, Vol. 19, No. 1, March 1993, pp. 6–28.

Simpson, Chris, 'The Undemocratic Game', *Africa Report*, Vol. 38, No. 4, July–August 1993, pp. 49–51.

Skjelsbaek, Kjell, 'Peaceful Settlement of Disputes by the United Nations and Other Intergovernmental Bodies', *Cooperation and Conflict*, Vol. 21, No. 3, 1986, pp. 139–54.

Smith, Anthony D., 'The Ethnic Sources of Nationalism', *Survival*, Vol. 35, No. 1, Spring 1993, pp. 48–62.

Smith, Patrick, 'Angola: Free and Fair Elections!', *Review of African Political Economy*, Vol. 55, November 1992, pp. 101–6.

Solarz, Stephen J., 'Cambodia and the International Community', *Foreign Affairs*, Vol. 69, No. 2, Spring 1990, pp. 99–115.

Somerville, Keith, 'Angola: An End to the Misery in Sight?', *The World Today*, Vol. 47, No. 5, May 1991, pp. 72–3.

Spence, J.E., 'A Deal for Southern Africa', *The World Today*, Vol. 45, No. 5, May 1989, pp. 80–3.

Stein, Eric, 'The United Nations and the Enforcement of Peace', *Michigan Journal of International Law*, Vol. 10, No. 1, Winter 1989, pp. 304–16.

Stevenson, Jonathon, 'Hope Restored in Somalia?', *Foreign Policy*, No. 91, Summer 1993, pp. 138–54.

Stoelting, David, 'The Challenge of UN-Monitored Elections in Independent Nations', *Stanford Journal of International Law*, Vol. 28, No. 2, Spring 1992, pp. 371–424.

Sullivan, Joseph G., 'How Peace Came to El Salvador', *Orbis*, Vol. 38, No. 1, Winter 1994, pp. 83–98.

Sweetman, A.D., 'Close Air Support Over Bosnia-Herzegovina', *RUSI Journal*, August 1994, pp. 34–6.

Thomas, Trisha, 'Into the Unknown: Can the United Nations Bring Peace to Cambodia?', *Journal of International Affairs*, Vol. 44, No. 1, Spring 1990, pp. 495–515.

Tickell, Sir Crispin, 'The Role of the Security Council in World Affairs', *Georgia Journal of International and Comparative Law*, Vol. 18, No. 3, Winter 1988, pp. 307–17.

Touval, Saadia, 'Multilateral Negotiation: An Analytic Approach', *Negotiation Journal*, Vol. 5, No. 2, April 1989, pp. 159–73.

'Why the U.N. Fails', *Foreign Affairs*, Vol. 73, No. 5, September/October 1994, pp. 44–57.

Turley, William S., 'The Khmer War: Cambodia After Paris', *Survival*, Vol. 32, No. 5, September/October 1990, pp. 437–53.

Tvedten, Inge, 'U.S. Policy Towards Angola Since 1975', *Journal of Modern African Studies*, Vol. 10, No. 1, 1992, pp. 31–52.

Umhoefer, Carol, 'United Nations: Towards a U.N.-Sponsored Cambodian Solution', *Harvard International Law Journal*, Vol. 32, No. 1, Winter 1991, pp. 275–85.

United Nations Department of Public Information, 'Towards Peace in Cambodia', DP1091, September 1990.

United Nations Department of Public Information, 'The Peace Process in El Salvador and the United Nations: Fact Sheet 1', DPI/1149A-40697, 1 July 1991.

United Nations Department of Public Information, 'Mozambique: Out of the Ruins of War', Africa Recovery Briefing Paper No. 8, May 1993 (New York: United Nations, 1993).

United Nations Briefing Paper, 'United Nations Observer Mission in El Salvador', DPI/1306/Rev.2, 31 October 1993.

Urquhart, Brian, 'The UN: From Peacekeeping to a Collective System?', in *Adelphi Paper 265, New Dimensions in International Security Part 1* (London: Brassey's and IISS, 1991/92).

van der Kroef, Justus M., 'Cambodia: Toward the Fourth Indochina War', *Asian Thought and Society*, Vol. 14, Nos. 41–2, May–October 1989, pp. 116–35.

'Cambodia in 1990: The Elusive Peace', *Asian Survey*, Vol. 31, No. 1, January 1991, pp. 94–102.

Waltz, Kenneth N., 'The Emerging Structure of International Politics', *International Security*, Vol. 18, No. 2, Fall 1993, pp. 44–9.

Weiss, Thomas G., and Meryl A. Kessler, 'Resurrecting Peacekeeping: The Superpowers and Conflict Management', *Third World Quarterly*, Vol. 12, No. 3, July 1993, pp. 124–46.

Wesley, Michael, 'The Cambodian Waltz: The Khmer Rouge and United Nations Intervention', *Terrorism and Political Violence*, Vol. 7, No. 4, Winter 1995, pp. 60–81.

'Blue Berets or Blindfolds? Peacekeeping and the Hostage Effect', *International Peacekeeping*, Vol. 2, No. 4, Winter 1995, pp. 457–82.

Will, Gerhard, 'The Elections in Cambodia: Taking Stock of a UN Mission', *Aussenpolitik*, Vol. 44, No. 4, 1993, pp. 393–402.

Young, Tom, 'The MNR/Renamo: External and Internal Dynamics', *African Affairs*, Vol. 89, No. 357, October 1990, pp. 491–509.

Zametica, John, 'The Yugoslav Conflict', *Adelphi Paper 270* (London: IISS, 1992).

Zubeck, Josephine M., Dean G. Pruitt, Robert S. Pierce, Neil B. McGillicuddy, and Helena Syna, 'Disputant and Mediator Behaviours Affecting Short-Term Success in Mediation', *Journal of Conflict Resolution*, Vol. 36, No. 3, September 1992, pp. 546–72.

Index

Accordos da Paz (Angola), 99–109
Addis Ababa Agreement (Somalia), 70, 75
Afghanistan, 5, 100
Agenda for Peace (1992), 68, 75
aid, foreign, 13, 59, 69, 70, 84, 86, 87, 89
Aideed, General Mohammed Farah, 68, 71, 73, 75, 77, 78
  manhunt for, 77–8
  see also USC-SNA
Ajello, Aldo, 89–90, 92
  see also ONUMOZ
Akashi, Yasushi (1931–), 114
  see also UNTAC
Ali Mahdi Mohammed, 68, 71–80
  see also Manifesto Alliance
alliances, 33
Alvor Agreement (Angola), 102
anarchy, 3–4, 8, 17–18, 23
Angola, 5, 82, 84, 87, 98–109, 126
  FNLA, 98
  MPLA, 98–99, 101–9
  Savimbi, Jonas (1934–), 101, 102, 105, 106, 108
  Unita, 87, 98–9, 101–9, 127
Anstee, Dame Margaret J. (1926–), 104, 108
  see also UNAVEM II
anti-imperialism, 71, 72, 73, 76, 105
Association of South East Asian Nations (ASEAN), 109, 110–11, 119
Australia, 111, 121
authoritarianism, 5, 51, 114

Baker, James A. III (1930–), 50
balkanisation, 11
banditry, 60, 68, 93
Bangladesh, 79
bargaining, 19–20, 90
Belgium, 73, 79
Besmertnykh, Alexander A. (1933–), 50
bloc conflict, 4, 5, 60, 98–9, 106, 110
Bosnia-Herzegovina, 31–49, 126, 128, 129, 130
  comparison to Somalia, 69
  government of, 35, 37, 42–4
  Muslim–Croat alliance, 38, 43, 45
  parliament of, 43
  Washington Agreement, March 1994, 38, 43
Bosnian Croats, 32, 37–8, 39, 40, 42–3
  Muslim–Croat alliance, 38, 43, 45
Bosnian Muslims, 32, 39, 40
  Muslim–Croat alliance, 38, 43, 45
Bosnian Serbs, 31–49, 127
  intractability of, 38–9, 44–5, 47–8
  Karadzic, Radovan (1945–), 38, 44
  Mladic, Ratko, 38, 48
  Republika Srpska, 42, 45, 48
  VRS (Bosnian Serb Army), 32, 38
Botswana, 83, 106
Boutros-Ghali, Boutros (1922–), 12, 14, 68, 69, 73, 119
Burundi, 106
Bush, George H.W. (1924–), 59, 60, 61, 69

CAC (Cessation of Armed Conflict Mechanism (Mozambique)), 86, 90
Cambodia, 5, 98, 109–24, 126, 130
  Coalition Government of Democratic Kampuchea (CGDK), 109
  Funcinpec, 109, 113
  Ieng Sary, 121
  Khieu Samphan (1932–) 121
  Khmer Rouge, 109–24, 127
  KPNLF, 109, 113
  non-Communist resistance, 111, 113
  Nuon Bunno, General, 114
  Pol Pot (1928–), 113, 119, 121

Cambodia – *continued*
Son Sen (1930–), 121
State of Cambodia (SoC), 112–13, 115
'Voice of the Greater Union Front of Cambodia' (Khmer Rouge Radio), 119, 121
Cameroon, 106
Canada, 100
cantonment of belligerents, 89, 118
Cape Verde, 100, 106, 108
Carrington Arbitration Commission, 36
see also Bosnia-Herzegovina
Castroism, 49, 55
CCF (Ceasefire Commission (Mozambique)), 86, 90
CCFA (Commission for the Formation of the Armed Forces (Angola)), 104
Central African Republic, 106
Central America, 50–1, 54, 60
Central Europe, 47
Chad, 106
China, People's Republic, 3, 109, 110–11, 119–20
military support/transfers, 83, 120
Qian, Qichen (1928–), 119
Christiani, Alfredo, 50, 51, 52, 57
civil war belligerents, 13, 14, 15–28, 30
calculations of, 15–21, 22–7, 30, 53, 67, 87–8, 90, 103, 105, 117
coercion of, 13, 14, 22, 41–2, 45, 47–8, 116–17
commitments, 31
cooperativeness, 3, 14, 22, 23–5, 26, 27, 28, 43–4, 53, 62, 73, 77, 89, 90, 104–5, 107, 110, 112, 117
expectations, 20, 72
incumbents, 13, 14, 16
insurgents, 13, 14, 16
leverage over, 16, 20, 22, 25, 26, 44, 45–6, 58, 68, 111, 120, 129
opportunism, 16, 17–19, 21, 23–5, 31
persuasion of, 13, 41, 43, 116–17
reincorporation to society, 56, 86, 96, 98, 104
self-reliance, 7–18, 21, 23, 27
supporters, 17, 52, 113, 114
veracity of undertakings, 43, 80–1
weaponry, 15, 37–8, 45–6, 76, 80, 120
civil war conflict dynamics, 1–2, 15–21, 26, 67, 96, 98, 125–32
in Angola, 122–4
in Bosnia, 31–2, 37–9
in Cambodia, 111, 114–15, 122–4
in El Salvador, 51, 57, 62
in Mozambique, 87–9, 93, 94
in Somalia, 69, 71–2, 73, 78, 81, 94
civil wars, 1–28
perceptions of, 7, 10, 15, 16, 22, 23–5, 27, 30, 47, 70–1, 75, 77–8
as security concerns, 4–5, 7, 8–9, 10, 14, 25, 32, 50, 52, 70, 83
clan warfare, 68, 71, 127
Clausewitz, Carl von (1780–1831), 18
Clinton, William J. (Bill) (1946–), 34, 69
CMVF (Joint Verification and Monitoring Commission (Angola)), 104
Coalition Government of Democratic Kampuchea (CGDK), 109
non-Communist resistance, 111, 113
cohesion, belligerents', 19, 27–8, 92–3
in the Bosnian Serbs, 47–8
extremism, 28
factionalism, 27–8, 48
in the FMLN, 61–2
in the Khmer Rouge, 113, 114, 121
in Renamo, 82
in Unita, 108
in the USC-SNA, 71, 80
cohesion, UN, 8, 9, 21, 22, 27, 46–7, 80–1, 88, 107–8, 120–1, 123, 128

Cold War, 4, 5, 50, 79, 98, 100, 128
  end of, 50, 51, 60, 107, 110
  post-Cold War era, 1, 2, 5, 6, 49, 96, 119
collective legitimation, 6, 7, 12, 13, 20, 132
Columbia, 59
Comision Nacional para la Consolidacion de la Paz (COPAZ) (El Salvador), 61
compliance, 9
  see also multilateralism
conflict
  bases of, 11, 12, 23, 29, 51, 97, 100
  de-escalation, 89
  international, 5, 10, 12, 13, 19, 127–8
  'ripeness' for resolution, 40, 51, 57, 62, 74, 87–8, 131
conflict analysis capability, UN, 130–2
conflict resolution, 1, 2, 3, 7, 8, 9, 11, 12, 13, 15, 29–31, 35, 74, 96, 110–11, 126, 130
  coercion towards, 13, 14, 22, 41–2, 45, 47–8, 116–17
  leverage for, 16, 20, 22, 25, 26, 44, 45–6, 58, 68, 111, 120, 129
  persuasion towards, 13, 41, 43, 116–17
  proposals, 10–12, 15, 16, 25, 30, 39, 67
conflict stakes/objectives, 15–20, 25, 30, 67, 71–2, 85–6, 113
  irridentism, 16
  power, 13, 15–20, 25, 67, 71–2, 85, 97, 102, 127
  secession, 16, 31, 37, 43
  survival, 13, 17, 24, 25, 67, 71–2, 86, 90, 97
  zero-sum, 101, 102
Congo, 106
CORE (Committee for Reintegration of Demobilized Personnel (Mozambique)), 86
correlation of forces, 58, 113, 115
Costa Rica, 60
Côte d'Ivoire, 100, 106
counter-insurgency, 4, 17, 49, 58, 84–5, 129
Croatia, 31 37, 38–40
CSC (Supervisory and Monitoring Commission (Mozambique)), 89, 90
Cuba, 49, 51, 57, 60, 100, 101
  military assistance/transfers, 99, 103, 106
Cyprus, 11

Dayton Accord (Bosnia), 32, 48
de Soto, Alvaro (1943–), 50, 57
  see also El Salvador; mediation
death squads (El Salvador), 49, 51, 52, 55, 57, 58, 61
demobilization, 2, 50, 56, 66, 70, 82, 84, 86, 87, 89, 90, 104–5, 106, 110, 112, 113, 114, 116, 118, 120, 127
  demobilization timetables, 89, 116
democracy, 5, 11, 96–8, 101–2, 112, 127
democratization, 55, 84, 85–6, 100, 102
Department of Peacekeeping Operations, 74, 88, 131
  Planning and Co-ordination Cell, 131
  Situation Monitoring Centre, 131
Department of Political Affairs, 131
diplomacy, 9, 34, 35, 38, 66, 129
diplomatic pressure, 25, 26
disarmament of belligerents, 50, 66, 70, 82, 84, 89, 93, 105, 110, 112, 114, 116
Djibouti, 70
Djibouti Accords (Somalia), 71
Dlakama, Afonso, 82, 92
Duarte, José Napoleon (1925–86), 49, 51

East Asia, 110
Eastern Europe, 51
Egypt, 73, 79
El Salvador, 5, 31, 49–65, 128
  ARENA Party, 51, 52, 54, 62
  Christiani, Alfredo, 50, 51, 52, 57

El Salvador – *continued*
death squads, 49, 51, 52, 55, 57, 58, 61
Duarte, José Napoleon (1925–86), 49, 51
FMLN, 49–62, 127, 128
government of, 49–53, 128
security forces, 52
election monitoring, 2, 66, 82, 96–124
electoral process, security of, 105, 116
endorsement of results, 105, 112, 118
inspection, 104
neutral environment, ensuring, 112, 116, 117
registration, 105, 113, 114, 117
violations/irregularities, 104
voter education, 113, 114
see also UNAVEM II; UNTAC
elections, 96–8
in Angola, 98–109
in Bosnia, 37
in Cambodia, 110–24
in El Salvador, 51
fairness/authenticity, 97
legitimacy through, 97–8, 101, 102
in Mozambique, 82, 84, 88
as procedural solutions, 96–7
in Somalia, 70
Esquipulas Group, 50
Ethiopia, 70
ethnic cleansing, 31–2, 36–7, 38, 39, 45
ethnic conflict/motivations, 4, 5, 11–12, 16, 35, 36, 46, 101, 102, 105, 113, 127, 128
ethnic division/cantonisation, 36, 48
European Union, 31, 32, 33, 42, 69
external interference, 50, 51, 82–3, 106–7
external links, 21, 25, 26–7, 45–6, 64–5
of the Bosnian Serbs, 45–6
of the FMLN, 59–60
of Frelimo, 90–2, 95
of the Khmer Rouge, 120
of Renamo, 82, 90–2, 95
of the Salvadoran government, 59–60
of Unita, 107
of the USC-SNA, 79
see also aid; diplomatic pressure; sanctions; self-sufficiency; weapons transfers; zero-zero option

fact-finding missions, 15
UNAMIC, 115
FMLN, 49–62, 127, 128
FNLA, 98
Four Friends of the Secretary-General, 59–60
France, 3, 33–4, 43, 51, 79, 111, 120
Frelimo, 81–7, 128
Funcinpec, 109, 113
Coalition Government of Democratic Kampuchea (CGDK), 109

Gabon, 106
General Assembly, *see* UN General Assembly
genocide, 5, 82, 91, 109, 111, 120
Germany, 33, 34, 43, 47, 51
Kohl, Helmut, 34
Ghana, 100
Goulding, Marrack I. (1936–), 131
great powers, 3, 40, 43, 45, 48, 83, 108, 109, 110
Greater Serbia, concept of, 44
Greece, 34, 35, 45–6
Guatemala, 50, 60
guerrilla tactics, 120
Guinea-Bissau, 106
Gulf War/Desert Storm, 6, 14, 35, 69, 81, 132

historical enmities, 12
Holbrooke, Richard C. (1941–), 32, 48
Honduras, 60
Howe, Admiral Jonathan T., 75
see also Somalia; UNOSOM II
human rights, 5, 11, 16, 39, 40, 62
humanitarian crises, 32, 69, 74, 79, 83

humanitarian intervention, 5, 40, 69, 72, 78

ideology, 4, 11, 19, 26, 114, 121, 128
Ieng Sary, 121
  see also Khmer Rouge
IFOR, 132
impartiality, 23, 39, 63, 73, 75, 76, 77, 87, 114, 120, 131
independence, demands for, 37, 52
India, 79, 111, 119
Indonesia, 111, 120, 121
infiltration, 113
insurgency, 17, 49, 76, 82, 84, 106
intelligence, 76, 117, 131
International *ad hoc* Commission (Angola), 108
International Committee on the Former Yugoslavia (ICFY), 32, 39–48, 62, 126, 127
international community, 6, 31, 37, 38, 45, 60, 104, 118, 120, 121, 123, 126, 127, 130, 132
International Donor Conference, Mozambique, 90–1
international isolation/condemnation, 39–41, 75–6, 108, 117, 119, 123
international law, 20, 36
  uti possedetis, principle of, 36
international order, conceptions of, 7, 22
international public opinion, 13, 20, 35, 51, 63, 69, 74, 77, 83, 111
international representation, 16, 113
intervention, 4, 6, 16, 29, 66
  in Angola, 99–101, 107, 108–9, 123
  in Bosnia, 33–4, 131
  in Cambodia, 109, 120, 123
  casualties of, 6–7
  collective, 5–7, 91, 126
  costs of, 4, 6–7, 8, 10, 12, 13, 14, 80
  in El Salvador, 49, 50, 51, 52
  humanitarian, 5, 40, 69, 72, 78
  in Mozambique, 81
  in Somalia, 68–71, 72–8
  as a UN response, 6, 7, 9, 11, 131
  unilateral, 4
Iran, 79
  Iran–Iraq war, 111
irridentism, 16
Islam, 34–5, 40, 45, 46, 47, 69, 77
Italy, 70, 73, 79, 83, 90

Japan, 111, 119, 121
JNA (Yugoslav National Army), 31, 37

Karadzic, Radovan (1945–), 38, 44
Kenya, 70
Khieu Samphan (1932–), 121
  Khmer Rouge, 109–24, 127
Khmer Rouge, 109–24, 127
  Ieng Sary, 121
  Khieu Samphan (1932–), 121
  Nuon Bunno, General, 114
  Pol Pot (1928–), 113, 119, 121
  quadripartite proposal, 113, 118
  Son Sen (1930–), 121
  split within, 121
  'Voice of the Greater Union Front of Cambodia' (Khmer Rouge Radio), 119, 121
KPNLF, 109, 113
  Coalition Government of Democratic Kampuchea (CGDK), 109
  Funcinpec, 109, 113
  non-Communist resistance, 111, 113
Krajina, 31, 39, 42, 46

Lake, N. Anthony (1939–), 5
law
  domestic, 16
  international, 20, 36
League of Arab States (LAS), 70, 78
Lebanon, 11
legitimacy, international, 115, 117, 121
lift and strike, policy of, 34

Macedonia, 45
Malawi, 83
Malaysia, 79
Mali, 106

mandates, UN missions, 2, 3, 8, 9, 10, 12, 14, 15, 22, 27, 29–30, 43, 70, 100–1, 112–13, 121, 127, 129–30
  in Angola, 99–102
  in Bosnia, 32, 35–7
  in Cambodia, 110–12, 116
  clarity of, 9–10, 22, 27, 47–8
  in El Salvador, 51–3
  in Mozambique, 82–4
  in Somalia, 71–5, 77, 81, 82
Manifesto Alliance (Somalia), 73, 76, 94
Marxism/Marxists, 52, 81, 98, 101–2, 109
media, 5, 35, 39, 78, 79, 83, 105, 112
mediation, 1, 2, 13, 24, 29–65, 111, 119, 129
  bargaining positions, 40–1, 56, 121
  Caracas Agenda (El Salvador), 54, 56
  Contact Group Plan (Bosnia-Herzegovina), 32, 42–4
  double veto in, 30–1
  Geneva Framework (El Salvador), 56
  mediation formulas, 41, 53, 56–7, 58, 64, 128: deductive mediation formulas, 41, 43–4, 56, 64
  mediation timetables, 56
  normative solutions, 44, 130, 132
  preliminary talks, 53, 56, 85
  Serb–Croat proposal (Bosnia-Herzegovina), 32, 42–3
  Vance–Owen Plan (Bosnia-Herzegovina), 32, 42
Mexico, 59
Mexico City Agreement (El Salvador), 50
middle powers, 5, 83
military balance, 18–19, 22, 24, 26, 27, 63, 114–15, 120
  in Angola, 103
  in Bosnia, 34, 37, 39, 40–2
  in Cambodia, 110, 114–15
  in El Salvador, 49, 52–3, 54–5
  in Mozambique, 81–2, 87–8
  in Somalia, 73–4
military stalemate, 24, 82, 87
Milosevic, Slobodan (1941–), 38
mission design, 15, 21–2, 24–5, 123
  in Angola, 104–5
  appropriateness of, 11–13, 21–3, 25
  in Bosnia, 41–2
  in Cambodia, 115–16, 117–18
  in El Salvador, 55–8
  in Mozambique, 88–9
  in Somalia, 74–5
mission durability, 27–8
  in Angola, 107–8
  in Bosnia, 46–7
  in Cambodia, 120–1
  in El Salvador, 61
  in Mozambique, 92–3
  in Somalia, 79–81
mission failure, 1–3, 20, 93–4, 108, 125–32
mission presence, 23–4, 126
  in Angola, 102–3
  in Bosnia, 39–40, 63
  in Cambodia, 114
  in El Salvador, 53–5
  in Mozambique, 86–7, 88
  in Somalia, 72–4
mission weaknesses, 1–3, 15, 20–1, 22–7, 29, 30, 33–48, 60–70, 79, 96, 98, 125–32
  in Angola, 105, 122–4
  in Bosnia, 33–7, 41, 44, 45
  in Cambodia, 110, 114, 115, 116, 118, 122–4
  exposure to attack, 20, 73–5
  mission security, 105
  in Mozambique, 82–4, 88, 89, 93–4
  in Somalia, 70–1, 74–5, 77, 78, 81, 94
Mixed Military Working Group (Cambodia), 117
Mladic, Ratko, 38, 48
  see also Bosnian Serbs
Montenegro, 45
morale, belligerents', 13, 26, 27–8
  in the Bosnian Serbs, 31–2, 37–9, 45
  in the FMLN, 61–2, 103
  in the Khmer Rouge, 114–15, 120

morale, belligerents' – *continued*
in Renamo, 82
in Unita, 103, 108
in the USC-SNA, 71, 80
Morocco, 108
Mozambique, 68, 81–93, 100, 101, 106, 128
Dlakama, Afonso, 82, 92
Frelimo, 81–7, 128
Renamo, 81–94, 128
MPLA, 98–9, 101–9
multilateralism, 4, 6, 8, 12, 14, 27, 132
minimization of costs through, 4–8, 35, 88, 100, 104, 107–8, 128–30, 131

Namibia, 84, 100, 106
National Electoral Council, Angola, 106
nationalism, 71
negotiation, 8, 15, 22, 26, 30, 55–6, 89, 118–19
Nicaragua, 5, 49, 50, 51, 57, 60
Sandanistas, 60
Nigeria, 106
Nkomati Accord (Mozambique–South Africa), 85
Non-Aligned Movement, 35, 47, 78
non-Communist resistance, 111, 113
Coalition Government of Democratic Kampuchea (CGDK), 109
Funcinpec, 109, 113
KPNLF, 109, 113
non-Western states, 6, 79
normative solutions, 10–12, 22
in Bosnia, 36–7, 39
in Cambodia, 111–12
North Atlantic Treaty Organization (NATO), 32, 33, 34, 40, 41
Norway, 79
Nuon Bunno, General, 114
see also Khmer Rouge

objectives, civil war belligerents', 15–19, 22–4, 25, 26
of the Angolan government, 102
of the Bosnian Serbs, 37–9
of the Bosnian government, 37–9
of the FMLN, 52–3, 54, 57
of Frelimo, 85
of the Khmer Rouge, 113–15
of the Manifesto alliance, 71–2
of Renamo, 85–6
of the Salvadoran government, 51–2, 53, 57
of the SoC, 112–13
of Unita, 102
of the USC-SNA, 71–2
objectives, UN, 8, 15, 16, 20, 21–3
in Angola, 99–102
in Bosnia, 33–7
in Cambodia, 110–12, 115
in El Salvador, 50–1
in Mozambique, 82–4
in Somalia, 70–1
ONUMOZ, 82–95, 127, 128, 129
see also Mozambique; peacekeeping
ONUSAL, 54
see also El Salvador; mediation
Operation Provide Comfort, 69
Organization of African Unity (OAU), 78
Organization of American States (OAS), 54
Organization of Islamic Conference (OIC), 47, 70, 78
Owen, Baron David A.L. (1938–), 42

pacification, 70, 75, 76, 87
Pakistan, 70, 79
Paris Agreements (Cambodia), 110, 111–12, 115, 116–17, 118, 119, 120, 121, 123
Paris Peace Talks (Cambodia), 115, 121
'peace dividend', 6
peace treaties/agreements, 22, 29, 126–7
Accordos da Paz (Angola), 99–109
Addis Ababa Agreement (Somalia), 70, 75
Alvor Agreement (Angola), 102
Dayton Accord (Bosnia), 32, 48
Djibouti Accords (Somalia), 71

peace treaties/agreements – *continued*
flaws in, 100–1, 111–12
Mexico City Agreement (El Salvador), 50
Nkomati Accord (Mozambique–South Africa), 85
Paris Agreements (Cambodia), 110, 111–12, 115, 116–17, 118, 119, 120, 121, 123
plan for Bosnia, 34, 42–4
plan for El Salvador, 51–3
Rome Agreement (Mozambique), 82–8, 93–4
Serb–Croat proposal (Bosnia), 32, 42–3
Vance–Owen Plan (Bosnia), 32, 42
Western Contact Group plan (Bosnia), 32, 42–4
see also mediation
peacebuilding, 1, 13, 24, 29, 70–1, 74, 76, 81, 84
peace-enforcement, 13, 14, 66, 75–8
peacekeeping, 1–3, 6, 13, 15, 16, 20, 24, 29, 66–95, 96
in Angola, 82, 87, 98–109, 126, 127, 128
attacks on peacekeeping missions, 73–4, 75, 77, 80, 81, 119
in Bosnia, 33, 34, 47
in Cambodia, 98, 110, 112–24, 126, 129, 130
capabilities, 39, 70, 71–2, 76, 81, 87, 129–30
ceasefire monitoring, 70, 73, 84, 86, 88, 93, 104
colateral damage, 76, 77
command structure, 14, 76–7, 80
components, 112, 117
consent to, 74, 75, 76, 80
contingents, 73, 77, 80
in Cyprus, 11
deployment, 10, 89, 93, 110, 115–16, 117, 130–1
diversity, 14, 76
doctrine, 74, 75, 76–7, 117, 122, 129
in El Salvador, 54
endorsement/authorization, 7, 14, 27, 121
equipment/weaponry, 10, 14, 15, 25, 71–2, 75, 76, 129
force posture, 74, 76, 112, 123, 129
as an international policy instrument, 1, 70, 125, 132
in Lebanon, 11
logistics/staff work, 14, 77
in Mozambique, 82–95, 127, 128, 129
multicomponent peacekeeping, 66
in Namibia, 108
peacekeepers taken hostage, 25
personnel, 2, 3, 8, 25, 27, 76, 129
Rapid Response Force proposal, 12
rate of dispatch, 132
resourcing, 2, 3, 7, 8, 10, 25, 79, 88, 92, 115, 123, 129
riot control, 76
rules of engagement, 14, 25, 75–8, 117
self-defence, 117
in Somalia, 68–81, 126, 127, 128, 129
Status of Forces agreements, 88
tenure, 8
withdrawal, 77, 80, 81, 95
see also individual peacekeeping missions
Perez de Cuellar, Javier (1920–), 55, 57, 59–60
Pol Pot (Saloth Sar) (1928–), 113, 119, 121
Khmer Rouge, 109–24, 127
popular/electoral support, 55–6, 88, 101, 105, 112–13
Portugal, 91, 98, 99, 100, 102, 105–6
power sharing, 52, 86, 92, 102, 110
preventive deployment, 13
propaganda, 13, 17, 71, 72, 73, 76, 79
proxy war, 5, 26, 50, 59, 79, 98, 99, 110, 126
public opinion, 5, 35

Qian, Qichen (1928–), 119

Radio Mogadishu, 71, 77
Reagan, Ronald W. (1911–), 61
Reagan doctrine, 83, 107

Realism, 17
  anarchy, 3–4, 8, 17–18, 23
  cost-benefit calculations, 4, 8, 15, 24, 30
  realpolitik, 12
  relative gains considerations, 9, 22, 33
recognition
  Bosnia-Herzegovina, 33, 36, 37
  Cambodia, 112, 113
  domestic, 53
  international, 13, 20, 31, 46
reconciliation, 101, 102
Redman, Charles, 38, 43
referenda, 31, 37
  in Bosnia-Herzegovina, 36
  in Republika Srpska, 42, 45
refugees, 5, 36
relative gains considerations, 9, 22, 33
religious conflict, 5, 12, 16
religious ties, 35, 46
Renamo, 81–94, 128
  Dlakama, Afonso, 82, 92
resource overstretch, UN, 88, 104
revolution, 17, 55, 58, 60
Rhodesia, 91
  Military Intelligence, 81
rollback, strategy of, 107
Rome Agreement (Mozambique), 92, 82–8, 93–4
Rowland, Roland W. 'Tiny' (1917–), 91
Russian Federation, 3, 34, 43, 45, 46, 106, 108
  Yeltsin, Boris N. (1931–), 34
Rwanda, 106

sabotage, 49, 82, 84, 85, 99
Sahnoun, Mohammed (1913–), 69
  see also humanitarian crises; Somalia
sanctions/embargoes, 13–14, 20, 22, 25, 26, 79, 117
  on the former Yugoslavia, 32, 34, 37, 45, 47
  on the Khmer Rouge, 117, 120
  on the Republika Srpska, 40, 41, 44, 45
Sandanistas, 60
Sanderson, Lieutenant-General John M. (1940–), 118, 121
  see also UNTAC
São Tomé and Principe, 106
Saudi Arabia, 70
Savimbi, Jonas (1934–), 101, 102, 105, 106, 108
  personality cult, 108
  see also Unita
secession, 16, 31, 37, 43
security, 4, 10, 24, 100
  as global stability, 4, 5, 6, 100, 112
  internal, 5, 16, 50, 84, 116
  regional, 84, 100, 112
Security Council, *see* UN Security Council
security threats, civil wars as, 4–5, 7, 8–9, 10, 14, 25, 32, 50, 70, 83
self-determination, 38, 39, 46, 52
self-sufficiency, belligerents', 14, 22, 26, 48, 120
Serb–Croat proposal (Bosnia), 32, 42–3
  see also mediation
Serbia, 31, 38–9, 42
  Milosovic, Slobodan (1941–), 38
Siad Barre, Mohammed, 68, 71, 73
Slovenia, 37
socialism, 52
socio-economic conflict, 16, 52, 55
Somalia, 68–81, 126, 130
Son Sen (1930–), 121
  Khmer Rouge, 109–24, 127
South Africa, 79, 84–5, 90–1, 99, 100, 101, 102, 106
  African National Congress, 91
  apartheid, 84, 100, 101
  Codesa talks, 84
  de Klerk, F.W., 91
  South African Defence Force, 81, 91, 99, 103, 107
sovereignty, 3, 11, 12, 13, 16, 38, 49
  Angola, 105
  Bosnia-Herzegovina, 33, 35, 36, 39, 43, 46
  El Salvador, 51, 52

Soviet Union, 51, 59–60, 61, 99, 105, 106–7, 110–11
  Besmertnykh, Alexander A. (1933–), 50
  military operations, 100
  military support/transfers, 60, 83, 98, 109
  'new thinking', 60
  Soviet bloc, 49
Spain, 51, 59
sponsoring coalitions, UN, 7–8, 9, 10, 11, 12, 15, 16, 25, 27
  for Angola, 99–101
  apathy of, 83–4, 88, 92, 100, 106–7
  for Bosnia, 33–9: divisions in, 44–5, 46–7
  for Cambodia, 110–14
  coalition-building, 7: use of side payments, 8
  cohesion of, 8, 9, 27, 33–5, 46–7, 61, 88, 108, 119, 121
  coincidence of interests in, 33–5, 62, 70, 83, 110–11
  concerted direction, ability to achieve, 128
  decision making, 8
  defection from, 9, 27, 79
  divisions in, 44–5, 46–7, 79–80, 128
  for El Salvador, 50–1
  leadership, 9, 83–4
  for Mozambique, 82–4
  Paris Conference Group, 111
  for Somalia, 69–70: divisions in, 79–80
  stability of, 9, 78–80
  support, 115–16
Standing Committee of the Countries of the Horn, 78
State of Cambodia (SoC), 112–13, 115
state-centrism, 9, 10, 11, 22, 111, 126, 128, 130
superpowers, 5, 50, 59, 83, 98, 100, 120
  client states/organizations, 5, 26
  proxy war between, 5, 26, 50, 59, 79, 98, 99, 110, 126
Supreme National Council (SNC) (Cambodia), 110, 113, 117, 119
Sweden, 79
Syria, 6

tactics, belligerents', 20, 22, 25, 58–9, 72, 77–8, 82, 89–90, 105–6
  of the Bosnian government, 37–8, 44–5
  of the Bosnian Serbs, 31–2, 37–8, 44–5
  of the FMLN, 49, 57–9
  of Frelimo, 84–5, 87–8
  of the Khmer Rouge, 112–14, 116–19
  of the Manifesto alliance, 68, 76
  of Renamo, 84–6, 90
  of the Salvadoran government, 51–2, 57–9
  of the SoC, 112–13
  of Unita, 105–6, 108
  of the USC-SNA, 68, 71–2, 74, 76–8
territorial holdings
  of the Bosnian government, 37, 42–4
  of the Bosnian Serbs, 38–9, 42–4
  of Frelimo, 89
  of the Khmer Rouge, 114–15, 117, 119
  of Renamo, 89
  of Unita, 99, 104, 108
territorial integrity, 11, 12
  Angola, 100
  Bosnia-Herzegovina, 36, 39, 43
  El Salvador, 51
terrorism, 75, 85, 91, 121
Thailand, 111, 115, 119, 120
  Chatichai Choonhavan, 111
  military, 120
transparency, 120
Turkey, 34, 47, 70

UN coalitions, 3, 4, 7, 8, 9
  perceptions of civil wars, 4, 5, 7, 8, 9, 10, 35–6, 75–6
UN General Assembly, 10, 53, 55
  resolutions, 13

UN member-states, 3–15, 26, 29
contributions to the UN, 10, 25, 29, 79, 93
governmental tenure, 4, 9, 10, 22
self-interest/motivations, 3–4, 5, 6, 7, 8, 9, 10, 12, 14, 15, 22, 26, 27, 30, 131
support for UN initiatives, 2–7, 26
UN responses, appropriateness of, 10, 11, 15, 16, 23–4, 35, 39, 54, 122
UN Rio Conference on Environment and Development, 119
UN Safe Havens (Bosnia), 47
UN Secretariat, 14, 15, 74, 75, 88, 131
Department of Peacekeeping Operations, 74, 88, 131
Department of Political Affairs, 131: Goulding, Marrack, 131
Planning and Co-ordination Cell, 131
Situation Monitoring Centre, 131
UN Secretary-General, 29, 30, 50, 74, 79
Boutros-Ghali, Boutros (1922–), 12, 14, 68, 69, 73, 119: *Agenda for Peace*, 68, 75
Perez de Cuellar, Javier (1920–), 55, 57, 59–60
Special Representatives of, 32, 92: Ajello, Aldo, 89–90, 92; Akashi, Yasushi (1931–), 114; Anstee, Margaret (1926–); 104, 108; de Soto, Alvaro (1943–), 50, 57; Howe, Jonathan T., 75; Owen, David (1938–), 42; Sahnoun, Mohammed (1913–), 69; Vance, Cyrus (1917–), 32, 42
UN Security Council, 3, 10, 26, 33, 36, 39, 46, 50, 53, 55, 61, 69, 74, 75, 76, 77, 80, 82, 84, 87, 88, 92, 99, 108, 115, 116, 120, 129, 131
Permanent Five, 33, 111, 120
Permanent Five Ambassadors, Phnom Penh, 121
Permanent Five Contact Group, 111
resolutions, 13, 45, 46, 121
UNAMIC, 115
see also Cambodia
UNAVEM I, 99
see also Angola
UNAVEM II, 82, 87, 98–109, 126, 127, 128
see also Angola
UNFICYP, 11
UNIFIL, 11
unilateralism, 4, 26, 27, 56, 59, 111
Unita, 87, 98–9, 101–9, 127
Savimbi, Jonas (1934–), 101, 102, 105, 106, 108
UNITAF, 69, 74, 81, 132
see also Somalia
United Arab Emirates, 79
United Kingdom, 3, 33–4, 43, 51, 111
United Nations
admission to membership: Bosnia-Herzegovina, 36
capacity for independent action, 3, 9
Charter, 20, 36: Chapter VII, 75
condemnations: of Aideed, 75, 77–8; of the Bosnian Serbs, 39–40
diagnosis of conflicts, 36, 39, 51, 53, 70–1, 83, 101, 111, 123, 125–6, 127, 130–1
headquarters, New York City: UNTAC liaison, 121
philosophy, 11
representation, Cambodia, 109
resolutions, 13, 45, 46, 121
as a scapegoat, 7
structure, 11
United States, 3, 6, 33, 43, 45, 46–7, 48, 49, 50, 59–60, 74, 77, 79, 83, 91, 99, 101, 102, 105, 107, 108, 119
Baker, James A. III (1930–), 50
Bush, George H.W. (1924–), 59, 60, 61, 69
Clark Amendment, 1975, 99, 107
Clinton, William J. (Bill) (1946–), 34, 69
Defence Intelligence Agency, 99
engagement, international, 5

United States – *continued*
  Holbrooke, Richard C. (1941–), 32, 48
  Iran–Contra scandal, 50
  lift and strike, policy of, 34
  military operations, 109
  military support/transfers, 52, 54–5, 59, 99, 107
  Rangers, 78
  Reagan doctrine, 83, 107
  Reagan, Ronald W. (1911–), 61
  Redman, Charles, 38, 43
  right wing groups in, 91
  rollback, strategy of, 107
UNOSOM I, 69
  see also Somalia
UNOSOM II, 68–81, 126, 127, 128, 129
  see also Somalia
UNPROFOR II, 33
  see also Bosnia-Herzegovina
UNTAC, 98, 110, 112–24, 126, 129, 130
  see also Cambodia
UNTAG, 108
urban–rural conflict, 12, 102
USC-SNA, 68, 71–80, 127
  Aideed, Mohammed Farah, 68, 71, 73, 75, 77, 78

Vance, Cyrus R. (1917–), 32, 42
Vance–Owen Plan (Bosnia), 32, 42
  see also Bosnia-Herzegovina; mediation
Venezuela, 59
verification, 54, 56, 66, 67, 88, 97, 103, 112
Vietnam, 110, 112, 115, 120, 121
  PAVN, 118
  Vietnam War, 109
Vorgan (Unita radio station), 104
VRS (Bosnian Serb Army), 32, 38

war
  abandonment of, 18, 19, 23–5, 57, 87, 90, 102, 127
  assumptions about, 10–12, 15, 22, 126, 130
  over disputed commodities, 12, 23
  escalation, 41, 77–8
  illegitimacy of, 10–11
  intensity of, 16–17
  political uses of, 16–19, 23, 58
  stalemated, 54, 87–8, 110
  war weariness, 27, 87–8, 111
  zero-sum struggles, 101, 102
war crimes, 35
weaponry
  of the Bosnian Serbs, 40, 48
  of the Khmer Rouge, 118, 120
  of Unita, 107
weapons transfers, 13, 45–6, 54–5, 79
Western Contact Group (Bosnia), 32, 43–4
  Western Contact Group plan, 32, 42–4
Western Europe, 33–5, 70, 100, 103
  see also European Union
western states, 6, 40, 69, 79, 109, 110

Yeltsin, Boris N. (1931–), 34
Yugoslavia, 31, 36–7

Zaire, 100, 107
Zambia, 81, 106
zero-zero option, 107
Zimbabwe, 81, 83, 91, 106
  intervention in Mozambique, 83, 90, 91